Cultural nationalism
in contemporary Japan

Cultural nationalism in contemporary Japan

A sociological enquiry

Kosaku Yoshino

London and New York

First published 1992
by Routledge
11 New Fetter Lane, London EC4P 4EE

Simultaneously published in the USA and Canada
by Routledge
a division of Routledge, Chapman and Hall, Inc.
29 West 35th Street, New York, NY 10001

Typeset in 10/12pt Baskerville by
Falcon Typographic Art Ltd, Fife, Scotland
Printed and bound in Great Britain by
Biddles Ltd, Guildford and King's Lynn

British Library Cataloguing in Publication Data
A catalogue record for this book is
available from the British Library

Library of Congress Cataloging in Publication Data
Yoshino, Kosaku, 1953–
  Cultural nationalism in contemporary Japan: a
sociological enquiry / Kosaku Yoshino.
  p. cm.
  Originally presented as author's thesis (Ph.D.) – London
School of Economics and Political Science.
  Includes bibliographical references and index.
  1. Japan – Civilization – 1945– 2. National
characteristics, Japanese. 3. Nationalism – Japan. I. Title.
  DS822.5.Y674   1992   91–47102
  305.8'0952 – dc20   CIP

ISBN 0–415–07119–4
      0–415–06157–1 (pbk)

Contents

Tables

Acknowledgements

The present book began as a Ph.D. thesis at the London School of Economics and Political Science, and I am sincerely grateful to Professor Percy S. Cohen, my supervisor, for his untiring patience, continuous encouragement and insightful criticisms. I am also deeply grateful to Professor Anthony D. Smith for arousing my interest in a sociological study of nationalism. The publication of this book has greatly benefited from his advice and encouragement. He and Dr James Fulcher read the text with great care and made many sensible criticisms. My warm appreciation is equally due to Professor Kazuko Tsurumi, who has at various stages helped me to formulate my ideas in Japan and read the final product. My thanks are also due to Brian Moeran, John Clammer, Kate Nakai and John Hutchinson for reading the entire work or chapters of it and offering me comments and encouragement. I also thank Professor Ian Nish and Mr Patrick Davis of the Publications Committee of the LSE for their kind support. My deep appreciation is due to Professor Arthur Stockwin whose invaluable suggestions greatly assisted my revisions for this book.

I should like to record my debt to the late Professor Masaaki Takane, without whose enthusiastic encouragement, this endeavour could not have begun. I deeply regret that he is no longer alive to read my work.

Thanks are also due to John Bowler for his tremendous help in improving my English on the two earlier versions of this work and saving me from many mistakes. Jeff Burton and Jon Marks made very useful suggestions on English style. Dan Stoner also edited portions of the work. My thanks also go to Shin Watanabe for his help and guidance in compiling statistics.

For the empirical materials I am indebted to the many school teachers, headmasters and businessmen who spent hours talking with me. I should like to thank in particular Mr Fukutaro Watanabe and Mr Junichi Kawashima, who took the trouble of initiating me into the 'communities' of teachers and businessmen in the 'field work' city. Hiroshi Takinami, a high school teacher whom I came to know very well and who showed a great understanding of my research, was killed in a traffic accident while the research was still in progress. It is sad that he is no longer alive to exchange cups of *sake*.

I would like to acknowledge the financial assistance received from several sources. The British Council provided me with a scholarship which enabled me to study in Britain from 1982 to 1984. The Japan Society for Promotion of Science granted me a fellowship for the two years 1987–89 which permitted me to continue my research in times of economic hardship. The Ministry of Education in Japan awarded me a Grant-in-Aid from 1987 to 1989, which helped to cover expenses during my field research.

There are many others to whom I owe a great deal and who are deserving of my heartfelt gratitude. Among them are my mother and my deceased father, whom I can never repay for everything they gave me. My daughter, Megumi, has been a source of inspiration to me since she came into this world. Finally, I gratefully acknowledge the help of my wife, Akiyo. She was untiring in her patience and understanding, without which this work could not have been completed.

Kosaku Yoshino
Tokyo

Note on Japanese names and works cited

Japanese personal names appearing in the text are given, as is the custom in Japan, with the family name first. This custom seems to have become accepted at least in academic works in Western languages. In other contexts, however, Japanese personal names generally follow the Western custom, with the family name last. Thus, for example, my name appears in the customary Western order (i.e. Kosaku Yoshino) on the title page, as it is expected to be processed according to the Western custom in bookshops and libraries.

Japanese works cited in the text appear in English translations without original Japanese titles. Full publishing details of works cited will be found in the bibliography.

Macrons indicate long vowels. But they are not used in words and place names commonly used in English.

Chapter 1

Introduction

There are two main lines of enquiry pursued throughout this study. One is a general examination of cultural nationalism and national identity; the other is an analysis of contemporary Japanese society.

As a study of cultural nationalism, this book assesses some of the assumptions and theories concerning cultural nationalism, nationalism and ethnicity. Cultural nationalism may provisionally be understood as follows. Cultural nationalism aims to regenerate the national community by creating, preserving or strengthening a people's cultural identity when it is felt to be lacking, inadequate or threatened. The cultural nationalist regards the nation as the product of its unique history and culture and as a collective solidarity endowed with unique attributes. In short, cultural nationalism is concerned with the distinctiveness of the cultural community as the essence of a nation. By contrast, political nationalists seek to achieve a representative state for their community and to secure citizenship rights for its members, thereby giving their collective experience a political reality. Cultural nationalism and political nationalism often stimulate each other, but the two should be distinguished for their different aims.[1]

Two groups are normally prominent in the development of cultural nationalism: intellectuals (or thinking elites), who formulate ideas and ideals of the nation's cultural identity, and intelligentsia (or social groups with higher and further education), who respond to such ideas and ideals and relate them to their own social, economic, political and other activities. Although both groups can, and indeed do, overlap in occupational category, an analytical distinction between the two is useful because, as will be seen, these two groups have different concerns. In this study I shall examine the roles of intellectuals and intelligentsia in the development of cultural nationalism and the relationship between these groups. It should be made clear at the outset that my emphasis will be on national identity and sentiment, not nationalist movements.

On the substantive level, our problem concerns Japan in the 1970s and 1980s. I have selected this period for enquiry for the following reasons. First, little, if anything, has been written on cultural nationalism in contemporary Japan or, indeed, on nationalism in Japan after the 1950s, except short articles in newspapers and magazines. This is in contrast to the abundance of literature on the previous periods. Confining ourselves to books in English, we find Delmer Brown's *Nationalism in Japan: An Introductory Historical Analysis* (1955) which discusses the development of Japan's nationalism (or ethnicism) from about the seventh century AD to the late 1940s; Maruyama Masao's analysis of pre-war and wartime nationalism and of the impact of Japan's defeat on post-war nationalism in *Thought and Behaviour in Modern Japanese Politics* (1963); and Ivan Morris's *Nationalism and the Right Wing in Japan: A Study of Post-War Trends* (1960), to mention a few. The second and main reason for selecting the 1970s and 1980s is that this period deserves special attention. The last two decades have witnessed a resurgence of cultural nationalism in Japan. This may be called Japan's 'secondary' nationalism in the sense that, as Maruyama Masao put it, Japan 'had completed one full cycle of nationalism: birth, maturity and decline' (1953: 7–8) before the beginning of the post-war period in 1945. (The term 'primary nationalism' will be used to mean original nationalism throughout this study.) Among the various manifestations of contemporary Japanese nationalism, I shall concentrate on that which bears a close relationship with 'intellectual nationalism', or what is generally called the *nihonjinron*.

The *nihonjinron*, which literally means 'discussions of the Japanese', refer to the vast array of literature which thinking elites have produced to define the uniqueness of Japanese culture, society and national character. Publications on Japanese uniqueness reached their peak in the late 1970s but continued into the 1980s.[2] This study is also concerned with the 1980s because it is in this decade that the effects of the *nihonjinron* were strongly felt among wider sections of the population, as it takes time for thinking elites' ideas to diffuse to other social groups. (This is not to suggest simplistically that the thinking elites' *nihonjinron* precede the other social groups' concern with Japanese uniqueness. There is, as will be seen, an interplay between the two.)

The *nihonjinron* should be distinguished from rigorous academic research on Japanese society and culture. Peter Dale remarks that the *nihonjinron* 'are concentrated expressions of an intense tradition of intellectual nationalism whose broader impact on both our general way of interpreting Japan and specialist studies remains to be analysed' (1986: ii). The content of the *nihonjinron* covers the whole range of Japanese culture, using as their illustrative materials everyday episodes, contemporary news, travelogues, folklore materials and so on. Since the competition for the *nihonjinron* market has been fierce, writers have used one attention-catching key concept after another to describe Japanese uniqueness in a way that appeals to the general educated public. In this sense Dale is quite right in characterising the *nihonjinron* as 'the commercialised expression of modern Japanese nationalism' (1986: 14).

The specific aim of this study is thus an examination of the *nihonjinron* (thinking elites' ideas of Japanese uniqueness) and their role in Japanese society from the perspective of the sociology of knowledge, a perspective which understands ideas in terms of the social, cultural and civilisational milieu which produces and consumes them. Given their pervasive impact on the intellectual life of the Japanese, a number of criticisms of the *nihonjinron* emerged among concerned scholars in the early 1980s.

Various criticisms of the *nihonjinron* will be assessed in chapter 9 after the content of the *nihonjinron* has been discussed and our empirical data have been examined, but a brief look at some of the literature may be taken here in order to point out certain limitations and to suggest where the contribution of the present work will lie as a study of the *nihonjinron*.

Sugimoto Yoshio and Ross Mouer (e.g. 1982, 1986) are two of the most conspicuous critics of the *nihonjinron*. The two sociologists devote themselves to showing the serious weaknesses of the *nihonjinron* as a social theory on methodological, empirical and ideological grounds. In particular, they point out the lack of rigorous methodology in the *nihonjinron* or their heavy reliance on convenient examples in the form of personal experiences and everyday episodes in support of one particular type of social theory, that is, the 'consensus model' or 'group model' of Japanese society, and indicate in turn the importance of the 'conflict model', which emphasises conflicts between different groups in Japanese society. The ideological implication of the conservative bias criticised by Sugimoto and Mouer is that it serves the interests of the ruling establishment in Japan. These themes are also dealt with by other scholars, albeit with differing emphasis. Kawamura Nozomu (1982), for example, concentrates on ideological criticism, arguing how the *nihonjinron*, which emphasise group cohesion and neglect classes, can serve as a dominant ideology in Japan. Cultural anthropologist Harumi Befu (1980, 1987) also writes profusely on the limitations of the 'group model' of the *nihonjinron*. He provides a symbolic anthropological interpretation of how the *nihonjinron* have developed to reassert a Japanese cultural identity threatened by Westernisation. Furthermore, Peter Dale (1986) has done a critical examination of the 'unique' characteristics of Japanese culture as discussed in the vast *nihonjinron* literature, both historical and contemporary. Aoki Tamotsu's (1990) study of the changing emphasis in the post-war literature on Japanese uniqueness is also of interest.

There are also many other criticisms and reviews of the *nihonjinron*,[3] but the existing literature is all seriously circumscribed in following two respects. First, they are chiefly concerned with the *nihonjinron* as an 'academic' issue, showing their limited academic value on methodological, empirical and ideological grounds. Although such a critique of the *nihonjinron* may be important in itself considering their impact on specialist studies, *scholars have confined themselves to a mere critique and failed to offer a sociological analysis of what it is that has occurred, and between whom (i.e. from whom and to whom) in Japanese society*.[4] In particular, it has failed to pay attention to the 'receptive' or 'consumption' side of the *nihonjinron*. (This may apply to much of the sociology of knowledge literature in general in which the analyst's focus is usually on the 'producers', not the 'consumers' of intellectual works.) Even Befu, who characterises the *nihonjinron* as 'mass consumption goods' (1987: 54–67) rather than academic works, fails to specify who he means by the 'mass' or who 'consumes' works on Japanese uniqueness. Which social groups have actively responded to the *nihonjinron* and why? What effect have the *nihonjinron* had on the other sections of the population? What sort of cultural nationalism have the *nihonjinron* fostered? This study attempts to examine these questions on the basis of mainly qualitative data obtained through my empirical research conducted among educators and businessmen.

There is another fundamental limitation in the existing criticism of the *nihonjinron*: namely, *the lack of a comparative perspective*.[5] Those who criticise the *nihonjinron*'s emphasis of Japanese uniqueness have made a similar assumption that such an intellectual activity itself is unique to Japan. We are tempted to remind them of Nietzsche's remark on nineteenth-century German intellectuals' preoccupation with German uniqueness: 'It is characteristic of the Germans that the question "what is German?" never dies out among them' ([1886] 1990: 174). Such an intellectual concern is not confined to nineteenth-century Germany but is, as will be seen, a widely observed phenomenon. This study attempts, wherever possible, to situate the contemporary Japanese experience of the *nihonjinron* and cultural nationalism in a broader comparative and theoretical perspective. Hence, this is where our specific aim of analysing Japanese society converges with our more general aim to contribute to the study of national identity and cultural nationalism.

On the basis of the specific case study, the book takes up five main issues concerning national identity and cultural nationalism:

1 a comparison of the ways in which intellectuals (or thinking elites) formulate ideas of national distinctiveness in different national and historical contexts;
2 an examination of the relationship between culture and race in perceptions of national identity and in cultural nationalism;
3 an examination of the ways in which the two other educated sections of the population (educators and businessmen), regarded in this study as relevant in the context of cultural nationalism, respond to ideas of national distinctiveness formulated by intellectuals (or thinking elites);
4 a reassessment of the view that regards educators as playing the major role in transmitting and diffusing ideas of national distinctiveness and an assessment of the role of businessmen in cultural nationalism;
5 an exploration of the characteristics of 'secondary' nationalism in comparison with those of 'primary' nationalism.

Considering that our case deals with 'secondary' nationalism – and we understand 'secondary' nationalism as that type which preserves and enhances national identity in an already long-established nation-state – and that most theories of cultural nationalism are based on cases of 'primary' or original nationalism, our findings will be used as the basis upon which to modify and qualify the conventional theories rather than to refute them simplistically.

Several terms may require provisional definition. First, the term 'nationalism'. Nationalism is not an easy concept to be defined in a few sentences.[6] For scholars like Hans Kohn, nationalism is basically a subjective 'state of mind' (1955: 9); for others such as A.D. Smith (1971, 1973) it is primarily an ideological movement. Also, nationalism can be a latent phenomenon expressed mainly as pride in the nation's history and way of life, or it may develop as a dynamic force demanding strenuous efforts and immense sacrifice on the part of the members of the nation. Whatever aspect of nationalism one refers to and whatever form nationalism may take, the common denominators of nationalism are the belief among a people that it comprises a distinct community with distinctive characteristics and the will to maintain and enhance that distinctiveness within an autonomous state. Nationalism may provisionally be understood in this broad sense for the purpose of the present study.

A second set of terms requiring definition is 'intellectuals' and 'intelligentsia', the two groups who normally occupy an important place in cultural nationalism.[7] The intelligentsia may be defined as those 'who possess some form of further or higher education and use their educational diplomas to gain a livelihood through vocational activity, thereby disseminating and applying the ideas and paradigms created by intellectuals' (Smith 1981: 108). They may also be simply referred to as highly educated sections of the population. The intellectuals are those who are devoted to the formulation of original ideas and engage in creative intellectual pursuits, thereby constituting, in a sense, a small, creative segment of the intelligentsia and providing the intellectual leadership for the rest of the intelligentsia. I prefer another term, 'thinking elites', to intellectuals in discussing the contemporary Japanese scene, though I admit that 'thinking elites' may be a somewhat inelegant term. I use this term for want of a more appropriate alternative. It is debatable whether those who engage in the discussion of Japanese uniqueness are 'intellectuals' in the sense defined above. Those who have participated in the *nihonjinron* include elites of diverse types ranging from academics to journalists, diplomats and even business elites. These occupational groups are not 'intellectuals' in that they are not devoted to creative intellectual pursuits. Writers on Japanese uniqueness are not 'ideologues' either, because I do not suppose that the majority of them are aware what specific ideology they are propagating. They may more appropriately be called 'thinking elites' in the sense that they are a minority which has influence on others by virtue of thinking about a particular subject.[8]

It must be emphasised that I do not intend to furnish an inclusive account of cultural nationalism in contemporary Japan. My purpose is much more limited: to highlight that dimension of cultural nationalism that has resulted from, and resulted in, the *nihonjinron* and to focus on the roles of the three groups – thinking elites, educators and businessmen – that I consider particularly relevant in the context of this dimension of cultural nationalism.[9] Furthermore, it should be borne in mind that perceptions of national identity are never static and that the main body of this study concentrates on the period of the 1970s and 1980s. I hope, however, that the conclusions drawn from this study will be used not merely as perspectives on the above period but as a basis for understanding any subsequent developments of Japan's cultural nationalism that may take place in future.

One chief aim of this study is to promote a dialogue between specialist studies on Japan and the general sociology of ethnicity and nationalism. Much of the literature on Japan, particularly on the present theme, lacks comparative and sociological perspective. This study seeks to analyse the phenomenon of the *nihonjinron* by dividing it into some generalisable theoretical issues and propositions in the hope of enabling comparative discussions and of stimulating further comparative studies. It also seeks to indicate some neglected areas in the sociology of ethnicity and nationalism. I hope that this study will suggest the type of enquiries that future Japanologists and sociologists might develop when considering the crucial questions of ethnicity, race and nationalism.

AN OUTLINE OF THE STUDY

This book begins with a general introduction as to the nature and content of the *nihonjinron*, an important intellectual basis of cultural nationalism in contemporary Japan (chapter 2). Before embarking upon a further examination of the Japanese experience, it is useful to introduce comparative and theoretical perspectives on issues concerning ethnicity, national identity and cultural nationalism. Chapters 3 and 4 deal with this task. We then return in chapter 5 to the substantive discussion of the Japanese case. (Students of modern Japan, not necessarily concerned with theories of ethnicity and nationalism, may skip chapter 4 and go straight on to chapter 5 and continue until it becomes necessary to clarify the terms and theories used in the discussion, and then turn back to this theoretical chapter for guidance.) Chapter 5 shows that the 'holistic' approach employed in the *nihonjinron* to apprehend the essence of Japanese social culture reflects an important intellectual tradition in both academic and politicised theories of modern Japanese society.

The empirical core of the study is to be found in chapters 6–10. An analysis is made on the basis of the data I have obtained through my research on educators (school teachers and headmasters) and businessmen, regarded in this study as relevant in the context of Japanese cultural nationalism. Methods of collecting data are discussed in chapter 6. The study aims not only to expound the empirical core of the research but also to relate it to the wider questions of national identity and cultural nationalism in Japan. Chapters 6 and 7 explore the social process that occurs between thinking elites who 'produce' works on Japanese uniqueness (the *nihonjinron*) and other educated social groups who 'consume' such works. Chapter 6 examines in detail the manners in which educators and businessmen, the two educated sections of the population chosen for study, perceive Japanese uniqueness. Special emphasis is given to an examination of the relationship between culture and 'race' in perceptions of national identity. Chapter 7 investigates which of the two social groups is more receptive to the *nihonjinron*, and why and how. In the course of the discussion in chapter 7 we find that businessmen actively responded to the *nihonjinron* (thinking elites' ideas of Japanese uniqueness). Chapter 8 expands on the role of businessmen and argues that leading members of the business elite have played an important role in diffusing such thinking elites' ideas as well as systematising their own ideas of Japanese distinctiveness. This chapter also outlines the changing role of business elites in the history of modern Japanese nationalism. Chapter 9 clarifies my position regarding the explanations of why the phenomenon of the *nihonjinron* has developed by critically assessing some of the prevalent explanations set forth by Japanese specialists. The book concludes with chapter 10 which discusses another type of nationalism found among our respondents, that is, 'prudent revivalist nationalism' which is concerned to eliminate negative images that have been attached in post-war Japan to some of the symbols and practices that had surrounded pre-war and wartime nationalism in Japan. The chapter compares and contrasts 'prudent revivalist nationalism' and 'resurgent cultural nationalism', that type associated with the *nihonjinron* and the main subject of this book, and concludes by considering the possibility of a 'merger' between the two.

Chapter 2

The *nihonjinron*: thinking elites' ideas of Japanese uniqueness

It is best to begin with a general introduction to the characteristic features of the world view of Japanese thinking elites as manifested in their writings on Japanese uniqueness. These writings are usually referred to collectively as the *nihonjinron*. The *nihonjinron* genre is so vast that a comprehensive discussion of its content is beyond the scope of this chapter. None the less, it is possible to focus on some of the themes frequently discussed in the *nihonjinron* and also the reviews of the *nihonjinron* literature that have subsequently appeared. As mentioned above, the term *nihonjinron* refers to the whole genre of such writings, but I will sometimes use the term to refer to a subgroup of the genre or to an individual essay.

The writers of the *nihonjinron* are not confined to academics but include thinkers of various occupations such as journalists, critics, writers and even business elites. However, the *nihonjinron* considered here are mainly the work of academics, who have discussed more systematically than other groups the uniqueness of Japanese culture and society. (Business elites' *nihonjinron* are discussed in chapter 8.) Academics occupy a respected position in Japanese society, where there is no conscious anti-intellectualism or antipathy towards sociology as one might encounter in England.[1] Academics are, in a sense, 'proxy spokesmen for the inarticulate soul of the national essence' (Dale 1986: 15). Japanese academics have published their *nihonjinron* in popular editions and occasional essays in newspapers and general interest magazines, rather than in limited scholarly editions or purely academic journals. The *nihonjinron* should be distinguished from rigorous academic study, but the two are not unrelated (see chapter 5).

CULTURALISM AND THE 'THEORIES' OF UNIQUE JAPANESE CULTURE

The mode of explanation in the *nihonjinron* is best characterised as that of culturalism (or cultural determinism or cultural reductionism). Culture is seen as infrastructural, and social, economic and political phenomena are often seen as symptoms of immanent culture. The following passage from Aida Yūji's *The Structure of Japanese Consciousness*, a typical work of the *nihonjinron*, is illustrative:

> It is not that overcrowding causes excessive [economic] competition [in Japan] but that the mental structure of the Japanese itself causes this peculiar kind of excessive competition. Is it then possible to rectify this defect? No, this is not so easy as it seems, since national characteristics (*minzokuteki tokushitsu*) are the product of racial, climatic and historical conditions. Moreover, it is not a question of 'good' or 'bad', but a matter of 'character'.
>
> (Aida 1972: 30)

The *nihonjinron* explain everyday occurrences and current news in terms of culture or cultural ethos considered peculiar to the Japanese. Virtually anything can become subject matter for the *nihonjinron*, and the *nihonjinron* explain what, in cultural terms, lies behind the topic chosen. For example, when trade imbalances between Japan and the USA first received public attention, Japanese critics tended to explain this issue in cultural terms, as the Japanese designation *bōeki masatsu* (trade friction) suggests. Whereas Americans perceived the issue largely in economic and political terms, Japanese opinion formers emphasised cultural differences, maintaining that, in contrast to American culture which encourages aggressive verbal confrontation, Japanese culture finds virtue in empathetic silence, which often results in failure to make the Japanese position understood well and causes international misunderstanding, of which 'trade friction' is an example. Others argued that the real cause of the problem was a difference in their attitudes towards group culture which resulted in a productivity gap. (As debates on trade imbalances continued over the years, the Japanese began to argue in less culturalistic terms.) Because of their heavy emphasis on culture, the *nihonjinron* (discussions of the Japanese) are also called the *nihonbunkaron* (discussions of Japanese culture).

The *nihonjinron* purport to demonstrate the uniqueness of Japan. There are various ways of saying that certain features are 'unique' to Japan in Japanese, such as *dokutoku* (distinctive), *dokuji* (original), *tokuyū* (singular), *tokushu* (peculiar), *tokusei* (characteristic) and *koyū* (intrinsic). None of these expressions corresponds exactly to the English word 'unique' which precisely means 'the only one of its kind'. These Japanese words run the range of connotation from 'very different' to 'unparalleled'.

The endless discussions of Japanese uniqueness are, if more precisely put, discussions of difference, but difference of a specific kind. Japanese identity is the anti-image of foreignness and, as such, can only be affirmed by formulating the images of the Other; namely, the West (or in a previous age, China). In general terms, ethnicity may be understood, to a certain extent, as the symbolic boundary process of organising significant differences between 'us' and 'them' (see chapter 4). Wallman, who adopts a strict boundary perspective on ethnicity, understands it as:

> the process by which '*their*' difference is used to enhance the sense of 'us' for the purposes of organisation or identification.
>
> (Wallman 1979: 3, emphasis added)

But is it '*their*' difference that is used? In the *nihonjinron*, it is normally '*our*' difference that has been actively used for the reaffirmation of Japanese identity. For example, the *nihonjinron* have often emphasised the 'non-logical', non-verbal and emotive mode of communication of the Japanese as opposed to the logical, verbal and rational mode of Westerners (see below). In such a discussion the Japanese mode tends to be assumed to be the exception and the Western mode to be the norm. Logic is most likely to mean Western Aristotelian logic, which tends to be regarded as the universal logic. This may seem a small point but it illustrates the manner in which Japanese thinking elites have perceived themselves and their culture in the world. The Japanese have long perceived themselves to be on the 'periphery' in relation to the 'central' civilisations where the 'universal' norm has been supposed to exist. China and the West have constituted the two 'significant others' from which the Japanese have borrowed models and against which they have affirmed and reaffirmed their identity. For the Japanese, learning from China and the West has been experienced as acquiring the 'universal' civilisation. The Japanese have thus had to stress their particularistic difference in order to differentiate themselves from the universal Chinese and Westerners. The *nihonjinron* or discussions of Japanese uniqueness are, therefore, discussions of 'particularistic' cultural differences of Japan from the 'universal' civilisation. The *nihonjinron* have rarely concerned themselves, at least until fairly recently, with the other non-Western societies and civilisations as their reference groups.[2] As long as the world view of the writers and readers of the *nihonjinron* is limited solely to Japanese culture and Western civilisation, Japan's 'particularistic difference' from others is virtually synonymous with its 'uniqueness'. It should be stressed that those ideas concerning Japan and the West emphasised in the *nihonjinron* do not necessarily represent empirical reality but rather images created to reinforce Japanese identity.

There are two theoretical pillars of Japan's cultural uniqueness, the first dealing with linguistic and communicative culture, the second, social culture. Obviously, the two are closely interrelated. But, since each has its characteristic themes, it is necessary to make this distinction.

Linguistic and communicative culture

Language and communication form a very important aspect of Japanese cultural uniqueness, frequently discussed in the *nihonjinron*. Considering that the uniqueness of the in-group is most directly felt in interactions with outsiders, the linguistic and communicative mode is the key area. As the scholar and television commentator Kunihiro Masao argues, the difficulty of communicating with a Japanese person is considered to be closely associated with the 'Japanese people's peculiar view of language and mode of language usage, the unique patterns of cognition and perception, and the system of logic' (1976: 4). This view is echoed by many others, not only by scholars of linguistics and literature (e.g. Kindaichi 1975; Suzuki 1975; Watanabe 1974; Itasaka 1978) and anthropologists (e.g. Ishida 1967), but by thinkers in various fields who are interested in intercultural communication. In fact, *ibunkakan komyunikēshon* (intercultural communication) was another popular theme of intellectual discussion in the 1970s along with the *nihonjinron*, and much was written on the uniqueness of Japanese patterns of communication as a possible obstacle to intercultural communication.[3] Although discussions on intercultural communication were intended to facilitate communication across cultures, it had the unintended consequence of obstructing communication by sensitising the Japanese excessively to Japanese uniqueness.

Intercultural communication studies and the *nihonjinron* were, therefore, two sides of the same coin.[4]

The linguistic and communicative mode of the Japanese is characterised in the *nihonjinron* by taciturnity, ambivalence, non-logic, situational ethics and emotionality. The Western mode, by contrast, is characterised by eloquence, dichotomous logic, rigid principle and rationality.

The unique Japanese patterns of communication are often characterised by comparatively light emphasis on overt linguistic expression and logical presentation. Kunihiro Masao is one of the most explicit contemporary exponents of this view, who states that 'Japanese tend to be taciturn, considering it a virtue to say little and rely on nonlinguistic means to convey the rest. Verbal expression is often fragmentary and unsystematic, with emotional, communal patterns of communication' (1976: 270). Kunihiro relates this linguistic behaviour to the cognitive behaviour of the Japanese which, he argues, is very different from that of Westerners, who employ the dualistic Aristotelian logic, which is, in simple terms, based on the dichotomy 'It is . . .' or 'It is not . . .'. Kunihiro states:

> Dualism still persists in the West. Even when groping for a third road of synthesis, the two-way contrast is used as the point of departure. For instance, atheists in the West are different from their counterparts in Japan, and the same is true of agnostics. They probe intensely within themselves to ask whether God exists or not.
>
> (Kunihiro 1976: 280)

The Japanese, on the other hand, do not rely on such a reasoning process. Kunihiro quotes anthropologist Ishida Eiichirō who argues that in an endogamous and homogeneous society like Japan, 'it is easy to follow what might be called a transrational route, which is weak in classification and categorization and avoids dichotomies such as god and the devil, good and bad, individual and whole' (Ishida, quoted in Kunihiro 1976: 277). The Japanese are thus described as relying less on logical presentation – and therefore the use of language – and more on affective means of communication.

There are a number of descriptions for this style of communication in Japanese such as *ishin denshin* (empathetic understanding) and *haragei*, although the former may be somewhat less appropriate as a name for something uniquely Japanese because it is also Chinese. *Haragei* ('the art of the abdomen', if translated literally) means the 'art' of communicating between persons – and often the way of achieving a difficult consensus – without the use of direct assertions and quite often on the strength of one's personality. The name derives from the fact that the *hara* (abdomen) has been traditionally considered to house one's courage, integrity, purity, genuine feelings and so on. *Haragei*, which Matsumoto Michihiro maintains, is 'the last bastion of Japanese uniqueness' (1984: 17), was one of the popular themes in the discussions on Japanese uniqueness and intercultural communication in the 1970s (e.g. Matsumoto 1975). Matsumoto remarks that '*hara*, although a bit too ambiguous for the uninformed Westerner to understand easily, is what the Japanese comfortably identify with' (1984: 31).

> For the Japanese, reality cannot be grasped through concepts and ideas. The reality of *hara* goes beyond the dichotomy of we and they, or subject and object, or sadism and masochism, and cannot be analyzed or comprehended by mind-logic, but can be 'experienced' by *hara*-logic.
>
> (ibid.)

Matsumoto provides the following fictitious example to show how a logically-minded Westernised woman with an American MBA and a 'hara-logical' Zen monk talk at cross-purposes, thereby pointing out a major Western–Japanese difference in logical and verbal presentation. Matsumoto's book is presented in a dual-language format, designed for both Japanese-language and English-language readers. The latter does not necessarily mean non-Japanese readers but is supposed to include those Japanese interested in explaining this 'uniquely Japanese' notion in English. Although the following dialogue seems somewhat unnatural, I quote it as written in English by Matsumoto:

> 'The purpose of my visit here is to seek your advice on my career choice. I want to be a professional business woman in Japan . . .'
> '. . . You are going to get married, aren't you?'
> 'Not for the time being, no. How many years do you think it will take before I establish myself, so to speak?'
> '. . . You are not going to get married for the time being. Why not?'
> 'Because I want to commit myself to work. I don't want to end up being just another housewife doing housework.'
> '. . . It'll take ten years.'

'Ten years? I don't understand. I'm an MBA. And I did far
better than many male students in school. When it comes to
problem-solving skills, I can hold my own . . .'
'. . . It'll take fifteen years.'
'Fifteen years?'
'You'll be getting married in the future, won't you?'
'What's that got to do with my career choice?'
'. . . Have a cup of tea.'

With this interjectory phrase by the monk, the woman realises that
she should calm down, but the conversation soon resumes and
continues at cross-purposes for another while until the monk says,
'You haven't drunk your tea yet'. Here is the rest of the dialogue.

> 'Never mind . . . You don't understand how seriously I'm com-
> mitted to becoming an influential business woman – useful for
> society.'
> '. . . Useful for society? It'll take thirty years.'
> 'I beg your pardon. . . . You don't know anything about busi-
> ness.'
> 'With that *hara* of yours, you'll never make it in Japan.'
> 'You never know.'
> '. . . I know by my *hara*. You didn't place your shoes properly at
> the entrance, did you?'
> 'How do you know?'
> '. . . The way you talked and the way you breathed.'
>
> (Matsumoto 1984: 29–30)

Matsumoto's conclusion regarding this conversation is that 'the
woman's heart told her not to see the monk again', whereas
'the monk's *hara* told him to wait until she came back again,
enlightened, balanced her breath regulated [because] he may have
liked her guts, contrary to his words' (ibid.: 31). Matsumoto explains
discommunication in this example as follows:

> The straightforward woman thought linearly that every problem
> has a solution, whereas the holistic monk thought non-linearly or
> rather circularly that the problem is the solution and conversely
> the solution is the problem. Worse still, the woman listened hard
> and responded strongly to every word expressed without hearing
> inaudible breaths, whereas the monk heard her breaths but
> barely listened to her arguments. . . . Westerners stress the need

for critical listening, whereas *hara*-logical Japanese emphasize non-critical 'hearing', or listening between and beyond the lines, so to speak. The interjectory phrase, 'How about tea?' during the conversation could mean, 'Take it easy', or more precisely, 'Regulate your breath'.

(Matsumoto 1984: 30–1)

This example, as Matsumoto himself admits, is grossly exaggerated and idealised; it is hard to imagine the average Japanese identifying comfortably with it. However, it is very illustrative of how an image of Japaneseness *vis-à-vis* Westernness is created in the *nihonjinron*.

Matsumoto's background is indicative of a type of thinking elite interested in discussing the Japanese patterns of behaviour and thought supposedly unique to Japan. Throughout his career, in which he held many different jobs such as an office worker in a large trading company, an English teacher, an American Embassy employee, an interpreter, a secretary to a top company director, a management consultant and a university professor, his chief concern was the mastery of communication in English with a strong emphasis on behavioural and mental differences between the Japanese and Americans for the practical purposes of international business. Such concerns are relevant to the question of which social groups play a major role in formulating and disseminating ideas of Japanese uniqueness.

It is frequently argued in the *nihonjinron* that essential communication is performed non-logically, empathetically and non-verbally. The sensitivity shown in the social interaction of the Japanese is considered to obviate the need for explicit and verbal communication, and the Japanese find aesthetic refinement in a person capable of non-verbal, indirect and subtle communication. Aida Yūji, a popular figure in the *nihonjinron*, quotes an anecdote recounted by another writer as an illustration of such subtle communication:

The husband comes home. He looks at the flowers in the alcove arranged by the wife. There is something disorderly about the arrangement and he senses that something is upsetting his wife – so he wonders what may have happened. Supposing that such a disorderly arrangement was deliberately made by the wife, I think that this [non-verbal style of conveying one's message] is very Japanese. For instance, the wife cannot possibly directly confront her mother-in-law and yet wants to make her husband aware of her trying experience [with the mother-in-law]. This difficult situation can be conveyed by such a means.

(Aida 1972: 100)

The non-verbal, empathetic and 'non-logical' mode of Japanese lin-guistic expression is a theme that has been touched upon frequently, dating well back to the eighteenth century. Motoori Norinaga (1730–1801), a scholar of *kokugaku* (national learning), labelled the Chinese approach 'pompous verbosity'. Motoori contrasted the Chinese rationality with the *mono no aware* (pathos of things),[5] the more intuitive and emotive approach, that was thought of as the symbol of the Japanese ethos. Later in early modern Japan, novelist Tanizaki Junichirō ([1934] 1974) reiterated a similar point in his *Bunshō Dokuhon* (Manual of Prose Composition). The objective, rational and verbal discourse of foreign speech was contrasted with the subjective, emotive and non-verbal nature of Japanese communi-cation. Tanizaki (1974: 118) attributed Japan's losing of the League of Nations' debate on Sino-Japanese conflict to the eloquence of the Chinese. Unlike the Chinese and Westerners who believe in the power of language, Tanizaki wrote, the Japanese respect the virtues of taciturnity.

Those patterns of communication of the Japanese which discour-age dichotomous logic and verbal confrontation are, as will be seen, closely related to their high evaluation of consensus and harmony in interpersonal relations, thereby reinforcing the view of Japanese society as group-oriented or 'interpersonalistic'.

Social culture

The Japanese social structure is characterised in the *nihonjinron* by groupism or 'interpersonalism' (or 'contextualism'), verticality and dependence (or other-directedness) in contrast to Western society which is characterised as having the opposite characteris-tics: individualism, horizontality and independence (self-autonomy). This aspect of Japaneseness has been most frequently and widely discussed in the *nihonjinron* of the 1970s and has developed into the most influential perspective on Japanese society. Among the many who have given a theoretical backing for this proposition, Nakane Chie (1967) and Doi Takeo (1971) are two of the most prominent.

Social anthropologist Nakane attempted to identify peculiarly Japanese forms of social organisation and interactions by using the key concept, 'vertical society'. By this, Nakane means, first, that 'the overall picture of society . . . is not that of horizontal stratification by class or caste but of vertical stratification by institution or group of institutions' (Nakane 1970: 87). The Japanese are thus described as a group-oriented people preferring to act within the framework of a group, typically, a company. Second, such a group is hierarchically organised based on the relationship between paternalistic superiors and their subordinates as well as the relationship between senior and junior group members or between members differentiated by the time of entry into the group (see chapter 5).

Psychiatrist Doi Takeo identified the psychological process supporting the vertical social structure as well as the socialisation process that enables the persistence of such social structural features and the transmission of such social culture. On the basis of his experience of treating Japanese and Western patients as a psychiatrist, Doi formed his conviction that *amae* is a key concept for exploring the essence of the Japanese personality. *Amae* is the noun form of *amaeru*, which roughly means 'to depend and presume upon another's goodwill'. The prototype of *amae* can be found in 'the feelings that all normal infants at the breast harbor toward the mother – dependence, the desire to be passively loved, the unwillingness to be separated from the warm mother–child circle' (Bester 1973: 7). It is Doi's contention that in Japanese society this attitude of dependence (*amae*) is prolonged into adulthood, thereby shaping the entire attitude of a Japanese person to other people. Dependence on another's benevolence is encouraged rather than discouraged during socialisation, so that a Japanese adult continues to seek emotional dependence in social relations other than the family, in the assumption that he has another's goodwill.

This type of dependency is considered to occur typically as a quasi-parent–child relationship in companies and political factions, where a person in a subordinate social position assumes the role of a child towards his superior who plays the role of a parent (see chapter 5). The child-role player can seek dependence (*amae*) upon the parent-role player for security and protection, and the latter is expected to display his benevolent *oyagokoro* (parental sentiment). The subordinate is expected to reciprocate his debt through loyal service. Reverse dependence of the superior on his subordinates is also possible just as parents seek affective and instrumental dependence upon their children when the parents are old.

Although literature on Japanese group orientation is immense,

Nakane and Doi are considered two of the most influential contemporary exponents of the 'group model' of Japanese society.[6] Nakane's
social structural theory has been supplemented by Doi's psychological theory, thereby constituting the two pillars of the 'group model'
which characterises the *nihonjinron*'s world view of Japanese society.[7]
In addition to the characteristics already discussed, 'groupism' or
'group orientation' (*shūdanshugi*) refers to a variety of phenomena
such as the individual's identification with and immersion into the
group, conformity and loyalty to group causes, selfless orientation
towards group goals, and consensus and the lack of conflict among
group members. A group in the context of industrial Japan means
primarily a company organisation. The term *shūdanshugi* began to be
used frequently in the late 1960s, especially in the context of business
organisation, management and industrial relations. Nakane, too,
devotes extensive discussion to social interactions, decision-making
and leadership within an enterprise.

Some argue, however, that the concept of groupism – often contrasted with individualism – does not accurately describe Japanese
patterns of behaviour and thought. Sociologist Hamaguchi Eshun
argues that the notion of *kanjinshugi* ('interpersonalism' or 'contextualism') is more appropriate.[8] Hamaguchi points out that
'what it really feels [to be part of the group for the Japanese]
in their everyday life is clearly different from [what is implied by]
the term "groupism"' and that it 'cannot be explained in terms of
group members' immersion into and loyalty to the organisation'
(Hamaguchi 1980: 37). He attributes this failure to the methodological problem that dichotomises the individual and the group. The
problem lies in the dichotomy between methodological individualism
and methodological holism, which regard the individual and the
group as analytical points of departure, respectively. Arguing that
such a Western-derived dichotomy cannot be applied to Japanese
society, where the fundamental form of human existence is neither the individual nor the group but rather the 'contextual' or
'interpersonal relationship', Hamaguchi introduces 'methodological
interpersonalism' as a perspective that transcends the dualism of the
individual and the group and thereby comprises what he regards as
a cogent analytical perspective on Japanese society (ibid.: 36–8).
Kanjinshugi (contextualism or interpersonalism) as a cultural value
is then set against individualism. Whereas individualism is characterised by such features as egocentricity, self-reliance and human
relation as a means, *kanjinshugi* (interpersonalism) is defined by

mutual dependence, mutual trust and human relation in itself (ibid.: 42–3). *Kanjinshugi* refers to 'the situation in which cooperation among group members is respected . . . or to the ideal which seeks symbiosis of the "individual" and the "group"' (ibid.: 38).

In *The Familial Society as a Civilisation*, Murakami Yasusuke, Kumon Shunpei and Sato Seizaburō (1979: 32) argue in a similar vein that the epistemological position concerning dualism between the individual and the group is the product of the Western experience of modernisation and, as such, does not fit the Japanese setting. The notion of groupism can imply unilateral influence or control by society over individual behaviour. Interpersonalism, on the other hand, gives the highest value to interpersonal relationship or inter-action, not to society as an entity. The notion of interpersonalism has thus been created to avoid Durkheimian sociologism which describes society as unilaterally determining the behaviour of the individual.[9]

The 'non-individualistic' nature of Japanese social culture is also discussed from a more psychoanalytic point of view, but this is too large a topic to be included in this chapter.[10]

Many writers of the *nihonjinron* attribute the group-oriented or 'interpersonalistic' nature of Japanese society to the earlier pro-ductive modes, maintaining that differences in productive base and dietary style have given rise to different cultural patterns in history: the Japanese, being agriculturalists (or rice cultivators), have developed a highly communal way of life; the Westerners, by contrast, are individualistic and aggressive because they are pastoralists and nomads.

Cultural anthropologist Ishida maintains that 'one clue to the dis-tinctiveness of Japanese culture is that it belongs to the rice-growing cultural sphere characterized by irrigated rice cultivation'. This, he says, is 'a basic factor from beginning to end' (1969: 110). Wheat culture is associated with pastoral economy. Rice cultivation, which requires cooperative labour, leads to the development of the family system and a close-knit community. The argument also quite often runs that the pastoral and nomadic mode of production leads to aggressive (masculine) interpersonal behaviour and bellicosity. An ideology of monotheism develops in order to fight against and to subordinate adversaries. The communal agricultural mode of Japan leads to opposite cultural traits. Aida Yūji (1962, 1972) is one of the scholars who has done much to popularise this type of thinking in the post-war period.[11] The following example is illustrative. Aida explains Japanese patterns of interpersonal communication in terms of ancient environmental conditions and modes of production:

> Hunting was the productive way of life of Europeans at the time when the European languages were being formed. Hunters must convey their messages clearly with one another in their coopera- tive work. If messages are put imprecisely and ambiguously, they cannot work together well and it is dangerous. [In this situation] the vocalised symbol – language – comes to refer to a specific object and to have a precise meaning.
>
> This is not the case with cooperation in food gathering and agriculture. Language formed under these conditions is intended to exchange the feelings of consideration, gratitude, encourage- ment and sympathy, which are unnecessary in hunting.
>
> (Aida 1972: 104–5)

This type of thinking also underlies Isaiah BenDasan's *The Japanese and the Jews*, the number-one best seller of all genres in 1970. The publication of this book was considered by many to have triggered the *nihonjinron* of the 1970s.[12]

BenDasan contrasts the geographical conditions of Japan and Israel as well as their earlier modes of production, agricultural and nomadic. He argues that Japan's modes of intensive rice production have caused the Japanese to master the virtues of cooperation and to value harmony and unanimous consent among the members of a community, whereas self-oriented behaviour was more suited to the nomadic lifestyle of the Jews. BenDasan then contrasts the Japanese and Jewish belief systems. Contrary to the religious Jews, BenDasan argues that 'the entire Japanese nation is a body of faithful followers of Nihonism [Japanism], which is based on human experience instead of on a covenant or body of dogma' (1972: 91). Nihonism in this sense is a 'secular religion'. As a humane religion, the principles of Nihonism are not articulated or codified into words and law. Nihonism allows the contradictions and ambivalences of 'human beingness' (*ningensei*). For the Japanese, *ningensei* is the primary source of moral value, and symbolic representations like words, reason and law remain of secondary significance. Whereas the Jews take words, reason and law literally, the Japanese attach utmost importance to 'words behind words', 'reason behind reason' and 'law behind law' (BenDasan 1970: 55–85). For example, BenDasan argues that, whereas religious dogma has intervened extensively into Jewish politics, political crises in Japan have been overcome by the 'restoration of mutual trust between man and man', and not by unilateral reliance upon a fixed law (ibid.: 73).

BenDasan's characterisation of the Japanese may be rephrased as the 'social preoccupation' and 'interactional relativism' of the Japanese (Lebra 1976: 1–21). The Japanese are described as being extremely sensitive to and concerned about social interaction and relationships and attach less importance to a more generalised criterion of judging conduct such as ideology or religious dogma.

'RACE THINKING'

The mode of thinking as manifested in the *nihonjinron* of the 1970s and the 1980s may be characterised not only as that of culturalism but also as what may be called 'race thinking'. At the base of the *nihonjinron* is an assumption concerning the 'racial' nature of Japanese identity. Built on this assumption is belief in the uniqueness of Japanese culture, the aspects of which have already been discussed. Let us now enquire into the 'racial' assumption in Japanese perceptions of their uniqueness.

In order to avoid possible misinterpretations, it is essential to clarify the way in which the concept of 'race' is used in this study. Historically, the term 'race' has been used in several different senses and can be quite misleading (see e.g. Banton 1983: 32–59; Van den Berghe 1978: 9–11).

Physical anthropologists used to conceive of races in the sense of sub-species of *homo sapiens* characterised by certain phenotypical and genotypical traits, such as negroid, mongoloid and caucasoid. But research over the last five decades or so has revealed that 'racial' boundaries are so blurred that no meaningful taxonomy of races is possible. Classification of numerous groups into distinct 'races' on the basis of phenotypical variation is an impossible task. There is also as great a genetic diversity within a supposedly distinct racial group as between supposedly different races. Thus, a biological concept of race has been refuted. None the less, the concept of race continues to be used in everyday social relations. Naturally, its usage is accompanied by ambiguities. For example, in the United States, a person of partially African ancestry is often regarded as black even though his outward appearance is white. The same person would be very likely to be called white in Brazil, where a black is someone of predominantly African ancestry. Also, Julian

Pitt-Rivers (1977: 318) provides an illustration in which a study was conducted in preparation for the 1950 census in Guatemala as to how an Indian should be defined. Having discovered that the definition of Indian had varied from one community to another, much of the census-taking had to be entrusted to local people who best knew how people were classified there.

The continued use of 'race' in everyday discourse has led social scientists to acknowledge the existence of socially constructed races, to define race by employing social actors' definition of the situation, and to use socially constructed races as analytical categories. Rex remarks that 'sociology being the kind of discipline it is, any attempt to define its field without taking into account actors' own subjective definitions of the situation must be seriously inadequate' (1970: 161). Similarly, Banton (e.g. 1977) uses socially constructed 'races' as analytical categories in his study of race relations.[13] Benedict Anderson's (1983) insight regarding nation as 'imagined community' (see chapter 3) may usefully be applied to 'race'. Like nation, 'race' is also imagined in the dual sense that it has no real biological foundation and that the members of the 'race' do not actually know most of their fellow members, 'yet in the minds of each lives the image of their communion' (ibid.: 15). Like the concept of nation, 'race' is also imagined as limited in that its members perceive its boundaries, beyond which lie other races. Like nation, 'race' is imagined as a community having a common and unified sense of comradeship. The only criterion of nation as 'imagined community' that does not apply to 'race' is sovereignty (Miles 1987: 26–7).

Socially constructed 'race' continues to exist in popular discourse when a person indicates 'difference that *seems to be* immutable'. By contrast, ethnicity signifies 'a possibility for change which "race" precludes' (Wallman 1986: 229). Here, ethnicity is regarded as an essentially cultural phenomenon, and culture can be acquired and changed.

The concept of 'race' is employed in this study with this understanding in mind: 'race' has no real biological foundation and is, first and foremost, socially constructed. 'Race' may thus be defined as a human group that perceives itself and/or is perceived by other groups as different from other groups by virtue of innate and immutable phenotypical and genotypical characteristics.[14]

There are two dimensions of what may be called 'race thinking' in Japan. The first concerns the notion of the 'Japanese race' itself; the second the relationship between 'race' and culture.

The invention of the 'Japanese race'

It has been widely held that Japanese society is uni-racial and homogeneous in its composition. Western society, by contrast, is poly-racial and heterogeneous in its make-up. The uni-racial (*tan'itsu minzoku*) and homogeneous composition of the Japanese has been widely assumed in the discussion of Japanese uniqueness. The uni-racial assumption may be divided into three related yet distinct aspects.

First, although there is no such entity as the 'Japanese race' in the objective sense, the Japanese have tended to perceive themselves as a distinct 'racial' group. 'Race', along with a unique culture, is an important element of Japanese identity. Perception of phenotypical difference is not the only basis upon which a group can be racialised, as Lee and DeVos state with reference to Koreans in Japan: 'although most Koreans are physically indistinguishable from Japanese, they nonetheless continue to be considered racially distinct by Japanese' (1981: 356). Imagination of 'genotypical' difference can also be a basis for racial categorisation. Kunihiro Masao remarks with reference to the Japanese view of Japanese nationality that 'what makes a Japanese, more than anything else, is "blood"' (1972: 34). He refers to this mode of thinking critically as *junketsu-shugi* (pure-blood-ism). The idiom 'Japanese blood' is used in popular speech to refer to that aspect of Japanese identity which tends to be perceived as immutable by the Japanese. (The word 'race' [*jinshu*] as such is not used to refer to Japanese people.) Belief in the 'immutable' quality of Japanese people is just as important as, if not more important than, belief in distinctive Japanese culture in Japanese perceptions of their national identity, as is typically shown in the statement '*You have to be born a Japanese* to understand Japanese mentality'. A Japanese expresses the 'immutable' or 'natural' aspect of Japanese identity through the imagined concept of 'Japanese blood'. Since a scientifically founded 'racial' classification of the Japanese and non-Japanese is meaningless, 'Japanese blood' is, first and foremost, a case of social construction of difference. But as Wallman remarks that the 'differences observed and the way they are interpreted say as much about the classifier as about the classified' (1986: 229), the fictive notion of 'Japanese blood' reveals much about the way in which the Japanese perceive their supposedly 'immutable' difference. My interest lies in analysing how and why this quasi-racial notion is used in the symbolic boundary process to define 'us' Japanese against 'them' non-Japanese, rather than encouraging the erroneous view of the Japanese as a distinct 'race'.

The second aspect of the uni-racial ideology is a constant emphasis on the homogeneous composition of Japanese people as if to disregard the historical process whereby many peoples fused with one another to form the 'Japanese race' in the past. Anthropologist Masuda Yoshio remarks that, unlike in Europe where there was the continual mixing of blood and culture, the Japanese, as a 'pure-blood people' (*junketsu no minzoku*), have peacefully protected and nurtured their homogeneity without engaging in conflicts with other peoples (*minzoku*) (1967: 42). Ethnologist Ishida Eiichiro similarly stresses that excessive consanguinity and endogamy within a people, which normally decreases ethnic vitality and vigor, have produced favourable results for the Japanese, enabling the Japanese to assimilate one new foreign culture after another without disruption (Ishida 1969: 156). The Japanese historically formed an image of themselves as a 'racially' distinct and homogeneous people. Despite this myth, the Japanese, like all other peoples, are the product of a long period of mixture. Archaeology and historical records show a flow of peoples from north-eastern Asia through the Korean peninsula into Japan before the eighth century AD when the northern part of the country was still inhabited by the Ainu. It is supposed that there was an earlier flow of people from more southerly regions such as South-east Asia and the South Pacific.[15]

The third aspect of the uni-racial ideology is a lack of adequate attention given to the presence in Japan of minorities such as Koreans, Chinese and Ainu. The existence of race relations in Japan have not generally been consciously felt until recently partly because Koreans, the largest minority,[16] are physically indistinguishable and partly because Japanese scholars have tended to refrain from touching upon minority groups in Japan in their writings.[17]

The *nihonjinron* literature quite often contains the phrase 'the Japanese are *tan'itsu minzoku*'. *Tan'itsu* means 'one' or 'uni', but *minzoku* is a multi-vocal term which, reflecting the Japanese situation, means not only race but ethnic community and nation. Racial, ethnic and national categories almost completely overlap in the Japanese perception of themselves. *Tan'itsu minzoku* is used as a convenient phrase to indicate the homogeneity of Japanese people without specifying whether one is referring to their racial or cultural features. In this connection, Kamishima Jirō maintains that, during the '*nihonjinron* boom', homogeneity has been used as an easy and erroneous explanation for so-called distinctively Japanese characteristics such as harmonious interpersonal relationships, group conformity and consensus (1980: 64–76). The homogeneous/heterogeneous contrast is often used to explain Japanese/Western differences in social and cultural characteristics, such as patterns of communication, social stability and so on.

It is also important to note that the uni-racial ideology of the Japanese was closely associated with the notion held before and during the Second World War of Japan as the family-nation (or family-state) of divine origin (see chapter 5). Members of the family-nation were perceived to be related 'by blood' to one another and ultimately to the emperor. The concept of the family-nation represents what Armstrong calls 'the racialisation of the imagined community' (1989: 338). Kinship, religion and race were fused with one another to produce an intensely felt collective sense of 'oneness'.

An additional remark may be made here on the notion of 'race' as an element of national identity in Japan. Race is a symbol that evokes strong psychological response. 'Race' for the Japanese is closely concerned with positive identification of the in-group. Here, I disagree with the proposition that, whereas ethnicity is concerned with positive identification of 'us', race deals with negative categorisation of 'them' (see Banton 1983: 106). While this may be largely true of British and American race relations, we should recognise the existence of such a notion as 'Japanese blood', which is used for the positive identification of 'us' Japanese. The distinction between two similar notions, sign and symbol, is useful here (Wallman 1981: 121). 'Japanese blood' is not merely a sign or the abstraction of the object it stands for – since it is an imaginary notion it does not stand for any object, anyway – but a symbol which 'stands for a complex set of emotional and intellectual dispositions' (Firth 1973: 228). 'To it are assigned meanings of a complex kind of which the individual is by all evidence unconscious or only partly conscious' (ibid.: 225). The symbol of 'Japanese blood' evokes the stable sense of 'us' and 'our' identity by representing a complex set of meanings and emotive associations concerning Japanese identity. If ethnicity is a collectivity of people defined by virtue of a belief in shared culture and history, race focuses upon, and exaggerates, a particular aspect

of ethnicity, that is, kinship and kin lineage.[18] Here, race is a marker
that strengthens ethnic identity. The symbol of 'Japanese blood'
generates, and is generated by, an image that 'we' are members of
the extended family that has perpetuated its lineage. Furthermore,
the notion of 'Japanese blood' assumes the existence of distinct
racial groups, which is predicated upon the assumption of breeding
isolation. This assumption enhances psychological distance between
the in-group and others, generating the sense that 'we' Japanese
people have been formed within 'our' own circles and in isolation
from others and that 'we' are the product of this special formative
experience. The symbol of 'Japanese blood' thus facilitates the image
that the Japanese possess unique qualities.

'Japanese blood', as suggested, is not so obviously a 'racial' concept
as the term 'blood' suggests. It is socially invented *not* to refer
to genetic traits as such *but* to mould and channel psychological responses concerning 'we'-ness and 'them'-ness. The difference
between race and ethnicity is not clear-cut. The ways in which the
Japanese perceive 'immutable' difference from non-Japanese tend to
fluctuate, as will be seen in chapter 6 where our respondents' views
often flowed unsystematically from one statement to another. Given
an opportunity to think about 'Japanese blood' consciously, the
Japanese would certainly deny its scientific value. But the symbolic
image it generates, and the collective sentiment expressed in it, still
make it an effective 'boundary marker'. Usage changes over time,
and the changes in the usage of the concept 'race' reflect changes
in the popular understanding of the *difference* of a people from
other peoples. It is quite possible that, when international contact
(especially international marriage) becomes more common and as
the myth of 'Japanese blood' loses its explanatory force, sociologists
will no longer have to use the notion of 'race' and may comfortably
replace it with that of 'ethnicity' to describe the Japanese perception
of their identity.

The preceding considerations already suggest that 'race' (or
quasi-race, to be more precise) is closely associated with culture
in the discussions of Japanese uniqueness.

'Race' and culture

The second aspect of 'race thinking' among the Japanese closely
associates unique Japanese culture with the 'Japanese race'. In

'race thinking' – not necessarily that of racism – racial and cultural differences are closely related. Such a relationship may be divided analytically into two separate propositions:

1 that genetically transmitted traits determine (or condition) cultural traits (genetic determinism);
2 that particular cultural traits should belong to, or are the exclusive property of, a particular group with particular phenotypical and genotypical traits ('racially exclusive possession of a particular culture').

For example, a nineteenth-century notion, which was used to rationalise British colonial expansion, claimed that 'the "inferior African races" lacked the capacity for self-government because of their supposedly inherent savagery and childishness' (Miles 1982b: 285). This notion refers to, or emphasises, the first aspect (genetic determinism). South African apartheid 'places an extreme emphasis on cultural difference in a situation of increasing acculturation and seeks to reverse the trend towards a common culture by policies of education and segregation' (Kuper 1974: 28). To say this is to emphasise the second aspect ('racially exclusive possession of a particular culture'). This is not to suggest, of course, that in South Africa the first aspect is lacking. I am simply maintaining that, although these aspects can overlap, it is analytically useful to make the distinction.

Genetic determinism or a deterministic relationship between biological characteristics and cultural attributes is the more familiar form of the association between race and culture and has often been equated with racism *tout court*.[19] The term racism itself is a relatively new one. One of the first scholars to have used the term critically and extensively was Ruth Benedict who wrote that 'racism is the dogma that one ethnic group is condemned by nature to congenital inferiority and another group is destined to congenital superiority' ([1942] 1983: 97). Michael Banton posits the kernel of this doctrine in the assertions: '(a) that people's cultural and psychological characteristics are genetically determined; and (b) the genetic determinants are grouped in patterns that can be identified with human races in the old morphological sense that envisaged the existence of pure races' (Banton 1970: 17–18). Banton then defines racism as 'the doctrine that a man's behaviour is determined by stable inherited characters deriving from separate racial stocks having distinctive attributes and usually considered to stand to one another in relations of superiority and inferiority' (ibid.: 18).

Returning now to the Japanese case, one might say that it represents racism in the sense of being genetic determinism, because the Japanese are strongly aware of their 'racial' and cultural distinctiveness from other peoples and because they closely associate 'race' and culture. In the 'race thinking' of the Japanese, the second aspect ('racially exclusive possession of a particular culture') predominates over the first (genetic determinism). The concept of 'property' suitably expresses that sense of Japanese uniqueness, since possessiveness is its main attribute.[20] Exclusive ownership is claimed upon certain aspects of Japanese culture.

The other point concerns the Westerners' sense of difference as fundamentally one of superiority. This is understandable as racism arose in the West as an ideology to rationalise colonial expansion and domination. The sense of difference of the Japanese from the others (Westerners) in the prevalent discussions of Japanese uniqueness has been basically that of horizontal difference or difference in kind. (This does not mean that the sense of superiority is absent among the Japanese as in the case of their attitude towards the Korean minority in Japan.) Many of the *nihonjinron* of the 1970s have presented the image of the Japanese as simply being very different without explicitly claiming superiority, though some literature has discussed the strengths of Japanese society, as will be seen in detail in chapters 7, 8 and 9. The important point to be noted here is that explicit claims of Japanese superiority have not been so common as non-Japanese readers, who may equate the Western style of racism with race thinking *tout court*, might have supposed.

The *nihonjinron* offer abundant examples that suggest that Japanese culture belongs exclusively to the Japanese people ('Japanese race'). Many writers of the *nihonjinron* have inferred in one way or another the 'uniquely Japanese' mode of thinking from Japanese phrases which, they assume, defy translation, suggesting that one has to be born a Japanese to be able to grasp the intricacy and delicacy of the Japanese language. For example, Watanabe Shōichi, professor of English Literature, writes that the spirit of the Japanese language is 'as old as our blood' (1974: 8). He observes that, though he knows of some Europeans whose Japanese is accurate and quite fluent, and though some Korean residents in Japan have won literary awards for their Japanese prose or fiction, he knows of no foreigner who can write good *waka* or thirty-one syllable Japanese poetry (ibid.: 105–6). He does not go so far as to say, however, that the spirit of the Japanese language is genetically transmitted. What he suggests is that it 'belongs exclusively' to the Japanese in the sense that it can be truly appreciated only by the Japanese. The analytical importance of the distinction I have proposed earlier may be illustrated here. In an attempt to reveal what he regards as the 'racistic' thinking of Watanabe, Wetherall summarises Watanabe as saying that 'the spirit of Japanese language and its poetic expression is all but *genetically transmitted*' (1981: 299–300, emphasis added), but this shows Wetherall's failure to distinguish the two distinct types of thinking.

One might argue that, if certain cultural features are claimed to belong exclusively to a particular race, it logically follows that such features are hereditary. But in reality this is not the case and the two should be distinguished. An explanation for this is provided based on a close analysis of respondents' perceptions of the different dimensions of the relationship between culture and race in chapter 6 (see pp. 115–21).

To argue that genetic determinism and 'racially exclusive possession of a particular culture' are distinct does not mean that genetic determinism is totally absent among the Japanese. There is a strong Japanese interest in the relationship between blood type and personality traits as a case of genetic deterministic thinking. Since this subject is not directly related to the *nihonjinron*,[21] it will suffice to focus only briefly on two post-war popularisers of the 'theory', Nomi Masahiko and Suzuki Yoshimasa, who produced a number of books in the first half of the 1970s (see Hayashida 1976).

In pre-war Japan, the study of blood types was closely associated with the classification of racial types and verification of the claim that the Japanese and the Koreans were of different races. But a theory also developed to link blood type with temperament and with ethnic character. Although the German influence on blood studies between 1900 and 1930 cannot be denied, the tradition of a study of blood had already existed in Japan.[22] Following Japan's defeat in 1945, the subject of blood types disappeared from the scholarly scene and the lull continued until the 1970s, when post-war constraints on some of the themes asserted in pre-war and wartime Japan were expected to have diminished. The fact that the re-emergence of this topic in the 1970s was not met with any significant criticism may suggest a difference in the way this topic was dealt with in the West and Japan. Japan's post-war intellectual history has lacked an *actively conscious* refutation of genetic determinism as has been the case in the West, perhaps because Japan's pre-war racialistic ideology did not formulate genetic determinism as explicitly and articulately as occurred in the West.

Most Japanese are favourably oriented to the topic of blood type and personality/temperament although they may be vague about the actual content of the relationship.[23] Blood type information is very frequently sought when a person's personality and temperament are discussed, and in this sense it is rather similar to the Western horoscope. Some of the popular subjects include: blood types and congeniality between sexes; the ways of developing one's latent talents deriving from one's blood type; skills required for dealing with persons with particular blood types in social and business settings.[24] Stimulated by numerous publications of books on this topic in the first half of the 1970s, it has become common for mass circulation magazines to carry information on blood type and its relation to various aspects of social life.

An emphasis is *almost always* given to the relation of blood types to the personality traits of individuals, not to ethnic character. But the former can suggest the latter, as Nomi himself states: 'Considering that blood type is reflected in temperament at the level of the individual, it logically follows that it has something to do with ethnic character' (1973: 53). Suzuki is even more explicit on this point. Suzuki remarks that the Japanese character has not changed very much for the last hundred years because

> blood type is hereditary . . . [and because] the relative proportion of four blood types for an ethnic group remains almost constant. This means that . . . national and ethnic character passes on in a heridtary manner from parent to child and from child to grandchild, thereby persisting indefinately.
>
> (Suzuki 1973: 222–3)

Nomi argues that, because the Japanese are a well-mixed ethnic group with a highly uniform distribution of blood types throughout the country and because type A has the largest representation, the A-type character may be strongly reflected in the Japanese character. Some of the characteristics associated with type A are: 'diligence, group consciousness, formalism, respect of tradition and customs, lack of individual assertion, superficial politeness and in-group exclusiveness, skills for practical improvements rather than creativity, and preference of situational ethics to ideology'

(Nomi 1973: 54). Suzuki, too, suggests a relationship between blood types and national character by taking an interest in the rank ordering of types A, B and O. (For example, AOB means that type A is most largely represented among a particular group followed by O and B.) Suzuki focuses on the two common patterns, OAB and AOB: the former is represented by the Americans and the latter by the Germans and the Japanese. He argues that the Japanese and the Germans have much in common; for example, they are both 'introverted, concerned with details, and emotional' (Suzuki 1973: 218).[25]

It has not been my intent to argue that most Japanese accept these ideas on blood type. However, these writings and ideas could not have emerged if there had been a conscious rejection of genetic determinism. An interest in blood type in general may be taken as one indication that genetic determinism exists among the Japanese, but this should not be conflated with what I call the 'racially exclusive possession of particular cultural characteristics' which best describes the Japanese perception of their uniqueness.

THE INTROSPECTION BOOM OF THE 1950s

The *nihonjinron* was not the only case of intense national self-appraisal in post-war Japan. The first such 'boom' occurred in the period immediately following Japan's defeat in the Second World War. Since the 'introspection boom' of the late 1940s and 1950s set the tone for the subsequent style of discussion of Japanese characteristics prior to the emergence of the *nihonjinron* in the 1970s, it is necessary to make at least brief mention of the 'introspection boom' of the early post-war years.

Of the literature on the peculiarities of Japanese society published during this period, Ruth Benedict's *The Chrysanthemum and the Sword* (1946, 1948) occupies a special place, with its significant impact on post-war Japanese studies. As a cultural anthropologist, Benedict is well-known for her *Patterns of Culture* (1934). At the time this was published, the dominant trend in anthropology was functionalism, represented by Malinowsky and Radcliffe-Brown. Functionalism may be called a holistic approach in that it explains social practices in terms of their contribution to society as a whole. Strange customs made sense when their total context was understood.[26] Benedict's approach was also holistic, but of a different kind. Unlike functionalists who assumed the commonality of human motivations regardless of the variety of cultures, Benedict maintained that motivations (or 'drives'), and the priority of motivations, varied from one culture to another. Benedict's main concern was to analyse the characteristic 'culture patterns' of various peoples, with special reference to value systems and corresponding personality types. Her approach was 'holistic' in the sense that she was concerned with a search of a rational whole – which she called 'patterns of culture' – behind complex, often seemingly contradictory, behavioural manifestations of a culture.

Benedict was assigned by the American government to study Japanese patterns of behaviour in 1944 and was forced by the situation to depend only on the data available in America. By interviewing Japanese-Americans in America and examining Japanese films and literature, Benedict explored the coherent 'patterns of Japanese culture' behind seeming contradictions in Japanese behaviour. In her attempt to grasp Japanese society as a rational whole, she stressed the hierarchical nature of order in Japanese society, arguing that one was expected to know one's place (*bun*) in society because the proper placing of people allows for dignity of behaviour in all strata of society, even in the lower strata. In order to describe and explain what she saw as the hierarchical nature of order among the Japanese, she further made an extensive analysis of the 'uniquely Japanese' concepts such as *on* (normative obligation) and *giri* (socially contracted dependence) in the context of the parent–child relationship and quasi-parent–child relationship. Probably the best-known of her conclusions concerning Japanese culture is the characterisation of Japan as a 'shame culture', in which individuals are controlled by social threats to personal honour and reputation, in contrast to the West as a 'guilt culture' in which individuals are controlled by internal sanction against the violation of a moral standard.[27]

The Japanese translation of *The Chrysanthemum and the Sword* was published in 1948, to which Japanese scholars were quick to respond. This itself illustrates the extent of its impact on Japanese scholarship. In particular, the journal *Minzokugaku kenkyū* (Ethnological Studies) (1950) carried reviews and criticisms by a number of prominent social scientists, including Yanagita Kunio, a pioneer of Japan's folklore studies, and Aruga Kizaemon, a leading sociologist. Criticisms were made on such grounds as her limited data sources; her simplistic generalisation about the patterns of behaviour of the Japanese on the basis of the behaviour of military officers (Watsuji 1950); her treatment of Japan as a monolithic whole and a neglect of stratificational and occupational differences (Minami 1950); and her ahistorical approach ignoring the aspects of change (Kawashima 1950).[28]

Benedict's theories of Japan are already well-known and a number of reviews of this work are available in English.[29] Despite criticisms, there is no question about the prominent place that *The Chrysanthemum and the Sword* has enjoyed in post-war Japanese studies. It not only stimulated subsequent discussions of the uniqueness of the Japanese patterns of behaviour both in Japan and abroad, but also suggested the type of enquiry that later scholars could develop. In particular, Benedict's holistic concern with 'culture patterns' strongly influenced post-war studies of Japanese society. John W. Hall remarks:

> Benedict was not, of course, the first to apply the techniques of anthropological study of Japan. John Embree was surely the real pioneer in that respect. But Benedict, because of her wide reputation and because of the ambitiousness of her effort to understand the Japanese people as a totality, came to symbolize an approach which was, and still is, of prime importance to American scholarship.
>
> (Hall 1971: 24)

The holistic concern fitted smoothly into Japanese intellectual culture, too, which had its own tradition of perceiving Japanese society in a holistic manner (see chapter 5).

The Chrysanthemum and the Sword may not be called a genuinely anthropological work because it is not based on fieldwork. But Benedict's contribution should probably not be assessed simply on grounds of scientific rigour. Empathetic insights are also necessary in a study of this sort, that is, a study of the cultural ethos and world view of a people. In fact, the intuitiveness of Benedict as a poet probably contributed much to her understanding of the Japanese people, as suggested by Margaret Mead, who remarks that the poetic side of Benedict's nature is evident in this work (1959: xvi). There is, however, only a thin line between intuition and speculation, and between creative work of an insightful scholar and the superficial observations of a second-rate scholar. Benedict certainly belongs to the first category, but she may have encouraged the emulation of this sort of 'intuitive' approach among later writers of Japanese uniqueness, whose intuition and insight may not necessarily equal those of Benedict. As Moriguchi and Hamaguchi indicate, Benedict showed Japanese scholars that the 'anthropology' of the everyday patterns of behaviour – rather than the more serious study of culture – could be an interesting and acceptable approach in Japanese studies (1964: 659).

In addition to *The Chrysanthemum and the Sword*, there are a series of works Japanese thinkers produced to identify the peculiarities of Japanese social culture and to characterise them as feudalistic obstacles to the democratisation of Japan. Numerous works of this kind were published from the early 1950s. Among the works by scholars were sociologist Kawashima Takeyoshi's *The Familial Structure of Japanese Society* (1950), anthropological geographer Iizuka Kōji's *The Mental Climate of Japan* (1952) and social psychologist Minami Hiroshi's *The Psychology of the Japanese* (1953).

One of the main characteristics of the 'introspection boom' of this period is the negative evaluation of Japanese peculiarities. Sakuta Keiichi points out that 'the most widespread and common theme among thinkers for three to four years following Japan's defeat was the criticism of the legacies of feudalism' (1971: 379) and that the theme of democratisation preoccupied the minds of thinkers of various disciplinary and ideological backgrounds. What is important is that the criticisms of the legacies of feudalism did not end with political and legal institutions but went far down to the social and cultural features and to national character. Iizuka Kōji's remark is illustrative of this mood of Japan's intellectual culture at that time: 'Democratisation has to be a serious spiritual revolution on the part of each individual rather than a reform of legal institutions' (1952: 217). Kawashima Takeyoshi (1950) argued that pre-modern and undemocratic social relations in Japan could be attributed to the pre-modern family institution and that reform of this institution would be a prerequisite for the democratisation of Japanese society. Similarly, Iizuka (1952) maintained that the traditional patterns of social relations such as a hierarchical relationship between a paternalistic leader and his followers and familistic nationalism based on feudalistic familism were at the root of the undemocratic nature of Japanese society. (On the family system and other social characteristics of pre-industrial Japan, see chapter 5.)

Probably the most typical work reflecting the self-critical mood of this period was Kishida Kunio's *A Theory of the Abnormalities of the Japanese* (1947), in which self-criticism went so far as to describe the Japanese mental character as 'abnormal' in contrast to the 'normal' mentality of Westerners. Several scholars warned against becoming too self-abusive for fear of the danger of ever abandoning the real virtues of Japan.[30] It may be said, however, that the negative view of the peculiarities of Japanese society characterised the attitude of the general educated public during this period. This is also shown by the fact that a book portraying Japanese character with a self-critical style became the number-one best seller in 1951. Contrasting Europe and Japan, journalist Tsukasa Shintarō (1951) criticised the Japanese for lacking a sense of self-autonomy and independence and urged them to develop rationality and a greater sense of independence.

In a study of best sellers in post-war Japan, Tsujimura Akira (1981), professor of journalism, contrasted the two number-one best sellers on Japanese character, Tsukasa's *On the Ways of Looking at Things* (1951) and BenDasan's *The Japanese and the Jews* (1970), and maintained that, whereas Tsukasa appealed to the reader by being critical of the Japanese character in the period immediately following Japan's defeat in the Second World War, BenDasan made a more favourable observation of the Japanese. Tsujimura argues that this is symbolic of the change that had taken place in these two decades. Unlike the self-critical 'introspection boom' of the late 1940s and 1950s, the *nihonjinron* of the 1970s threw a more positive light on some of those features previously regarded as defects of the Japanese. However, the explicit assertion of Japanese superiority was rare. Most of the *nihonjinron* simply focused on Japanese *difference*. One of the reasons for this was that the earlier introspective and critical mood of post-war opinion had long set the style and tone for subsequent discussions of the Japanese, creating a norm that inhibited the explicit expression of superiority.

CONCLUDING REMARKS

The *nihonjinron* is an important intellectual pillar of cultural nationalism in contemporary Japan, but this does not mean that those scholars discussed in this chapter can simplistically be regarded as 'nationalists'. Whether or not the writers of Japanese uniqueness are themselves cultural nationalists depends on the way in which the term nationalism, which has diverse connotations, is used. If cultural nationalism is understood in a rather 'positive' sense to mean a set of ideas and activities which regenerates the national community by creating, preserving or strengthening a people's cultural identity when it is felt to be lacking, inadequate or threatened, it is probably appropriate to regard almost everyone quoted in this chapter as having promoted cultural nationalism, either consciously or unconsciously.

Nationalism can also acquire negative connotations, and cultural nationalism in contemporary Japan, too, can and often does produce what many probably agree to be undesirable effects. Ideas about Japanese distinctiveness can have negative effects depending on the manner and the context in which they are discussed. Particularly important in this regard is neglect of commonality between Japanese and non-Japanese. Mere emphasis of the Japanese difference from, and neglect of similarity with, other peoples as a way of defining Japanese identity promotes a strong and problematic feeling of 'unique us'. The assumption that uniquely Japanese modes of thinking and behaving are incomprehensible for non-Japanese tends to hinder social communication between Japanese and foreign residents and the latter's integration into social life in Japan. Furthermore, emphasis of Japan's cultural distinctiveness as an explanation of Japan's economic, social and other strengths also results in the enhancement of nationalist sentiment. This is especially so when such phenomena as Japan's economic productivity, comparatively few overt industrial disputes, relatively low unemployment rate and relatively low rate of serious crimes are explained solely by the supposedly unique and harmonious culture of Japan, thus being considered as examples of the 'cultural victory' of the Japanese. This hinders a more balanced understanding of Japanese society.

The writers of the *nihonjinron* should not simplistically be called 'nationalist ideologues' because most of them were probably not aware of what specific ideology they were propagating and of the effects their activities might have on the rest of the population. For example, it has been pointed out earlier in this chapter that one motivation behind the thinking elites' concern with Japanese uniqueness in the 1970s (and 1980s) was to promote better communication between the Japanese and non-Japanese through the exploration and articulation of the peculiarities of Japanese behaviour, which were assumed to be a possible obstacle to intercultural communication. Conscious recognition of the peculiarities of Japanese behaviour was therefore considered to be a step towards better intercultural understanding. The good intentions of many discussants of Japanese uniqueness (e.g. Kunihiro) should be mentioned here. The many thinkers who participated in the exploration and discussion of Japanese distinctiveness included those who – reflecting on ultra-nationalism in the Second World War and determined not to repeat the errors of narrow-minded nationalism – wanted to see the emergence of internationally-minded Japanese who could communicate effectively with foreigners and could make real contributions to understanding between people of different cultures. However, the resulting large increase in the discussions of Japanese uniqueness had the effect of emphasising the Japanese difference to the extent that commonality between the Japanese and non-Japanese was forgotten, and that foreign residents were assumed from the beginning not to understand Japanese people because of the latter's supposedly unique mode of thinking and behaving. What started as a well-intentioned activity to facilitate international understanding thus often had the unintended and ironic consequence of obstructing communication by sensitising the Japanese excessively to their distinctiveness. Criticism of the *nihonjinron* became noticeable in the early 1980s, and many writers and commentators have become more cautious about the manner in which characteristics of Japanese society and culture are discussed. Some of those writers whose ideas have been introduced in this chapter can no longer be classified as participants in the *nihonjinron*. The time factor must be taken into account. Perceptions and expressions of national identity are never static and are constantly changing.[31]

Moreover, different scholars had different reasons for discussing Japanese peculiarities, and even when scholars emphasised the same peculiar aspects of Japan, it does not necessarily mean that they shared the same political orientation. This applies not merely to the writers of the *nihonjinron* but also to students of Japanese society in general interested in analysing characteristics of the society in cultural terms. Japan, like any other society, is different from – and at the same time similar to – other societies, and culture certainly explains part of the difference. In fact, some of the ideas of Japanese characteristics lead to interesting insights about Japanese society and may be pursued seriously in further comparative, if not contrastive, studies.

The aim of this study is not to attempt to identify 'nationalists' among the thinking elites, but rather to explore the effects, intended or unintended, which the thinking elites' ideas of Japanese uniqueness (*nihonjinron*) have had on the rest of the Japanese population regarding the promotion of cultural nationalism.

Chapter 3

Ideas of national distinctiveness: comparative perspectives[1]

Most of those scholars who criticise the *nihonjinron* assume the Japanese preoccupation with national distinctiveness to be unique to Japan's intellectual culture – thereby arguing on the same plane as many of those engaged in the endless discussion of Japanese uniqueness. In fact, national distinctiveness as a theme of intellectual enquiry is widespread, and ideas of national distinctiveness need to be examined in general terms to provide a comparative framework within which to locate the contemporary Japanese experience of the *nihonjinron* and cultural nationalism.

In general, two groups are prominent in cultural nationalism: intellectuals or thinking elites, who formulate ideas of the nation's cultural identity, and the intelligentsia who respond to such ideas and relate them to their own social, economic and political or other interests and activities. This chapter first examines the part played by intellectuals in exploring and formulating ideas of national distinctiveness in various national and historical contexts and, second, enquires into the ways in which ideas of national distinctiveness, once formulated, are diffused in society.

INTELLECTUALS AND IDEAS OF NATIONAL DISTINCTIVENESS

Intellectuals' concern with ideas of national distinctiveness is by no means unique to Japan's intellectual culture. As the discussion proceeds, however, some differences will be observed in the ways in which intellectuals formulate ideas of national distinctiveness depending on different national and historical settings. Through international and historical comparisons and contrasts of various types of intellectuals' concern with national distinctiveness, the contemporary Japanese experience of the *nihonjinron* and cultural nationalism will eventually be properly located in a broader comparative and theoretical perspective.

At the outset and on the basis of two historical examples (those of Turkey and India), some generalisations will be attempted concerning the activities of intellectuals who articulate ideas of national distinctiveness. It is important to include the Indian case because the experience of colonisation was more of a rule than an exception in non-Western countries and the Indian case was typically anti-colonial. By contrast, Turkey, like Japan, was not subjected to formal political control by Western powers during the formative period of becoming a nation-state. Also, although nationalism took very different forms in very different circumstances in Japan and Turkey, the Turkish case may usefully be considered for our purpose in that cultural nationalists in these two cases were concerned to separate 'culture' from 'civilisation' or to define nationality *vis-à-vis* 'civilisation'. Turkey confronted not only Western civilisation but also had experience of another 'great civilisation', that of Islam. (The Japanese also confronted two great civilisations – China and the West – in their attempts to define national identity.)

Example 1: Turkish cultural nationalism

The Turks had long been well aware and proud of their place in the history of Islam, but this was 'as Ottomans, not as members of a Turkish nation' (Kushner 1977: 1). Early sporadic signs of Turkish ethnic consciousness were seen in the fourteenth century and the first half of the fifteenth century, when Anatolian poets sought to go back to pure Turkish expressions without Arabic and Persian elements and the official Ottoman history cited stories of early Turkish history (ibid.: 2).

The distinctiveness of Turkish culture became a major focus among Turkish scholars particularly in the 1890s, when 'Turkism' emerged emphasising the ethnic past of the Turks themselves rather than the territorial and political nature of the empire or the Islamic past of the Muslim–Turkish Ottomans, which Ottomanism and Islamism, the previous ideological movements of the mid-nineteenth century, had emphasised in their turn.[2] Turkish culture was viewed as the nation's own creation, reflecting its distinctive history. Numerous books and newspaper and magazine articles were written on

Turkish writers, poets, musicians, artists and scholars. Although earlier works did not clearly distinguish Turkish from Islamic heritage, distinct attempts emerged to assert the Turk's own cultural heritage and creations.[3] Language was the main preoccupation but was viewed as only one element of the national culture which also included, among other things, literature, poems, music and visual arts (ibid.: ch. 7)

Turkists such as Necib Asım argued that the Turks had already possessed their own distinct language and literature before Arabic and Persian influences became dominant, thus calling attention to the Turks' previous neglect of their own indigenous language and literature. This Turkist movement led to a call for language reform based on the language of the people. In the area of prosody, some writers argued that the *aruz* meter, taken from the Arabs and Persians and used in Ottoman poetry, did not suit the distinctive structure of Turkish and advocated the use of the original Turkish syllabic meter, based on that used in folk poetry. Moreover, Necib Asım emphasised the existence of indigenous classics not only in Ottoman but in Chagtay and other Turkic languages, some of which he regarded as superior to those of Europeans (Kushner 1977: 82–5). Some musicologists and writers also called attention to an indigenous Turkish music with its distinctive melodies, meters and harmonies that could be found among the people despite foreign influences, especially from Persian music. The Turkish musicologist, Rauf Yekta sought to establish a theoretical basis for distinctively Turkish music, to write its history and to record it (ibid.: 85–6). In visual art, too, Celâl Esad regarded Turkish art as possessing its own original character despite influences from Arabs, Persians and Byzantines. The realms of daily behaviour, morals and customs were also discussed as part of national culture (ibid.: 86).

In 1908 the scholarly Turkish Society (*Türk Derneği*) was founded to study and make known the history, culture and society of the Turks. A more systematic and political form of Turkism emerged with the appearance of the journal *Türk Yurdu* (Turkish Homeland), founded by literary figures. In 1912 Ziya Gökalp (1876–1924), a poet and prominent theoretician of Turkism, became its editor, and under his leadership it became an influential journal for theoretical issues of Turkism (Lewis 1968: 349–51).

With the help of Durkheimian sociology and notions derived from Romanticism, Gökalp systematised ideas, hitherto expressed only in a scattered manner, into a coherent doctrine of Turkism. His analysis centred on what he perceived to be the basic malaise in Turkish society, which he attributed to a lack of adjustment between the two essential but distinct aspects of social life, civilisation (*medenîyet*) and culture (*hars*). For Gökalp, civilisation refers to rational modes of action composed of what he calls the 'traditions' which are imposed upon individuals by their common civilisation, whereas culture consists of 'mores' which represent the specific ethos of a particular nation and which are, consequently, unique. Civilisation 'never penetrates into the inner life of a people'; it assumes meaning and role in the life of people only when it serves culture (Berkes 1954: 384). As Berkes put it, theocratic civilisation in Turkey and perhaps in other Muslim countries 'had come to be a mere skeleton corroding and annihilating all cultural flesh and blood of the social body' (ibid.). The impact of Western civilisation added another problem, but the basic question was the same dichotomy between civilisation and culture. Gökalp argued that the remedy lay in 'discovering the basic social unit which is the source of cultural values', and that this was the 'nation' (ibid.). The modern nation, according to Gökalp, is 'a community in a unique complex of cultural values, on the one hand, and a society based on organic solidarity, division of labour and functional differentiation, on the other' (ibid.: 385). Nations do not come into existence out of nothing but must have an ethnic basis. Only cultural remains 'are capable of giving cohesion and orientation to the life of the nation' (ibid.: 386), and for this reason it is necessary to discover the original ethnic basis of distinctive Turkish culture.

One of the common Turkist arguments was that the Turks had drifted away from their ethnic traditions and adopted the cultures of Persians, Arabs and Europeans. Gökalp maintained that the basic cultural traits which had long been associated with the Turks such as polygamy, the subordinate status of women, fatalism, asceticism and the concept of a transcendental God were not Turkish and had 'never got a strong hold over the Turkish ethos' (Berkes 1954: 388–9), thereby pointing out the necessity to go back to pre-Islamic origins. Gökalp's essays exalted the ancient Turks who, to him, were distinguished by excellent moral, cultural, political and other qualities. He regarded language as the pivotal element of nationality and considered it essential for Turks to have a common, national language, based on the spoken language of Constantinople (Hostler 1957: 106–7).

Example 2: Indian cultural nationalism

The period from the early nineteenth century to the 1880s saw the Indian cultural revival, which emerged out of religious reform movements and was directed against the English cultural dominance in India. Indian national identity was associated with the glory of the Aryan civilisation (c. 1,000 BC).

Hindu cultural nationalism began to develop in the 1870s with many educated Hindus falling back upon their ancestral culture in the wake of English and Western cultural penetration.[4] Editorials in the *Indian Mirror* often dealt with this theme and argued that foreign manners and customs, modes of thought, speech and action and various other aspects of foreign culture introduced by the English ruined the original ways of life of the Hindus (McCully 1966: 240–4). The glory, genius and vitality of Hindu India ended and its spiritual and cultural degeneration started with the influx of foreigners which began in Alexander of Macedon's time (ibid.: 251). Modern Hindus then accelerated their cultural decay under British rule. Norendranath Sen remarked in a speech that 'our nationality and our spirituality, the two most important elements which contributed so much to the glory of Ancient India, [had] departed' through English education (1883, quoted in ibid.: 253). An article in the *Indian Mirror* proclaimed that under the impact of utilitarian Western civilisation, India must 'reassert its vitality through the development of a purely Hindu culture' (11 June 1876, quoted in ibid.: 242). But Hindu cultural nationalism was 'much more than an indictment of foreign ideas and practices' (ibid.: 244).

Hindu cultural nationalists stressed the achievements of their ancestors, the ancient Aryans. Surendra Nath Banerjea (1848–1926) was one of the prominent intellectuals who declared the importance for Indians of studying the history of their own country. Indian thinkers discussed the greatness and the uniqueness of the Aryan civilisation in journal and newspaper articles, and speeches. They emphasised the unique creativity of Aryan India: Aryan India was the mother of philosophy, science, art and literature, and responsible for the high standard of spiritual, moral and ethical life of the Aryans.

It was also a free country and it was the originator of civilisation, its light spreading to the other parts of the world such as Egypt, Greece and Rome (McCully 1966: 244–50).

Sri Aurobindo Ghosh, a religious thinker and important spiritual leader of Indian nationalism, wrote profusely in a journal called the *Arya* which he began to publish in 1914 on India's great cultural heritage and achievements in various spheres of human activity. *Foundations of Indian Culture*, the collection of his articles, is an analysis of the unique and original foundations upon which Indian civilisation was built and upon which it survived through the centuries. The book challenged the criticisms and misinterpretations of Western literary commentators frequently directed against the quality of Indian culture in Ghosh's day (Singh 1963: 92–8). Hindu cultural nationalism thus included the programme of restoring the Aryan spiritual and cultural life which Indians had lost through centuries of foreign rule. The revival of Sanskrit language and literature was encouraged because it was thought that the study of Sanskrit, the most enduring monument of the past greatness of the country, would assist Hindus in preserving their nationality and their love of national greatness (McCully 1966: 244ff).

Generalisations

These two examples show, first, that the role of intellectuals in exploring and articulating ideas of national distinctiveness is an essential part of cultural nationalism. Parallels are found in many other parts of the world, as will be seen from more examples later.

Both cases are typically those of 'primary' or original nationalism which is concerned with creating a nation and/or 'nation-state', rather than 'secondary' nationalism which preserves and enhances national identity in an already long-established nation. In fact, most of the literature on nationalism focuses on primary nationalism. Limiting our discussion to primary cultural nationalism, we may make two further generalisations.

The first of these – and our second broad generalisation – is that the examples suggest a tentative answer to the question with which we shall be concerned in the rest of this study: to what extent ideas of national distinctiveness are formulated on the basis of a nation's historical memory, and to what extent on the spatial boundary differentiation of 'us' and 'them'. The Turkish and Indian examples indicate the *primary* importance of historical memory in the formulation of national identity. In other words, intellectuals' formulation of ideas of national distinctiveness centres around the emphasis of a shared history and the discovery and articulation of the uniqueness of the ancestral culture. A sense of common history unites successive generations, and a sense of having a distinctive ancestral culture provides a sense of communal uniqueness. Indian nationalist scholar Banerjea's remark is illustrative:

> Approach reverentially the sacred records of your sires. Remember that you are studying the sayings and doings of your revered ancestors, of those for whose sake alone you are now remembered, for whose sake alone the intellectual elite of Europe even now feel a deep and an ardent interest in your welfare.
> (Banerjea 1880, quoted in Kedourie 1971: 62)

Kedourie remarks that 'Banerjea's argument only articulates and makes explicit the fundamental assumption of nationalist literature, namely, that it is the past of a "nation" which gives it an identity, a meaning, and a future' (1971: 62). Kushner similarly points out, with reference to the Turkish case, that looking upon and sharing of memories of a glorious past are essential for a nation's existence (1977: 7). The historical memory of a nation is at the base of the sense of national uniqueness in primary nationalism. The emphasis on contemporary differences between this nation and others is of secondary significance. This is, as one would expect, because contemporary culture is normally 'contaminated' with foreign cultural influences (as in the case of Turkey and India) and, for this reason, a return to the 'uncontaminated' ancestral culture is the only viable source with which the claim of uniqueness can be made and upon which communal regeneration depends. Here, the time orientation precedes the spatial one. The demonstration of spatial difference between 'us' and 'them' depends on 'our' historic memory. (The time and space orientations in theories of ethnicity and nationalism will be discussed in chapter 4.)

The third generalisation concerns the types of intellectuals who systematise the identity of a national community. Among the various types of intellectuals, historians and artists (frequently poets) are prominent in discovering and presenting the foundations in time of communal regeneration. This is understandable because, as discussed, it is by recovering the history of the nation that its members rediscover its authentic purpose. This is evident in the work of nationalist historians such as Palacky of the Czechs, Hrushevsky of the Ukrainians and Iorga of the Romanians.[5] Banerjea says that 'the study of the history of our own country furnishes the strongest incentive to the loftiest patriotism' (Banerjea 1880, compiled in Kedourie 1971: 235). What matters in the historical approach is 'not the authenticity of the historical record' but 'the poetic, didactic and integrative purposes which that record is felt to disclose' (Smith 1986: 25–6). For this very reason, we need artists, poets in particular, whose creativity derives from the collective and historical experience of the people, and who dramatise the people's collective vitality for the present (Berlin 1976: 203–4). One might mention the role in cultural nationalism of poets and authors like Kolar of the Slavs, Lönnrot of the Finns or Mickiewicz of the Polish.[6]

The last two generalisations concern primary nationalism. Whether they are valid in the case of secondary nationalism or, to be more specific, in the light of contemporary Japanese material is the subject of enquiry in the rest of this study.

THE PROTOTYPE OF CULTURAL NATIONALIST IDEOLOGY IN JAPAN

An analysis of the prototype of cultural nationalist ideology in Japan opens the way for the *nihonjinron* – a resurgent, contemporary version of Japan's cultural nationalism – to be located in a truly comparative framework.

The Japanese thinkers' exploration and emphasis of Japanese distinctiveness go well back to the beginning of the eighteenth century, when *kokugaku* (national learning) originated.[7] *Kokugaku* was essentially a nativist reaction against the sinophile intellectual atmosphere in Tokugawa Japan (1600–1867) and an affirmation of the indigenous culture of Japan. *Kokugaku* began as a philological study of ancient poetry. Keichū's (1640–1701) philological study of the *Manyōshu*, an eighth-century anthology of Japanese poetry, gave an important impetus to the later scholars of national learning. Kada no Azumamaro (1669–1736) was more concerned with the revival of Shinto as the 'ancient way' (*kodō*). These two concerns, concerns with ancient literature and the 'ancient way', find different expressions in the work of later scholars. Kamo no Mabuchi (1697–1769) went further than Keichū and resurrected the *Manyoshū* for the purpose of demonstrating how this eighth-century anthology could vividly evoke the sentiments of the ancient Japanese. Influenced both by the tendency of Confucian scholars to react against formalism and to return to a study of the old classics and by the studies of the Mito school of Japanese history,[8] Mabuchi paved the way for the study of antiquity (*kogaku*) and left important suggestions for later *kokugaku* scholars in *Kokuikō* (Consideration of the National Will) of 1765. The main thesis of this work was to point out the archaic simplicity and purity of people in Japan prior to the importation of foreign learning:

> In ancient time, when men's dispositions were straightforward, a complicated system of morals of the people was unnecessary. It would naturally happen that bad acts might occasionally be committed, but the straightforwardness of men's dispositions would prevent the evil from being concealed and growing in extent. So that in those days it was unnecessary to have a doctrine of right and wrong.
>
> (Mabuchi 1765, quoted in Brown 1955: 55–6)

Following Mabuchi's recommendation that a close reading of the *Kojiki*, Japan's earliest surviving written 'history' (compiled in AD 712)[9], would supply valuable information for understanding the language of the *Manyoshū* and the life of the ancient Japanese, Motoori Norinaga (1730–1801), reckoned as the chief luminary of *kokugaku*, devoted his scholarly energies to the study of this historical record and completed a voluminous commentary (*Kojikiden*) in 1759. His theory of Shinto or the 'ancient way' is one of his major contributions to the maturity of *kokugaku*. Norinaga also carried forward the study of ancient poetry started by Keichu.[10]

By way of provisional summary, *kokugaku* may be characterised by its reaction against the formalism of Confucianism dominant in the Tokugawa intellectual world and by its philological method of studying the way of life of ancient Japanese, exploring words and facts from an earlier age, and describing them as they were. Norinaga's following remark in *Kojikiden* is illustrative of the approach of *kokugaku*: 'Men have deliberated on the age of the gods (*kamiyo*) from a human perspective. I have sought to understand human affairs from [the perspective] of the age of the gods' (quoted in Harootunian 1978: 82). Norinaga viewed Confucianism or *karagokoro* (the Chinese mind) as 'an attempt to understand modalities and existence in terms of the rational activities of human beings' (ibid.). In rejection of this 'rational' thinking, Norinaga proposed the basis of true understanding, *magokoro*, the 'pure mind' that 'apprehends reality in its essential uniqueness and comprehends it sentiently and emotionally' (ibid.). *Magokoro* was to be achieved by a return to the pure meaning of words.

Harootunian explains the *kokugaku* scholars' concern with archaic words and poems by using the language of Kenneth Burke:

> Since languages develop by 'metaphorical extension', by borrowing words from the 'realm of the corporeal, visible, tangible and applying them by analogy to the realm of the incorporeal, invisible, intangible' they will in time lose contact with their original source of tangible meaning. In the end all that will survive is the intangible, the 'metaphorical extension', and only because the 'very conditions of living that reminded one of the corporeal reference have so altered that the cross reference no longer exists with near the same degree of apparentness in the "objective situation" itself', Burke reasons that *an apprehension, found usually among poets, prompts the effort to regain the original relation* by revising the procedures from intangible to tangible equivalents, which results in an inversion of 'metaphorical extension'.
>
> (Harootunian 1978: 79, emphasis added)

This would explain the strong concern of some, if not all, *kokugaku* scholars with language and emphasis on archaic words and syntax unspoilt by the Chinese influence and, above all, their concentration on poetic studies or, what Burke calls 'poetic realism' (ibid.: 80). Harootunian (1978: 81) argues that, although scholars of *kokugaku* reacted against the 'Chinese heart', it was not so much an attack against things Chinese as against civilisation itself in favour of the simple and basic sentiments of archaic life – particularly so in the work of Mabuchi.[11] It is for this reason that poetry occupied such an important place in *kokugaku* and that the resurrection of the *Manyōshu* was so vital to their project.

In its early stage, *kokugaku* was chiefly concerned with the study of ancient poetry. Even with Mabuchi and Norinaga, who came increasingly to establish a specific research perspective which they called *kodō* (the ancient way), their considerations were profoundly academic and apolitical. But in the course of academic enquiry into the ancient texts, *kokugaku* came to embody a nativistic reaction against sinophilism, thereby acquiring an ideological tone. This was, in a sense, a natural development because poetic 'intuitivism' was not simply a matter of literary renovation but was asserted in opposition to the rational approach of Confucianism. Matsumoto Sannosuke argues that the *kokugaku* scholars viewed the intuitive and sympathetic approach as 'the spirit intrinsic to the "Imperial Land" and distinct from the mode of thinking in the "Foreign Land"' (1973: 360). In other words, 'poetic intuitivism' itself was an expression of national consciousness. It contained what was to be a highly politicised ideology.

While the earlier *kokugaku* scholars respected the philological studies of ancient traditions, Hirata Atsutane (1776–1843) was not merely content with such textual analysis. He emphasised the normative role of *kodō* (the ancient way) or Shinto, an approach which clashed with the intuitivism of earlier scholars and their criticism of the normativeness of Confucianism. Atsutane was strongly concerned with the formulation of a religious world-view that emphasised reward in the afterworld for living a moral life in this world. He gave 'Shinto' a more concrete religious and normative content than earlier scholars and expressed the superiority of the Shinto religion in relation to foreign religions and philosophies. With Atsutane Shinto gained a more active ideological force, a force that was later to be used for the creation of greater national unity around the divine emperor. Atsutane's theory of religion and normative Shinto exerted a strong influence on many thinkers in the late Tokugawa period. His disciples laid a stronger emphasis on the importance of the practice of Shinto and the centrality of the divine emperor, thereby playing an important role in the *sonnō* ('revere the emperor') movement and in the rise of State Shinto, a main component of nationalist ideology in pre-war and wartime Japan (see Haga 1963; Matsumoto 1957; Koyasu 1977).

PRIMARY AND SECONDARY CULTURAL NATIONALISM

Two interim conclusions may be drawn here. First, intellectuals' concern with ancestral history and archaic poetry (and sometimes also language) unblemished by foreign elements, which has been discussed in the context of Turkish and Indian primary nationalism, finds an interesting parallel in *kokugaku* in the eighteenth century in Japan. Kamo no Mabuchi (1697–1769) would not have known about his contemporary Giambattista Vico (1668–1744), but we are struck with an amazing similarity in their approach: a concern with myths (history), and early poetry and language. We find here a historicist concern with national distinctiveness, that which centres around the discovery of the uniqueness of the ancestral culture and the emphasis of a shared history. Breuilly summarises the historicist argument as stating that 'history is the only way to apprehend the spirit of a community' (1982: 338).

In its contemporary version, the *nihonjinron*, a historicist (or primordial) concern is given less weight. We may say that in secondary nationalism a sense of belonging to a 'historical nation' is already taken for granted and that, therefore, an affirmation of the presence of a nation's original ancestral culture is not such an important intellectual concern as in primary nationalism. By contrast, the differentiating boundary approach increases its relative importance in that it reaffirms a sense of difference in a way that appeals to the contemporary audience. This accounts for the relative lack of historicism in the *nihonjinron*. Its main concern is to discuss systematically how the Japanese behave differently from foreigners (Westerners), thereby marking the symbolic boundary between 'us' Japanese and 'them' foreigners. This is not to suggest, however, that historical memory has lost its relevance in the contemporary discussions of national identity, as will be discussed in chapter 5. My argument here is that both historical memory and spatial differentiation are the essential sources of national identity but that the relative weight given to either of the two may vary depending on the stage and/or type of nationalism.

Corresponding to this shift of emphasis is a change in the composition of the types of intellectuals (or thinking elites) who formulate ideas of national distinctiveness. Primary nationalism is the domain of historical scholars and artists, typically poets, and also art scholars who explore a nation's origin and its 'original' culture. Study of the *nihonjinron* suggests that in secondary nationalism another important category of thinkers emerges to take much of the place formerly occupied by historical scholars and, in particular, artists.[12] The writers of the *nihonjinron* are, as it were, 'popular sociologists', who, by experience or expertise, are interested in theorising about contemporary Japanese society and culture and in formulating ideas of the distinctive Japanese patterns of behaviour and thought compared to those of non-Japanese. 'Popular sociologists' have very little to do with academic sociology in the sense that, although sociologists participated in the *nihonjinron* as individual writers, the *nihonjinron* did not become a sub-field of academic sociology. 'Popular sociologists' may be thinkers of any professional background – academics from any discipline, journalists, critics, diplomats, writers and business elites – who are interested in the 'study' of society and culture.

It may be appropriate to reflect further on our findings on the comparative perspective of national identity in the contemporary world. Scholars of nationalism normally confine themselves to the classic cases of 'old nationalism' or to the more recent cases of ethnic separatisms and 'neo-nationalisms' without paying adequate attention to the subsequent development of national identity in the dominant nations of the developed West. For this very reason the contemporary Japanese experience cannot be compared with the experience of other countries in any systematic manner. But looking around the well-established nations of the world today, we find that the thinking elites' active concern with national distinctiveness is not unusual, although we cannot generalise about the background of such a concern. Post-war England, for example, has witnessed two periods during which opinion leaders concerned themselves with the identity (or state) of the nation.[13] One of these periods was the first five to ten years following the end of the Second World War when the 'decline' of the British Empire was evident; the other was the 1970s during which discussion centred around the so-called 'English disease'.

While these conditions are peculiar to Britain (or England), it is not implausible to suggest that there is a common denominator for an active concern with national identity in some countries of Western Europe – the increasingly multiracial and multi-ethnic nature of their societies. Van Heerikhuizen points to the recent revival of interest among the Dutch and specifically among Dutch sociologists in the qualities that make their nation unique. He attributes this revived interest to the 'changing composition of the Dutch population' caused by the influx of a large number of immigrants from the former Dutch colonies of Indonesia and Surinam and migrant labourers from Italy, Turkey and North Africa (Van Heerikhuizen 1982: 120). In *De Nederlandse natie* (The Dutch Nation) published in 1981, which exemplifies this resurgent interest in the Dutch national character, sociologist P. Thoenes remarks that 'the multiracial aspect, in its present dimensions, is more of a valuable counterpoint than a threat to the national character' (quoted in Van Heerikhuizen 1982: 121).

The Netherlands does not stand alone in this experience. In England, too, racial issues stimulated discussion of immigration, the state of the country and, above all, the notion of nationality. Wallman describes 'English racial rhetoric' as follows. The symbol of race evokes the sense of 'us' and 'our identity', because race symbolises a whole chain of items and events: 'race' is associated with 'them', 'them' with immigration, and immigration with unemployment, deteriorating urban conditions and lower living standards. Race and 'they' are associated with economic and social problems, and 'they' are 'the indication that things are not perfect' (Wallman 1981: 120). Wallman offers an illuminating remark on the changing background against which national identity is reformulated and reasserted:

> In a post-imperial, post-industrial, no longer powerful era, we cannot define ourselves the way we used to. There is, as there was in the thirties, a demand for new meanings and ideologies that will explain and justify the way we are now.
>
> (Wallman 1981: 133)

One of our findings concerning national identity in contemporary Japan is that a historicist concern is largely replaced by a symbolic boundary concern with differences between 'us' and 'them'. It is possible to illustrate a predominantly 'boundary' concern with an example from another well-established nation. The 'linguistic' nationalism that emerged or re-emerged in France in the 1970s (and is still prevalent today) against the 'invasion' of Americanism in the field of popular culture (fast food restaurants, movies, music, etc.) is primarily concerned to mark the symbolic boundary between 'very French' realms of French culture and Americanised realms. In the 1960s and 1970s this coincided with a fear of the Americanisation of Europe in the corporate business field (see e.g. Servan-Schreiber 1968).[14] Content analysis of London-based newspaper editorials from 1945 to 1984 suggests that the distinctiveness of the English is discussed in a 'lay-sociological' manner, rather than in a 'historicist' manner, so as to point out the characteristics of their social culture. End-of-the-year editorials in British newspapers are full of words and phrases describing the English national character and reaffirming a sense of difference in such a way that appeals to the contemporary audience. Among the descriptions used in the period 1945–84 are: creative and inventive, courageous and adventurous, individualistic, industrious, tolerant, forward-looking and optimistic, kindly and friendly, conscientious, orderly, rational, stoic, confident, introverted, good humour, fair play, genius for improvisation, and so on.

The Japanese experience also suggests that, whereas historical scholars, art scholars and artists (typically poets) played a primary important role in primary or original nationalism, present-day writers on Japanese uniqueness are, as it were, 'popular sociologists', who theorise differences between contemporary Japanese society and other societies or between the patterns of behaviour of the Japanese and other peoples. Although this has very much to do with the conditions surrounding contemporary Japan as indicated in this study, parallels may be found elsewhere, albeit with differing emphases. Van Heerikhuizen points out that it is what he calls 'lay sociologists' who exhibited a keen interest in the subject of the Dutch national character:

> Pondering the differences between the Dutch and people in other countries is a very popular pastime among sociologists and non-sociologists alike, especially immediately after a vacation abroad. If the more academic studies of this subject were banned from the realm of 'serious' sociology, this would sever a potential link between sociologists and 'laymen'.
>
> (Van Heerikhuizen 1982: 122)

Here, the term 'lay sociologists' is expected to mean any type of social commentator such as journalists, critics, writers and travellers who discuss the Dutch national character and, by so doing, reaffirm a sense of difference in a way that appeals to the contemporary audience.

HOLISTIC AND INSTITUTIONAL APPROACHES TO NATIONAL DISTINCTIVENESS

Let us now examine from yet another perspective the ways in which intellectuals express and formulate ideas of national distinctiveness. It is possible to classify the two main approaches to national identity as 'holistic' and 'institutional'. The first regards a nation as a whole and assumes that the members of a nation share a common 'soul' or character. By contrast, the second approach expresses national identity in terms of differentiated institutions and artefacts without necessarily inferring from them a distinctive national 'spirit' or character common to the members of the nation.

The holistic approach

The holistic approach deals with the identity of the nation as a whole and sometimes by an analogy with the individual. Just as each individual has a unique personality and spirit, each nation is also described as possessing a distinctive characteristic and/or soul. This cultural core of the nation is often referred to as national character and/or *Volksgeist*, each of which will be discussed with examples in specific national contexts.

National character

In the history of the West a systematic comparison of the characters of different peoples occurred at the time of the formation of national consciousness. National (or ethnic) character became more than an object of curious casual observers. In the eighteenth century, national character was a popular subject particularly among French and German philosophers and writers. For example, Kant commented on the polite, amiable, vivacious and frivolous character of the French, the capriciousness of the English, and the seriousness and haughtiness of the Spaniards. He characterised Germans by their phlegm, honesty, love of order and diligence without ingenuity (see Kemiläinen 1964: 64–5). Montesquieu's *De L'esprit des Lois* of 1748 became a widely-read and influential work on the differences in mankind. He wrote on the influence of many causes on *l'esprit général* of a nation such as climate, history, the form of government, religion, laws, and manners and customs, but did not consider the influence of heredity and held to a rationalistic philosophy that people were originally the same (see Kemiläinen 1964: 67–8).

Eighteenth-century writers on the whole remained cosmopolitans, but in reality an increasingly strong national consciousness was becoming conspicuous. At the end of the eighteenth century, Herder put forward a new theory of the organic differences between nations. Because the struggle of the cosmopolitans against national sentiment was so great, Herder's stress on national individuality was especially significant and had an important influence on the nationalist ideology of the nineteenth century (ibid.: 72–3).

Intellectuals' attempts to express national distinctiveness in terms of national character have persisted and continued up to the present, and can be seen today in various countries. An interesting example may be cited from the Dutch intellectual scene in the 1930s and 1940s (see Van Heerikhuizen 1982).

If cultural nationalism creates, preserves and strengthens a people's cultural identity when such identity is felt to be lacking, inadequate or threatened, this example typically deals with the preservation and promotion of *threatened* national identity. Jan Romein shows that, whenever a threat to Dutch unity arose, there was an increase in the number of publications on the Dutch national character:

> This might very well mean that the crises of approximately 1600, 1672, 1787, 1795, 1813, 1830, 1870 and 1914 gave rise to the *illusion* that there was unity based on one and the same character, without this character really having existed, but it might just as well mean that there is definitely one national character but that it only clearly expresses itself in times of crisis, and on the basis of my experiences in the past few months I tend to favour the latter idea.
>
> (Romain 1941, quoted in Van Heerikhuizen 1982: 119)

Van Heerikhuizen (1982) reports that more was written about the Dutch national character in the 1930s and 1940s than ever before or since. The war had much to do with it. S.R. Steinmetz, J.P. Kruijit, J. Huizinga and J. Romein are some of the well-known writers who contributed to the topic during this period. These scholars cited various Dutch character traits such as

> the love of freedom, individualism (particularism) with its counterpart of licentiousness (indiscipline), unemotionalism (not very romantic or imaginative), sobriety, domesticity (a great amount of interest in family life, very little interest in public social activities), reserve ('secondary functioning', phlegmatic), commercial spirit, bourgeois mentality, tendency to maintain a show of respectability, an aversion to violence (peace-loving, not cruel to animals), awkwardness (stiffness), seriousness, honesty, a critical attitude, tolerance, thriftiness (economical, stingy), cleanliness (but, as was often noted, not with respect to personal hygiene), interest in religious questions.
>
> (Van Heerikhuizen 1982: 108)

In explaining national character, some scholars like Steinmetz mentioned heredity, while others such as Romein and Huizinga refuted biological interpretations and were chiefly interested in the social and natural environment (e.g. the struggle against the sea) and the history of the Dutch people (ibid.: 109–11).

It was suggested that the Dutch, unlike the Germans, could not be led into a totalitarian political system because of their national character traits. (In reality, a great deal of evidence points to the contrary, such as the results of the provincial elections of 1934 which favoured the Dutch National Socialists.) However, articulation of ideas of the Dutch national character certainly had a political meaning in the first few months of the Second World War. Romein was called upon to counteract the then prevailing theories legitimating the German occupation of the Netherlands on the grounds of racial, linguistic, historical and geographical affinities between the two peoples, and he made the most of the notion of the unique Dutch character (ibid.: 119–20). Van Heerikhuizen states that 'the notion of a typically Dutch national character was revived between 1940 and 1945, and had a special attraction for Dutch people who abhorred the German occupation' (ibid.: 119).

It should be noted that this example does not deal with the original, primary nationalism of the Dutch people, which is normally classified as 'political' nationalism.[15] Rather, this example deals with the intellectual dimensions of cultural national sentiment in the 1930s and 1940s.

Volksgeist

The notion of *Volksgeist* (folk spirit), which personifies the nation, is characteristic of German Romanticism. Romanticism, which in many ways was a reaction against the Enlightenment, was originally an aesthetic movement. In Germany, unlike anywhere else at that time, romantic poets and thinkers influenced political and social thought.[16] By emphasising the great depth of the German mind and German uniqueness, German Romanticism encouraged the development of nationalism in Germany after 1800 just as the Enlightenment shaped the form of nationalism in Western Europe. Among the individual harbingers of Romanticism are Vico and Shaftesbury, Justus Moser and Edmund Burke, but the one who exercised the most profound influence on the development of German Romantics and cultural nationalist ideology was Johann Gottfried Herder (1744–1803) (Kohn 1960: ch. 2; Reiss 1955: 1–11).

Fearing the disappearance of national individualities in Europe, Herder developed the notion of God-ordained organic cultural differences between nations. Herder's central idea is that the proper base of a sense of collective identity is not the acceptance of a common sovereign power but the sharing of a common culture. Whereas the former is imposed from outside, the latter is the expression of an inner consciousness, in terms of which each individual recognises himself as an integral part of a social whole. He calls a community with such a common culture *Volk*.

Language occupies an important place in Herder's ideas of nation,[17] because language, he thinks, is an internal experience in that it expresses people's innermost thoughts and feelings. What is more, language can only be learnt in a community. Those who share a common understanding of linguistic meanings may be said to constitute a nation. Language also links them with the past:

> By means of language he [man] is able to enter into communion with the way of thinking and feeling of his progenitors, to take part as it were, in the workings of the ancestral mind. He, in turn, again by means of language, perpetuates and enriches the thoughts, feelings and prejudices of past generations for the benefit of posterity. In this way language embodies the living manifestation of historical continuity and the psychological matrix which man's awareness of his distinctive social heritage is aroused and deepened.
>
> (Barnard 1969: 22)

Although language is important to Herder, he does not regard it as the only criterion of national identity. Herder includes other cultural traits such as myths, folk songs, ritual and customs as clues to people's collective 'personality' and manifestations of the unspoilt folk spirit. Language, culture and community are inextricably interwoven in Herder's thinking. As Breuilly puts it: 'If language is thought, and can be learnt only in a community, it follows that each community has its own mode of thought' (1982: 337). The argument can then be extended further by understanding other human activities as akin to language.

> Dress, architecture, customs, ceremonial, song, law: all these and many other activities can be understood in the same way. Ultimately 'community' is understood as the sum total of these modes of expression. Furthermore, this sum total is itself more than a collection of items and must be grasped as a complex unity . . . Each element in a society only makes sense in terms of the whole, which, in turn, is manifested only through these various elements.
>
> (Breuilly 1982: 337–8)

German Romantic scholars viewed the culture and history of a *Volk* through the metaphorical concept of *Volksgeist*,[18] inspiring research into the nation's traditions, folk poetry and other folk traditions as well as an interest in common people. The Romantics attempted to enrich the present by reviving the past. Fighting against the principles of the French Revolution, German Romanticists longed for a true, harmonious organic folk community, the ideal of which seemed to them to have existed in the Germanic Middle Ages, which then became a fountain-head of national culture. They also praised and edited the medieval poetry and stories, folk songs and fairy tales. Even nature became an attribute of national identity. Although Herder laid the foundations of German nationalism when he emphasised the communal bond woven by a common language and demanded a German national literature, he himself remained an enlightened humanitarian and pacifist. Following Herder, however, German Romanticism became largely a revolt against reason. Herder's theory of folk spirit was then incorporated into the more elaborate ideology of nationalism by the scholars of German Romanticism such as Fichte, Schlegel, Arndt, Schleiermacher, Brockhaus, Jahn and Müller.

The German Romantic version of nationalism may also be called the 'organic' version. From the external traits of language, customs and institutions is inferred a distinctive 'spirit' of the nation with its own independent power. Such a spirit turns the parts of a nation into an 'organic whole', which is more than the sum of its parts, and the nation stands over and above the individuals who compose it. The folk state was not a societal organisation based on human-made law, but an organic personality and God's creation (see Smith 1971: 16).

A brief mention may be made of some of the non-German contexts in which this idea was adopted. Since there is abundant literature on the impact of the German experience on eastern Europe, we might look for an example elsewhere, such as in northern Europe. In northern Europe, Denmark was particularly receptive to German intellectual movements, where the notion of *Volksgeist* appeared in nationalist thinking.[19] But it was in Norway, where language was a major concern, that 'folk spirit' was of particular relevance.

The main element of Norwegian cultural nationalism in the second half of the nineteenth century was the language question. When in the early sixteenth century Norway was downgraded to the status of a Danish territory, the old Norwegian–Icelandic written language was discarded and Danish adopted as the written language. The idea of linguistic revival began in the 1830s and gained a steady increase in popular support in the second half of the century. The notion of *Volksgeist* asserted itself in the thinking of linguistic cultural nationalists. National language reformers were confronted with a choice between the two types of the new written language: *Landsmål*, a wholly new written language based entirely on Norwegian dialects, and *Bokmål*, the result mainly of Norwegianising the existing Danish language. *Bokmål* seemed a practical choice but cultural nationalists opted for *Landsmål*. This new language was based on the foundation laid by a peasant's son, Ivar Aasen, who studied the Norwegian dialects (Haugland 1980: 21–9). In essence, the *Landsmål* movement was the core of Norwegian cultural nationalism. When the supporters of *Landsmål* rejected the compromise idea of Norwegianising the Danish language, they argued that, since language was 'a living organism' with its own identity based on the history of the nation, it must be rooted in national life. The romantic and organic concept of culture and a marriage of language and *Volksgeist* are clearly evident in this example (ibid.).

Institutional approach

Cultural nationalism is often equated with the German Romantic and organic version, but can be extended to include a wider range of sentiment and ideological movement that centre around national cultural distinctiveness. Take, for example, the ideas of national differences of Rousseau, Burke, Bolingbroke and Jefferson. In the writings of Rousseau, often regarded as the doctrinal founder of political nationalism, a nation's individuality occupies a central place. When Rousseau asserted in his well-known advice to the Poles in 1772 that there should be only Poles within the boundaries of their state, his real concern was for the individuality and cohesiveness of the community. Plamenatz goes as far as to conclude that 'there is no trace of political nationalism in his writings' because Rousseau 'argues only that members of a political community, if that community is to be united and strong, must share the same fundamental values. He does not argue that people who share the same culture should be united in one political community the better to preserve it' (Plamenatz 1976: 25).[20] Also, in his typology of nationalist ideologies, Carlton Hayes (1931) classifies scholars as different as Herder, Bolingbroke and Rousseau together into what he calls 'humanitarian nationalists', humanitarian because they not only respected national cultures but also possessed enthusiasm for mankind.

Kemiläinen, while basically approving of Hayes' contention, points out the difference in the ways in which the different writers thought of the determining factors of national differences. He maintains that 'the difference between on the one hand Bolingbroke and Rousseau, and on the other hand Herder was not only the fact that the former did not define nationality distinctly, while Herder did, but the dissimilarity between their conceptions of the origins of national individuality'. Whereas it is 'the *organic* and genetic factors which finally created in Herder's eyes an individual national character', 'Bolingbroke and Rousseau and many others acknowledged the importance of nationality and favoured national *institutions*' (Kemiläinen 1964: 168, emphasis added).

Cobban (1964: 108) makes a similar point in his study of Rousseau's notion of the nation. He shows how eighteenth-century Europe was evolving alternative conceptions of national identity to the German Romantic and organic notions. Rather than such extreme concepts as *Volksgeist* later to be prominent in the nineteenth century, some more moderate idea of the identity of a state or a community was felt to be required. To this Rousseau offered a solution. Rousseau believed that institutions were the key elements in creating a sense of national identity:

> It is national institutions which form the genius, character, tastes and manners of a people, which make it what it is and not something else, which inspire in it an ardent love of country based on customs which cannot be uprooted.
>
> (Rousseau 1772, translated and quoted in Kemiläinen 1964: 73)

In other words, Rousseau brought under 'the dominion of the human will forces that most previous and contemporary thinkers had treated as autonomous', that is, national character (Cobban 1964: 111). The relation between national character and institutions is complex, which Rousseau admits. The nation was shaped by the institutions, while simultaneously the institutions had to be adapted to the nation. But Cobban maintains that 'in so far as it was possible to attribute any priority it was to the institutions that he gave it' (ibid.).

The Indian case may be a good example of cultural national-ism in which the approach to national distinctiveness is highly 'institutional'. (This is, of course, not to suggest that Rousseau's ideas had any influence here.) Hindu cultural nationalism was based on the glory of the culture of the ancient Aryans. What is discussed in much of the literature in the name of Indian culture might even be designated as civilisation,[21] as the following sentence suggests:

Aryan India was the cradle of the sciences and arts, and it was from Aryavartha that light spread to other parts of the world.
(*Indian Mirror*, 9 April 1884, quoted in McCully 1966: 246)

McCully takes up this point, remarking further that

the exponents of Indian cultural nationalism maintained that the cradle of humanity was marked with a clear and brilliant civilization. . . . Philological research had proved beyond doubt a close relation between the Greeks, Romans and Indo-Aryan people. Comparative philosophy had shown that this relationship existed also in thought. That Indo-Aryans (now called Hindus) were the originators of civilization, and that Egypt and, Greece and Rome were their pupils and recipients had been plainly revealed by the fact that the light of knowledge first dawned on the minds of the Rishis of Aryavartha.
(McCully 1966: 247–8)

Thus, the Indian heritage is not something intrinsic to the Indians but the glorious civilisation which the ancestral Aryans created. Indian thinkers, therefore, expressed the uniqueness of the Hindu nation largely in terms of objectifiable traits of civilisation such as institutions, practices, objects and artefacts of the Aryans, who could 'manufacture cotton and silk fabrics', 'display in the preparation of their dishes culinary skill of a high order', 'work skilfully in metals and fashion elegant jewelry', 'form and highly refine a language, write elaborate works on its grammar, and compose hymns and prayers', 'discuss abstruse questions in theology and metaphysics,' 'make a code of civil law on just and humane principles', 'lay down rules of moral conduct which anticipated by many centuries the ethics of Christianity', and above all, 'form a clear conception as to the nature and attributes of the Supreme Being, while other peoples on the surface of the earth were hardly able to form any notion of their maker' (A Hindu, 'The national character of the Hindus of Bengal', *Bengal Magazine*, 1875–1876, quoted in McCully 1966: 250). Also, in L.H. Bilas's '"What we were" and "What we are"', national distinctiveness is expressed in terms of the richest, most abundant, interesting and morally sublime literature, the unprecedented high standards of the arts and sciences, the thriving nature of commerce, and so on (Bilas 1884–1885, quoted in ibid.: 248).

India's institutional approach is understandable, given the heterogeneity of its population and the absence of holistic ethnic culture embracing the entire population. Cultural nationalists in India were likely to stress common but differentiated 'external' institutions and customs. What they had to emphasise was the commonness of the Hindus of every part of India: that they resembled one another in all essential respects, in their customs and social institutions; that they had common ancestors and worshipped the same gods and goddesses; and that they used the same scriptural language, Sanskrit (McCully 1966: 244). Hindu nationalism not merely suggested the need for the writing of a national history which should remind Hindus of their past greatness but had to evoke the concept of India as the 'Motherland'. This represented an effort to develop a religious basis for nationalism on the assumption that the religious sentiment of the Hindus was much easier to arouse than their ethnic feeling based on a common cultural ethos. It should be noted, however, that, as Brass (1979) claims, once Hindu Indian nationalism developed in opposition to Muslim nationalism, the Hindus and Muslims began to form their cultural symbols into unified and distinct complexes of meaning.[22]

Summary and conclusion

We have observed a difference in the ways in which intellectuals express national distinctiveness. The fundamental difference between the holistic and institutional approaches may be summarised as follows. The holistic view of national identity can lead to, or is based upon, the notion that a particular cultural trait is *intrinsic* to a particular people. In some cases this may imply the notion that national 'character' or 'soul' is hereditary. F.M. Barnard argues that, whereas Rousseau looked to external agents, in particular, to the role of a legislator in the fashioning of a nation, Herder favoured *internal* development. This notion of Herder may best be seen in his conception of language as well as his idea of the nation as family. Herder compared the 'most natural state' to an 'extended family with one national character' (Barnard 1983: 241).[23] The important point as regards the holistic approach is that the cultural bonds which link the members of a nation into a relational whole are 'not *things* or artifacts' but 'living energies (*Kräfte*) emanating from within, shared meanings and sentiments which in time form a people's collective soul' (ibid.: 242).

Japanese thinking elites' ideas of Japanese uniqueness (*nihonjinron*) are highly holistic. Their primarily concern is, on the assumption of Japanese society as a homogeneous and holistic entity, to explore and describe the cultural ethos or collective spirit or, to be more exact, the characteristic mode of behaving and thinking of the Japanese that underlies objectified institutions and practices. In chapters 5 and 6 I shall enquire further into this holistic view of modern Japan and attempt to explain why and how it has become the essential view of Japanese identity.

DIFFUSION OF IDEAS OF NATIONAL DISTINCTIVENESS

Like many other 'isms', cultural nationalism has its originators – intellectuals or thinking elites who formulate ideas of national distinctiveness – and what Weber (1948: 269–84) called its social 'bearers' – a group or groups to whom a given set of ideas has a particular appeal or gives a particular purpose and who relate it to their material and ideal interests and activities, thereby diffusing cultural nationalism in society. (In reality, the distinction between originators and bearers cannot clearly be drawn, as will be argued in chapters 7, 8 and 9.)

Not much has been written on this aspect of cultural nationalism. An emphasis is normally given to the content of the ideology of cultural nationalism and not to the social process whereby its ideology is diffused in society. Nevertheless, a reading of the specific literature on nationalism as well as sociological literature in general points to the role of educators. Here, we are specifically interested in the role of formal education or the school.

The school as a political instrument for injecting national spirit

One prevalent view of cultural nationalism identifies the school as the main agent in injecting 'national spirit'. This view has been explicitly formulated by Elie Kedourie (1960, 1971), who equates the German 'organic' version of nationalism with nationalism in general. Nationalism, according to Kedourie, is a doctrine that holds that 'humanity is naturally divided into nations, that nations are known by certain characteristics which can be ascertained, and that the only legitimate type of government is national self-government' (1960: 9). Kedourie's ideas of nationalism and his conclusion regarding the role of the school in nationalism are drawn largely from Fichte's notions of national self-realisation through political struggle and absorption of the individual's will in that of the organic state. For Fichte the school becomes a political instrument for injecting national spirit. As an admirer of the French Revolution, Fichte valued the idea of a state in which, as he thought, individual freedom would have meaning only in the collective being. Fichte stated the goal of education in his *Addresses to the German Nation*, delivered in Berlin in 1806:

> By means of education, we want to mould the Germans into a corporate body, which shall be stimulated and animated in all its individual members by the same interest.
>
> (Fichte 1922: 15)

The new education is thus to mould the people's will in order to create an organic state, as Fichte remarks: 'if you want to influence him at all, you must do more than merely talk to him; you must fashion him, and fashion him in such a way that he simply cannot will otherwise than you wish him to will' (ibid.: 21). Following Fichte's conception, Kedourie maintains that this is why education must have a central place in nationalist theory.

Here, we have to remind ourselves of the two closely related but distinct dimensions of cultural nationalism: romantic and organic. The romantic dimensions are concerned with the (re)discovery and emphasis of the cultural distinctiveness and historic heritage of the nation. The organic dimensions deal with the organic state – which is itself an expression of the national spirit – and with the notion that individuals are free when they are absorbed into the will of the organic state, thereby dealing with the politicised aspect of *Volksgeist*. Based on this distinction, we find that Kedourie's thesis deals with the organic aspect of German cultural nationalism. As Kedourie himself remarks:

> The purpose of education is not to transmit knowledge, traditional wisdom, and the ways devised by a society for attending to the common concerns; its purpose rather is wholly political, to bend the will of the young to the will of the nation. Schools are the instruments of state policy, like the army, the police, and the exchequer.
>
> (Kedourie 1960: 83–4)

In other words, it is not simply the activities of educators but the policy of the state that should concern us, too.

Political nationalism also emphasises the importance of education. In fact, the idea of national education goes back to a demand for general education of the people under the auspices of the national state in France. La Chalotais's *Essai d'éducation nationale ou plan d'étude pour la jeunesse* (1763) was the first major document that articulated the notion of public education associated with the revolution (see Katsuta 1973: 12–13). Many other works followed, among which Condorcet's report on proposed reforms in education was presented to the National Legislative Assembly in 1792 and adopted as the basis of policy concerning a national system of public education (Ulich 1961: 146ff). However, what distinguishes cultural from political nationalists is that, whereas for the political nationalist, nations are simply political units, the cultural nationalist rests the nation not merely on consent or law but, first and foremost, on the human ties and passions nurtured by nature and history (Berlin 1976: 158–63).

Except for the well-formulated theory of Kedourie, not much of the literature on nationalism proper explicitly discusses the role of formal education. Nevertheless, one finds that this role of education is, from a different perspective, frequently touched upon in general sociological literature. In fact, this view is taken for granted in sociology. If society is to survive, its culture must be handed down from generation to generation. The schools are used to provide young people with knowledge, values and skills that a society considers important. The inculcation of national values has been especially apparent in modern societies. The emergence of nation-states and the growth of nationalism in nineteenth-century Europe resulted in an increasing emphasis on indoctrination in formal education. This description of modern national education tells us about the two closely-related aspects of formal education: cultural transmission and social control, which, in their fundamental aspects, correspond to the romantic and organic dichotomy pointed out previously. Since social control (and, therefore, social solidarity) presupposes the transmission of a society's cultural traditions, the two aspects cannot be separated from each other. This leads us to the second aspect of the role of the school in cultural nationalism: the school as an institution which transmits and diffuses the nation's distinctive cultural traditions articulated and 'invented' by intellectuals.

The school as main agent in transmitting national culture

Although there is no systematic study of this aspect of formal education, there are a number of scattered accounts of the schools as the main agent in transmitting ideas of a nation's cultural distinctiveness. Particularly noteworthy is the Danish invention, the folk high schools. This institution, first opened in Rødding in 1844, originated in the idea of a Danish poet and cultural nationalist, Nikolai F.S. Grundtvig (1783–1872). The folk school movement played an important role in maintaining and transmitting the Danish folk culture and folk spirit in the face of national and international threats in the first half of this century. The idea of the folk high school spread to other Scandinavian countries such as Norway, Finland and Sweden, and also to the United States, and in the twentieth century, Germany and England.

In Norway the folk high schools (*folkehögskolane*) played a particularly important role in promoting *Landsmål*, a movement to create a genuinely Norwegian written language and the core of Norwegian cultural nationalism. The folk high schools were designed to protect and enhance the national elements of language and way of life and to instil a sense of national history. Many teachers of the folk high schools held important positions in the Norwegian cultural nationalist movement in general and in the promotion of *Landsmål* in particular. Cultural nationalism was also part of the social struggle against upper strata in cities. The folk high schools were supportive of the values of the rural community and employed a pedagogical method based on 'the living word' (Haugland 1980: 27–9).

Parallels may be found in various parts of the world. In Turkey, especially since the Kemalist reforms emphasised 'Turkicisation' of the national culture, the curriculum of the schools, especially secondary schools, sought to implement the principles of the revolution by consciously teaching about the Turks' unique cultural heritage and pre-Islamic past (Kazamias 1966). In India, the basic conception of education was founded upon the social philosophy of Gandhi, itself inspired by Hinduism, and almost all public discussions of education linked the present to the Hindu past (Kabir 1956). In Tanzania – and other African countries – school curricula since the 1960s have been designed to Africanise the content of education. Swahili, national history, traditional values, traditional songs and crafts, and so on have been stressed (Dood 1971: 589–90).

In summary, literature on the diffusion and transmission of ideas of national distinctiveness is scarce and sporadic. Yet, there is no literature, either, that denies the role of formal education in spreading cultural nationalism. In fact, such a view on education is fundamental to modern sociology, which tends to identify society as coterminous with the boundaries of the nation-state.[24] The role of educators is generally dealt with in terms of such concepts as socialisation and enculturation. It may be concluded, then, that the major role of formal education in disseminating ideas of national distinctiveness is widely recognised. This view will be assessed in chapters 7 and 8 in the light of the Japanese material. It will be shown that another social group becomes of considerable importance in Japan's secondary cultural nationalism.

Chapter 4

Theories of ethnicity and nationalism: a critical review[1]

The main reason for engaging in a critical review of theories of ethnicity is that the Japanese view of nationality and nationalism is very much an ethnic one. The issues of Japanese nationalism centre around those relating to ethnicity rather than territoriality, although this is not to suggest that the territorial factor is unimportant. It is undeniably an important determining factor of Japanese national identity in that the territory of the Japanese nation is clearly defined within the Japanese consciousness, even though it has slightly expanded or contracted over time and there are areas of some ambiguity both to the north and the south.[2] The Japanese archipelago has been almost entirely immune from territorial wars. In other words, the territorial question is not an issue of which the majority of Japanese are actively conscious. The issues of Japan's nationalism have centred around the notion of the uniqueness of Japanese ethnicity shared by its members, a uniqueness which is a function of culture, religion and race.

A qualification on the concept of ethnicity is necessary at the outset. Usage of ethnicity and ethnic communities falls into two broad categories. The first of these is that of ethnic minorities and/or immigrant groups such as Basques in Spain, Chinese in Malaysia and Pakistanis in Britain. Second, many social scientists now extend the use of ethnicity beyond a mere synonym for a minority or subgroup to a historical prototype or substratum of national community such as England in the Shakespearean era, pre-colonial Vietnam, and so on. An ethnic group in this sense is 'a nation which has not yet become fully conscious of itself' (Francis 1974: 398). In the Japanese context, this can mean pre-Meiji Japan, which was characterised by ethnic sentiment and an ethnic state but was not fully conscious of itself as a nation. The concept of ethnicity can also theoretically refer to a substratal sense of difference among the contemporary Japanese based on culture and descent (though ambiguities surround the boundaries between 'ethnic' and 'national' sentiment). A.D. Smith understands nation – in the case of the first nations of Western Europe and several other leading states – as being based on ties of ethnicity, remarking that 'the nation arises upon ethnic foundations or is constructed out of such ethnic materials as are to be found' (1973: 26). Ethnicity understood as such is a key concept to enquire into the nature of nationalism, and it is in this sense that the concept of ethnicity is employed in this book.

There has been considerable sociological debate in the last decade or two on the underlying causes of the resurgence of ethnicity and nationalism in the modern world. Although the debate has helped to broaden our perspectives on the subject, it has at the same time created unnecessary theoretical divisions, as mutual criticisms have proceeded without recognising the different levels of analysis, and various theoretical proponents have continued to argue at cross-purposes. The limitations of the debate also derive from the assumption held by most participants that various theoretical alternatives are mutually exclusive.

This chapter first provides a critical summary of the various perspectives on ethnicity and, in so doing, elucidates the characteristic strengths and weaknesses of each perspective and also seeks to indicate the areas of mutual inclusiveness and compatibility among various perspectives. The discussion then shows that the diversity of theories of ethnicity and nationalism is not necessarily a basis for conflict. Rather, analysis reveals the potential for a 'pluralistic' approach to theoretical understanding of the subject in which the relationship among theories is complementary rather than competitive. The 'pluralistic' approach will be evaluated in the light of the Japanese case: it will be shown that supposedly contradictory theoretical perspectives can complement one another to explain the continuous development of Japanese nationalism.

THEORIES OF ETHNICITY: A REVIEW AND ASSESSMENT

What follows is a reorganisation of the complicated debate on theories of ethnicity in which I identify three different levels of analysis and examine a logically appropriate set of theoretical perspectives at each level. By so doing I do *not* suggest that the paired perspectives are mutually exclusive.

'Primordialism' and the 'boundary approach'

The first is the level of analysis concerning the essential nature of ethnicity: it seeks to examine the mechanism whereby an ethnic group constitutes and perpetuates itself, asking the question how it is that ethnicity exists and persists as durable ties. The logically appropriate set of perspectives that should be examined on this level consists of 'primordialism' and 'the boundary approach'. The primordialist approach places primary importance on the role of primordial ties for an ethnic group to constitute and perpetuate itself over time. The boundary approach, on the other hand, finds the primary condition of ethnicity in the symbolic boundary process differentiating between 'us' and 'them', which is considered essential to enable the group to constitute and maintain itself. Primordialism and the boundary approach emphasise the 'time' and 'space' dimensions of ethnicity, respectively.

Primordialism is the classic perspective on ethnicity, but it has undergone a conscious reaffirmation, both as a result of the confirmed recognition that primordial sentiment is not destined to decline in the wake of social structural differentiation and in response to the provocative challenge from the boundary approach. This classic view holds that 'primordial ties' form the 'natural' basis of an ethnic group. 'Primordial ties' as used by Edward Shils refer, first, to the ties, real or imaginary, relating to the historical origin of the community or the ties of kinship that bind a community's members to their common ancestors and, second, to the ties of culture shared by members of the community, which tend to be regarded as naturally given (1957: 113–45). Primordialism is, thus, a primary tendency to identify an ethnic group in terms of kinship, which implies ancestry and culture. The primordialist approach attaches supreme importance to the continuity over time of the ethnic community by emphasising these two aspects of the primordial ties. Primordial ties are considered essential to the sentiment of the ethnic community as they symbolise the starting point of the community. Furthermore, culture transmitted intergenerationally within the community promotes its integration. It is for these reasons that analysis of the cultural traits defining an ethnic community becomes the chief focus of enquiry for the primordialist. The primordialist approach is also exemplified by Clifford Geertz (1963) and Harold Isaacs (1975), who adopted Shils's usage.

Although Fredrik Barth is the most explicit exponent of the boundary approach, it should be remembered that there are also those before him who held the 'boundary perspective' in a prototypical manner, such as Edmund Leach (1954) and Max Gluckman (1940). Leach's study of the Katchin may be regarded as an earlier challenge to a primordialist – or, to be more precise, 'culturalist' – understanding of an ethnic group. Leach was probably the first to call attention to the *sine qua non* of defining one's own group in its relationship to other groups. In *The Political System of Highland Burma*, he brought a new perspective to show that the identity of the Katchin as a group could not be established in terms of their shared cultural traits, but only by considering their relationship with neighbouring groups. Leach remarked that 'the ordinary conventions as to what constitutes *a* culture and *a* society are hopelessly inappropriate' (Leach 1954: 28). In the field of sociology, it would appear that Max Gluckman was the first to place ethnicity within the purview of self/other relations. Taking an insight from Evans-Prichard's study of witchcraft, he introduced the concept of 'situational selection' in his study of European–Zulu relations in the South Africa of the 1930s. Gluckman (1940) showed how an individual's behaviour in a specific group setting varied according to the situational factors involved, such as values, beliefs, personal interests, technology and so on. His idea then developed into the concept of 'situational ethnicity', which pays much attention to the fluidity of ethnic boundaries.[3]

It is Fredrik Barth who made the boundary perspective an established perspective on ethnicity. Barth argued that 'the critical focus of investigation from this point of view becomes the ethnic *boundary* that defines the group, not the cultural stuff that it encloses' (1969: 15). He is not concerned with fixed cultural characteristics, but rather his analysis aims at understanding the boundary process by which the in-group is distinguished from the out-group. The Barthian approach has developed out of his criticisms concerning the classic view on the relationship between culture and an ethnic group. Barth argues that if the culture-bearing aspect of ethnic groups is regarded as their primary characteristic, 'the classification of persons and local groups as members of an ethnic group must depend on their exhibiting the particular traits of the culture' and the 'differences between groups become differences in trait inventories', thereby suggesting that it is necessary to explain why an ethnic community persists in the situation in which communities share with one another increasing numbers of cultural items (ibid.: 12). He thus proposes to draw attention to the analysis of *ethnic organisation*, not of the contents of shared culture.

Since problems with primordialism have already been suggested, let us assess the boundary approach. One major limitation of the boundary approach is its lack of concern with cultural content, for what makes ethnicity if culture does not matter? The difference between Jews and non-Jews and between Muslims and non-Muslims is not an arbitrary boundary: what makes them different is their religion and its accompanying culture. The members of an eth- nic group are concerned with the boundary not to maintain the boundary *per se* but to perpetuate their culture, religion and race. Commitment to their culture and religion is not simply for the sake of maintaining a boundary, but rather because they wish to maintain and perpetuate their culture and religion. There are cases, however, in which boundary appears to be a primary issue. When the Zulu and the Swazi came to town and began to interact, they were concerned with boundary marking. But again it is not an arbitrary boundary: it is based on *their* belief in possessing a different culture (e.g. the absence of Queen mother in the former and its presence in the latter).[4] To outsiders, their cultural difference may appear to be insignificant, but to them this is an important distinction. Moreover, the belittling of the 'contents' enclosed within the boundary results in a failure to distinguish ethnic solidarity from other forms of collective solidarity (e.g. regionalism, religion and class).

There is another, neglected, problem of the boundary approach. In its challenge of primordialism, the boundary approach takes up only one of the two principal concerns of primordialism – its concern with constitutive cultural traits – and discards the other concern regarding the historical origin of the community, thereby failing to do justice to the primordialist. The boundary approach concerns itself only with the spatial dimension of ethnicity – 'spatial' in the symbolic sense – and ignores the time dimension, failing to prepare its own answer to the question of why an ethnic community clings to its own past and traditions. By contrast, primordialism tends to be wedded to the time dimension, thereby also failing to convince fully. The one-sided clinging to either the time dimension or the space dimension is a major problem of the current theoretical debate, as will be discussed in more detail later.

'Expressivism' (affectivism) and 'instrumentalism'

This level of analysis delves into the characteristic role of ethnicity in modern life, or the question of what it is that ethnicity has to attract modern people. At this level, I consider 'expressivism' (or 'affectivism') and 'instrumentalism'. Ordinarily, it is primordialism and instrumentalism that are set against each other (e.g. McKay 1982), but this is the result of a failure to distinguish levels of analysis. More will be said concerning this error later. The controversy revolves around the question of whether ethnicity is to be seen merely as an expressive experience of affects, or whether it should be understood as a political means of interest groups.

The expressive or affective role of ethnicity has long been considered the mainstream view. The recent resurgence of ethnicity has led to a reaffirmation of this point of view. For example, J. M. Yinger (1976: 206) has written that in the modern world of rapid social change and a high degree of mobility, a world increasingly dominated by universalism, rationalism and instrumentalism, ethnicity provides a name and an identity to the lonely crowd living in this *Gesellschaft*-type modern society.

Instrumentalism, by way of contrast, understands ethnicity as a means of achieving specific ends. Glazer and Moynihan's analysis (1963) of the behaviour of New York ethnic groups from the viewpoint of interest groups may be regarded as a pioneering work. But it was with the work of Abner Cohen (1969, 1974) that the instrumentalist approach gained full acceptance. In his study of the Hausa of Ibadan in West Africa, Cohen defined ethnic groups as informal political interest groups. He analysed the process whereby people inhabiting certain areas of the city formed an ethnic organisation as a political means of pursuing their economic activities and livelihood. In Cohen's own words, 'tribes . . . are everywhere becoming integral parts of new state structures and are thus being transformed into ethnic groups with varying degrees of cultural distinctiveness' (1974: ix). It is worthy of note that Geertz (1963: 105–57), with his primordialist stance, interprets the same sort of phenomenon in an opposite direction, as being various expressions of the primordial tie of ethnicity, such as linguism in India, regionalism in Indonesia and racialism in Malaysia.[5]

Instrumentalism may be criticised from various angles (see e.g. Epstein 1978: 93–6). Its first problem is its inability to explain the persistence of the ethnic group itself despite continual changes in the contents of the group's interests. Hence, in order for a group to be defined as an ethnic group, there has to be some other factor which is antecedent to the interests of the group. Similarly, over-emphasis on the instrumentality of the group's behaviour results in failure to recognise the expressive aspects characteristic of ethnic behaviour. Glazer and Moynihan themselves modified their position in a later work, stating that 'one reason that ethnicity has become so effective a means of advancing interests is that it involves more than interests', and quoted a remark by Daniel Bell that ethnicity 'has become more salient [than class] because it can combine an interest with an affective tie' (Glazer and Moynihan 1974: 37). Accordingly, then, provided that instrumentalism is regarded not as an approach to define ethnicity as an interest group but as an approach to illuminate the effectiveness of ethnicity in promoting the interests of 'ethnic groups', the contribution of this approach merits recognition. It has provided a vital perspective from which to understand the complexity of contemporary society through the analysis of the dynamic interrelationships between politics and economy, on one hand, and affects, on the other (Ebuchi 1983: 517).

'Historicism' and 'modernism'

On the third level of analysis exists the opposition between 'historicism' and 'modernism'.[6] On the previous two analytical levels, explanation of the resurgence of ethnicity was sought through understanding of the essential nature and role of ethnicity; on this level the focal point of enquiry becomes the historical depth of the ethnic/national phenomenon. The two opposing perspectives are set against each other in the attempt to explain the emergence and resurgence of nationalism in the modern era. On the one hand, we find the view that the emergence and resurgence of nationalism are the inevitable results that derive from the very make-up of modern industrial society ('modernism'); opposed to this is the view that there is no intrinsic causal link with the process of industrialisation and modernisation, but rather that nationalism is rooted in a long, continuous historical process antedating the modern era ('historicism'). The significance of the enquiry on this level of analysis is that it represents a general condensation of the basic attitudes and assumptions of ethnicity and nationalism researchers. Thus, it is, in effect, the 'applied version' of the previous two levels.

I shall take up the three sub-varieties of the historicist perspective here. The first school, represented by Charles Tilly (1975), Gianfranco Poggi (1978) and John Breuilly (1982), regards the development of a competitive state system in Europe from the Middle Ages as an independent variable in the analysis of the basis of the national community. According to this perspective, from about the thirteenth century, rulers began to establish their independent sovereignty against the Church and Emperor by consolidating their own territory, centralising authority and standardising culture within this territory. In this historical process, the state began to assume a 'national' character; and in parallel with the spread of the idea of popular sovereignty in the eighteenth century, modern nationalism was born at the hands of political and secular rulers as an ideology legitimating their triumph over the dynastic state. This explanation considers the post-eighteenth-century formation of the modern nation-state and nationalism exclusively from the viewpoint of political institutions.

The second type of historicist views is contained in the theory of Anthony D. Smith (especially 1971, 1981, 1986), who introduces sociological variables, thereby advancing this line of thought into a more comprehensive theory of ethnicity and nationalism. Smith's basic contention is found in his emphasis on the historical depth of ethnicity, on the basis of which he shows how modern nations – to be more precise, the first nations of Europe and several other leading states such as Russia, Japan, China, Burma, Egypt, Iran, Turkey and Ethiopia – were reconstructed from the older ethnic ties. Smith argues that such a perspective reintroduces

> the much longer time-spans of pre-modern *ethnie* [ethnic community], and the survival of ethnic ties and ethnic mosaics from these periods into the modern world; and thereby makes it possible to explain the durability and widespread appeal of nations, and the intensity of ethnic aspirations today.
>
> (Smith 1988: 10)

Smith regards nationalism in the first nations of Europe as the modern manifestation of a much older cycle of ethnic resurgence in history. He maintains that the salience of ethnicity waxes and wanes in a recurring historical cycle. The ancient Greeks, for instance, possessed a firm ethnic identity in terms of culture, religion and institutions, but during the Roman imperial era such ethnic feelings diminished. Later, from the thirteenth century onwards, cultural ethnicism once again began to grow stronger in Europe as the rivalry for power among the various kingdoms intensified. (The Tudor dynasty, for example, made use of the growing sense of an English national identity in the resistance against Spain.) Smith, like Tilly and others, argues that the emergence of national consciousness in the early modern era in northern and western, and also in parts of eastern Europe, was induced by the recurrence of interstate wars, but advances a historicist explanation still further.

Smith links the revival of ethnicity in the modern era with the advance of science and the decline of religion. With the expansion of the realm of the secular 'scientific state' and the erosion of the religious colouration of the community, people are confronted with the dilemma of rationality versus communality (religiosity), with the consequent necessity of choosing one over the other or somehow managing a satisfactory integration. Smith's argument concerning solutions to this 'crisis of dual legitimation' is too extensive to be fully dealt with here; suffice to summarise his contention as stating that ethnic historicism arose as an attempt to solve this dilemma. The goal of ethnic historicism is to revive the ethnic community through a rediscovery and renewal of ethnic communal identity and a reconstruction or mores and attitudes that had existed at some time in the past. Particular attention is paid to the role of secular intellectuals undergoing an 'identity crisis' who serve in the vanguard of an ethnic historicist revival.[7]

A third school of historicism is represented by John Armstrong (1982), who holds that ethnicity, while indeed existing as long as human history itself, does not possess the character of primordial ties with relatively fixed 'naturally given' internal characteristics. He shows that ethnicity is the cumulative result of repeated boundary processes in the past.[8]

In contrast to historicism, modernism interprets the emergence and resurgence of ethnicity and nationalism as the product of the characteristic features of modern industrial society. Presented here is a summary of the viewpoint of modernism, with attention focused on the two representative issues concerning the relationship of nationalism to industrialisation and to modernisation. First, a heated debate surrounds the question: are nationalism and nation, the basic constituents of the modern international system, attributable to the process of industrialisation and modernisation? Or are they deeply rooted in human history itself? Second, it was previously a commonly held view among social scientists that the twin forces of industrialisation and modernisation, which were giving birth to 'the nation', would at one and the same time bring about an atrophy of ethnicity among minority regions left behind by these forces. In reality, however, there has been a marked resurgence of ethnicity among minority regions within the confines of the modern nation-state, and thus the relationship between industrialisation (and modernisation) and ethnicity has demanded an explanation in this other context. Thus, when we refer to the relationship between modernisation and ethnicity (and nationalism), there are actually two different dimensions to the problem.

The modernist approach may also be divided into three sub-varieties. First, there is what may be called the 'communications approach'. Karl Deutsch's (1966) classic thesis explains the rise of nationality in terms of cultural assimilation (typically, linguistic homogenisation) that occurs as a result of increasing social communication and economic exchange in modern society. According to this thesis, the process of 'social mobilisation' and the uprooting of villagers and small townsmen results in the cultural assimilation of smaller ethnic communities into a central or dominant region, that is, a nation. There are a number of objections to the 'communications perspective'. First, it gives too much weight to the volume of communication, thereby losing sight of the framework in which communication takes place, namely, the historical framework of an existing state. Second, although it may be granted that social communication may result in a new type of social integration, the theory does not explain why this integration must take the form of an ethnic nation. And third, in the modern era, ethnic separatism would seem to be rather more common than nation-building.[9]

Ernest Gellner (1973, 1983) also sees the emergence of nationalism as inseparable from industrialisation. That is to say, modern industry requires a mobile, literate and homogeneous population. This mobile population extending over a wider area becomes increasingly uprooted from basic social units such as kinship, and a new type of social integration based on language and culture becomes possible and necessary. Since regional mobility is limited to a particular region with a particular language or culture, nationalism will tend to arise as the integrative force for that particular linguistic-cultural region. Pre-industrial society, on the other hand, had no room for nations or nationalism because of its internal cultural division between elites and masses and the lack of integrative ideology.[10]

There is a second version of modernism formulated and presented by Benedict Anderson in *Imagined Communities* (1983). Anderson's viewpoint derives from another essential feature of modern society: the extensive use of the printed word under the new technology of 'print capitalism'. His main point is that the decline of religion and the rise of the printed word have both necessitated and enabled anonymous individuals, who do not socially interact with one another, to form an 'imagined' linkage among themselves and eventually a sense of belonging to an 'imagined' community of nationality sharing the same homogeneous time and space. *The Invention of Tradition* edited by Hobsbawm and Ranger (1983) may also be considered in this connection. This perspective indicates the recent emergence of many of what we now regard as time-honoured traditions and symbols of nation[11] (e.g. the Scottish tartan and kilt and the Welsh love of music) and throws light on the process whereby traditions are invented in order to establish a sense of continuity with the past (see pp. 82–3). The implications of this approach to the study of nationalism are significant, as Hobsbawm remarks that 'the national phenomenon cannot be adequately investigated without careful attention to the "invention of tradition"' since these modern concepts of 'France' and 'the French' must include an 'invented' component (Hobsbawm 1983: 14). It is in the sense that they pay no attention to pre-existing ethnic ties and their impact on the development of nations and nationalism that Gellner, Anderson and Hobsbawm are classified as 'modernists'.

The other major issue to be examined from the modernist point of view deals in terms of centre–periphery models with the phenomenon of ethnicity and nationalism of peripheral communities. This is usually focused on groups within the confines of the modern nation-state such as the Welsh and Scottish, Breton, Flemish, Basque and Catalan, although this theory also applies to the international scene involving many countries in Asia and

Africa, as Wallerstein remarks: 'The creation of strong states within a world system was a historical prerequisite to the rise of nationalism both within strong states and in the periphery' (1974: 149). This school of modernism, sometimes referred to as the 'internal colonial model', challenges the functionalist prediction of an inevitable decline in the salience of ethnicity with the increase of cultural homogenisation of the population in step with industrialisation and modernisation. In his analysis of nationalism in Wales, Scotland and Ireland, Michael Hechter (1975, 1978) links the resurgence of ethnic solidarity to the situation of an internal 'cultural division of labour' resulting from an uneven diffusion of industrialisation, and sees the revitalised solidarity as the reaction of the underdeveloped but culturally distinctive 'periphery' against the socially and economically dominant 'centre'. Ethnicity becomes revitalised as a means by which the 'periphery' may break out of the bondage from 'internal colonialism'. Tom Nairn (1977) advances a theory along a similar line. In this model, ethnic solidarity is conceived as a political instrument to be used by elites in peripheral zones for them to appeal to the masses to counter the political dominance contained in the uneven expansion of capitalism.

This model performs well in elucidating the economic background of the collective behaviour of specific groups, but in other areas problems abound. Some of the shortcomings of this model as a 'general' theory are, first, the invalidity of the model insofar as it posits the 'cultural division of labour' as the independent variable of ethnic resurgence, because an exactly opposite model exists in which the *lack* of a 'cultural division of labour' is given as the cause of ethnic revival (see Hannan 1979; Nielsen 1980; Ragin 1979). Second, underdeveloped regions by no means all undergo a resurgence of ethnicity (e.g. the southern region of Italy). A third difficulty with the model is that, although underdeveloped regions may be nationalistic (Brittany is a case in point), it is more often the case that regions which are more developed than the 'centre' (Catalonia, for example) are nationalistic. The problem seen in all of these examples stems from reducing the problem to the factor of underdevelopment and reducing the problem to mere regional differences. The model also fails to address adequately other crucial questions such as why ethnic ties are so effective. (These points are related to criticism of instrumentalism, discussed earlier.) The historical dimension – the existence of received traditions, values, cultural forms and so on – must be considered.

The relationship among the three analytical levels

It is now appropriate to clarify some areas of mutual compatibility and the relationship among the various theoretical approaches. First, I shall consider the apparent opposition between primordialism and the boundary approach and between expressivism and instrumentalism. Traditionally, an ethnic group has been understood as a group with a shared culture and belief in the community's origin. Both primordialism and expressivism, albeit from somewhat different perspectives, are based on a reaffirmation of this understanding, and are therefore compatible with each other. Instrumentalism and the boundary approach are often mistakingly lumped together but must be kept clearly separate. Instrumentalism presupposes the boundary approach, but not vice versa. Instrumentalism sees ethnicity as an effective and attractive means by which to mobilise masses of people in the pursuit of political and economic interests in mobile modern society in which a variety of groups are in mutual competition. For individuals, ethnic affiliations and loyalties fluctuate considerably and change their meanings depending on the generations and situations, as in the case of cross-generational American ethnic groups and 're-tribalised' African immigrants (Smith 1984: 452). Instrumentalism presupposes the boundary approach precisely because of this fluidity of ethnic identity. It may be critically said of instrumentalism that 'to see ethnicity as essentially a political phenomenon . . . is to make the same kind of methodological error as those who earlier defined it in terms of culture' (Epstein 1978: 95–6). By way of contrast, the boundary approach provides a more general conceptual framework (that is, the boundary process), thereby enabling debate on a higher conceptual level of analysis. Hence, this approach should clearly be distinguished from instrumentalism. If this is done, the boundary approach will be swept up willy-nilly in the harsh criticism of the instrumentalist's overstress on the political aspect of ethnicity, with the result that the real importance of boundary process analysis will be overlooked. Analysis will then tend not to go beyond a one-dimensional understanding of durable ethnic ties.

What of the relationship between the historicism/modernism

pair and other perspectives? First, modernism presupposes the instrumentalist and boundary approaches. This is so because the reduction of ethnicity to a structural feature of modern industrial society involves a process whereby particular social strata emphasise boundaries that set their own group off from their neighbouring groups and make use of their sense of belonging to a particular region as an instrument of competing with the other groups. Another noteworthy point is that primordialism, which sees ethnicity as a natural and persistent component of human societies, leads easily to the historicist's viewpoint which understands modern nationalism as one variation of the ethnic phenomenon rooted in history. But, the reverse does not hold true. One version of historicist theory (i.e. Armstrong's) accepts the view that ethnicity long antedates modernity, but does not regard it as a 'naturally given' primordial tie but as the product of repeated boundary processes in the past.

THE THEORETICAL DEBATE AND THE CASE OF JAPANESE NATIONALISM

What relevance does the theoretical debate have to an understanding of Japanese nationalism? What contribution does the study of Japan make to a theoretical understanding of ethnicity and nationalism? The Japanese example shows, as has been seen and as will be demonstrated further, much complementarity among the supposedly mutually contradictory theories and reveals that the continuous development of Japanese nationalism can appropriately be studied by adopting a pluralistic theoretical approach.

A large part of the theoretical antagonism that exists in a variety of forms can be boiled down, if not reduced, to a theoretical conflict between approaches focusing on the dimensions of the time and space of ethnicity. Primordialism and historicism, for the most part, attach supreme importance to the time dimension in explaining the nature, formation and persistence of ethnicity, stressing the sense of stability in time which is derived from shared beliefs in a distinct historical origin and communal life history. On the other hand, the boundary approach, instrumentalism and modernism are fundamentally space oriented, explaining the durability of ethnic ties by a boundary process or by the subjective or instrumental use of the 'us' and 'them' dichotomy.

The question of the 'time' and 'space' orientations, which reflects a fundamental point of argument in the theoretical debate, is also a question of how intellectuals engaged in cultural nationalism formulate ideas of national distinctiveness, as already suggested in the previous chapters. Bearing in mind that one is inclined to see a selected slice of reality by holding a particular perspective, it may be said that the space-oriented and time-oriented perspectives are analytically useful for different phases of nationalism, and that both provide valuable insights when applied in their proper contexts, respectively. Primordialists and historicists regard myths of descent and historical memories as primarily important components of ethnic identity. This is, as we saw, a useful perspective especially on the initial phases of Japanese nationalism. *Kokugaku* in particular suggests that the historical memory of a nation is at the core of the sense of national identity (see chapter 3). In the case of Japan's 'secondary nationalism', or resurgent cultural nationalism in the 1970s and 1980s, the primordialist/historicist perspective is given less weight, and a symbolic boundary concern increases in relative importance.

Focusing on the most basic analytical level where the primordial and boundary approaches appear to offer mutually opposing explanations, the 'invention of tradition' perspective proves useful for an understanding that the two need not, in fact, be mutually exclusive. The 'invention of tradition', as presented by Hobsbawm and others (1983), refers to the process by which societies, in response to the experience of rapid change and in order to maintain and establish a sense of continuity with the past, 'invent' traditions by employing old materials for new purposes in new conditions.

What this perspective suggests to the space-oriented boundary approach is that boundary items are often selected in such a way that the group may be able to ensure its sense of historical continuity. The use of 'our tradition', which is supposed to be long known to the group, effectively serves to maintain and enhance the secure, time-oriented sense of the identity of the ethnic group. Take, for example, the concern of Japanese scholars with the pre-industrial village community (*mura*) as the prototype of 'modern' Japanese social groups (see chapter 5). Group solidarity and group-oriented practices in the company and political party in modern Japan (e.g. the communal decision-making and consultation style, vertical social relations, age-group mentality), depicted as 'peculiarly Japanese' traits in the *nihonjinron*, are explained as deriving from peasants' solidarity and patterns of behaviour in the pre-industrial village community of Tokugawa Japan (1600–1867). Modern Japan is characterised positively in terms of an enlivened traditional structure and culture. Historical memories are not completely irrelevant in secondary nationalism. Meanwhile, the perspective of 'invention of tradition' urges a primordialist to reconsider the nature of 'primordial' ties in that many of the 'naturally given' primordial ties are not fixed entities but selected symbols of 'tradition', selected as appropriate to the particular group at particular phases of its history. Such symbols, selected with the aim of securing the comforting sense of time-oriented continuity between the group's present and its past, enhance the sense of significant difference between 'us' and 'them', and herein lies an important association with the boundary approach. The emperor system as a tradition 'invented' in the late nineteenth century is a good example in this regard (see chapter 5). Also, the non-rational, non-verbal and intuitive approach of the Japanese as discovered by Tokugawa *kokugaku* scholars in the ancient poetry became a source of self-identity of the Japanese as opposed to the supposedly rational and eloquent (or verbose) Chinese and later Westerners (see chapters 2 and 3).

Another fundamental issue of theoretical controversy concerns whether nationalism is a specifically modern phenomenon or has deep roots in history. The Japanese case exemplifies both sides of the debate without necessary contradiction. The Japanese experience of nation-formation is likely to validate the historicist theory. Grounding an understanding of modern nationalism on the much longer time-spans of pre-modern ethnic community, Smith points out the importance of investigating 'how far its themes and forms were pre-figured in earlier periods and how far a connection with earlier ethnic ties and sentiments can be established' (1986: 13). There is little question that, prior to the beginning of the Meiji era in the late nineteenth century, a large section of the population inhabiting the central and southern parts of the Japanese archipelago had possessed an 'ethnic' identity in the sense of a belief that Japan comprised a distinct cultural entity (as opposed to China). Furthermore, pre-modern Japanese history can be described as a process of developing an ethnic state through a series of attempts at centralisation.

The adoption of the *ritsuryō* system (state-governing system) in the eighth century brought about a high degree of political, administrative, military and economic centralisation in Japan. But by the twelfth century political and military power gradually devolved away from the centre (i.e. the imperial court of Kyoto) along with a degree of economic autonomy. A series of wars in the twelfth century, in particular, was instrumental in transferring the locus of administrative power from the court nobles to the military chiefs, bringing about feudalism in Japan. The ensuing centuries witnessed confrontations over military and administrative power among rival military families and factions, between the ruling military family and the civil nobility, and then among regional warlords. In particular, the age of civil wars in the sixteenth century witnessed hundreds of regional warlords fighting one another for the aggrandisement of their fiefs, with the ultimate aim of ruling the whole country. The civil warfare created alliances, thereby eventually reducing the number of fighting families to a small number of the most powerful ones. Feudal Japan also saw such attempts to restore a degree of central administration as the establishment in 1185 of the Kamakura bakufu government and the shogunal dynasty of the Minamoto, of the Ashikaga government in 1338, and finally of the Tokugawa government in 1600. Reunification and the establishment of a lasting military hegemony was carried out by Oda Nobunaga (1534–82), who gained control of most of the central provinces of Japan, and by Toyotomi Hideyoshi (1536–98), who succeeded in extending control to most of the southern island of Kyūshū and other strategically important regions of the country, and finally by Tokugawa Ieyasu (1542–1616), who established the Tokugawa shogunate that controlled Japan from 1600 to 1867. The chief concern of Hideyoshi and the early Tokugawa shoguns was to achieve political and economic unification. Hideyoshi carried out a number of measures such as a monopoly on mining, minting of coins, the standardisation of weights and measures, abolition of customs barriers,[12] a land survey and so on. The subsequent Tokugawa government imposed Confucian principles of social order on the whole society to consolidate the unification ideologically. Furthermore, the early Tokugawa shoguns carried out various measures to weaken the military, economic and political power of the daimyō (feudal lords), thereby consolidating their own power (see Lehmann 1982: ch. 2).

This sketch of pre-modern Japanese history provides support for the historicist argument – particularly that of Smith – that these centralising attempts in the pre-modern era were not 'motivated by nationalism, or by ideas of cultural autonomy' (1986: 91). Smith's view of the late-medieval and early-modern attempts to homogenise the population and to produce an 'ethnic state' is pertinent here:

> They [ethnic states in England, Sweden, Russia, Spain and Japan] stemmed from the needs of rulers and factions of the ruling classes to preserve their positions against rivals. . . . Yet as a by-product of these concerns, the growth of definite ethnic polities is evident, that is, polities whose majority is formed by a single *ethnie*, one that to varying degrees incorporates some of the lower and dependent strata into the culture and symbolism of the dominant elites. . . . In this way, they [administrative and religious elements of these elites] help to stabilize the polity, and enable it to weld the population together in a manner that favours the territorial integrity of the state. It was from this base that nations and nationalism emerged.
>
> (Smith 1986: 91)

What has just been said must not be taken to suggest that the formation of the Japanese nation has nothing to do with modernity. The course of nationalism in Japan has some bearing on modernist theory as well. The communications perspective in general is a necessary one to explain the spread of national sentiment in early-modern Japan. Japanese society for the first three decades following the Meiji Restoration of 1868 came gradually to be closely tied together by greater political, administrative and educational centralisation, and economic growth. An equally important factor in this regard was increasing communication facilitated by the growth of the popular press and other means of communication. It is during the decade leading to around 1895 that we find the type of collective sentiment that may properly be called modern nationalism. In the years prior to that, there existed nationalist ideas and action, but they were chiefly confined to intellectuals and a section of the ruling class.

A particularly relevant modernist perspective for our Japanese case is Benedict Anderson's theory of 'imagined community', according to which 'imagined' communities have replaced 'real' communities with the decline of religion and the rise and extensive use of the printed word in the modern period. I do not suggest that this theory alone explains the *origins* of the nation and nationalism, which should be understood, as has just been discussed, by taking account of pre-modern developments, but if the use of the theory is extended to include the enhancement of the already existing ethnic/national sentiment, it has some very relevant points to make. There is little question that extensive printed works on Japanese uniqueness (the *nihonjinron*) have been a key factor promoting imagination among 'the Japanese' (or at least educated Japanese) that they comprise a 'community' sharing a uniquely Japanese cultural ethos, despite the fact that those who inhabit the 'Japanese space' comprise diverse groups and cannot see for themselves how people in social groups and regions other than their own feel, think and behave. The promoted image is that of modern Japan as an extension of the traditional village community, as has been discussed earlier with reference to the 'invention of tradition' – another modernist perspective. This issue will be discussed fully in chapter 5.

The Japanese case does not necessarily support all modernist theories. It gives rise to questions concerning the views that explain the formation of the nation exclusively in terms of modern capitalism and industrialisation. Furthermore, the contemporary Japanese experience may be presented as a strong counter-example against another type of modernist theory that attributes the resurgence of ethnicity and cultural nationalism to economically deprived regions. This modernist and instrumentalist theory sees the resurgence of ethnic sentiment and solidarity as the reaction of the economically underdeveloped but culturally distinctive 'periphery' against the economically and politically dominant 'centre'. The validity of this theory is challenged by the presence of the example of contemporary Japan, one of the most economically dominant countries in the contemporary world. The Japanese (business) elites' reassertion of cultural uniqueness has nothing to do with the condition of economic deprivation and threat caused by the uneven expansion of capitalism, but is largely a response to Japan's perceived industrial strength (see chapter 8).

Chapter 5

Modern Japanese society as *Gemeinschaft*: the holistic tradition in theories of modern Japan

Japanese thinking elites tend to view the uniqueness of Japanese social culture in a holistic manner, as was seen in chapter 2 and as will be discussed further in the following chapters. The aim of this chapter is to enquire further into the holistic view of society which has been an important intellectual tradition in both academic and politicised theories of modern Japanese society. I also wish to show that some of the core academic theories of modern Japanese society, which have affected the theoretical tone of the *nihonjinron*, focus on peasant traditions rather than samurai traditions as the main historical roots of modern Japanese society. The choice of peasant traditions exemplifies, and has a particular bearing on, the characteristic features of cultural nationalism in contemporary Japan.

Many of the following descriptions of modern Japanese society represent an idealised interpretation of that society rather than a rigorously constructed representation of reality.

THE HOLISTIC APPROACH TO INDUSTRIAL SOCIETY

The explanation of order and cohesion in society has been a central concern of social theory. The question of order, or of what holds society together, has been explained in various ways. Two of the main explanations are, first, order by commonly-held *conscience collective*, and second, order by structural integration or interdependence in the division of labour. (Another explanation may be order by the use of coercion, physical, symbolic or moral.)[1]

The attempt to explain order in a highly differentiated industrial society as a whole is called holism, which is often equated with functionalism. I shall introduce another type of holism here, which I propose to call 'reproductionism' or 'extensionism'. This perspective regards order in industrial society as a reproduction or extension of order which is characteristic of *Gemeinschaft* or pre-industrial, communal society.

Functionalism regards a society as a system of interacting parts and aims to analyse order in a highly differentiated industrial society mainly through structural integration. Some forms of functionalism also regard commonly-held values as a necessary element of social order. Talcot Parsons (1937, 1951), for example, supplemented structural integration by indicating the importance of common sentiment and values for order through Durkheimian emphasis on collective consciousness as well as Weberian stress on ideas and values. But this does not deny the fact that structural integration or interdependence among differentiated parts of society is the primary concern of functionalism as a perspective to understand industrial society. Industrial society is described as differentiated and essentially segmentary and, in this sense, is contrasted sharply with pre-industrial communal society (*Gemeinschaft*) where members are tied to one another by common sentiment and values.

'Reproductionism' (or 'extensionism'), as I propose here, is another type of holism which attempts to explain order in industrial society primarily by *conscience collective* reminiscent of pre-industrial society. According to this perspective, industrial society is not contrasted with pre-industrial society but portrayed as an extension of *Gemeinschaft*-type pre-industrial society. Industrial society is orderly because the traditional realms of communal conscience collective have expanded to the level of the total society. 'Modernisation' is thus viewed as a process by which the bases of social order characteristic of pre-industrial social units become the prototype of order in industrial society.

The 'reproductionist' (or 'extensionist') theories hold that 'familial' and 'communal' industrial society has been formed in the 'modernising' process of Japan. Such a view has been a dominant intellectual tradition in academic as well as politicised theories of modern Japanese society. In fact, many ideas advanced in the *nihonjinron* are not necessarily original but quite often the popularised versions of these theories. It is therefore meaningful to look into those theories which have influenced the more popular literature on the distinctiveness of Japanese society.

In simple, small, pre-industrial society, kinship and community are normally the basic units of the social system. Kinship relations may be so extensive and significant that they often constitute the social system itself, but community is the more comprehensive concept in referring to a pre-industrial social unit. In simple, pre-industrial societies, order is usually understood to result from *conscience collective* or solidarity of resemblance (Durkheim [1893] 1960). According to 'reproductionism', the *conscience collective* characteristic of pre-industrial kinship and community has expanded beyond its original sphere to form the solidarity principle of the industrial society of modern Japan. The following discussion will describe the main characteristics of the kinship institution (*ie*) and the village community (*mura*) in pre-industrial Japan and show the ways in which such characteristics are explained, in the 'reproductionist theory', as having expanded their spheres throughout the modern, industrial society of Japan.

THE FAMILY AS A PROTOTYPE OF MODERN SOCIETY

The family system in pre-industrial Japan

The indigenous kinship institution that existed in pre-industrial Japan was the 'stem family' in which the eldest son (or the eldest daughter in the absence of sons) married and stayed in the parents' family to continue the main family (*honke*), while younger sons split off to establish their own branch families (*bunke*). These branch families thereafter continued to perpetuate themselves in the same lineal way (Aruga 1943, 1950). The main family and numerous branch families composed *dōzoku* (literally, 'the same lineage'), a clan system sharing a common ancestor and surname. Aruga Kizaemon points out that 'the main function of the *dōzoku* was worship of the family gods, and from that followed all types of cooperation in matters of everyday life' (1943: 102). This lineal family constituted the basic unit of social organisation in pre-industrial Japan. Unlike the Chinese stem family, the members of which were restricted to blood relatives, the Japanese *dōzoku* could include persons unrelated by blood to the family as its members (Aruga 1959: 175).[2]

Although it was generally the eldest son who succeeded to the position of the head of the household and inherited the family property, this primogeniture inheritance pattern was not an absolute rule among peasants during the Tokugawa period (1600–1867). It was the Meiji government that strengthened this system by law, using the samurai institutions as the basis for their concept of family. The head of the household had great power because he represented the lineal continuity of the family, directed rites of ancestor worship, directed family business (in the form of agriculture, commerce or craft work), and controlled the income the family had earned and the family property (Fukutake 1982: 26–9; Tsurumi 1970: 106).

Fukutake Tadashi indicates that the Japanese word *ie* (family) referred to a phenomenon that transcended the notion of a family as simply a group of living members:

> It was conceived as including the house and property, the resources for carrying on the family occupation, and the graves in which the ancestors were buried, as a unity stretching from the distant past to the present and occupying a certain position in the status system of the village or the town. The *ie* in that sense was far more important than the individuals who were at any one time living members of it, and it was seen as natural that the individual personalities of family members should be ignored and sacrificed if necessary for the good of the whole.
>
> (Fukutake 1982: 28)

This notion of *ie* gave birth to the notion that each family – including eventually the nation as a family – has a unique character just as an individual has his/her own personality.

Extension of the sphere of the 'family' in modern Japan

William Kornhauser (1959: 74–5) classifies three types of groups: the primary group (which means the family), the state (which includes the whole population of a society) and the intermediate group (which is located between the primary group and the state). It is commonly held that modern Japan saw the extension or reproduction of the organisational and ideological constitutive principles of the family into the other levels of society: those of the state and the intermediate group.

'The family-state'

The process of state-building in Japan was the process of the familistic ideals being expanded to the level of the state. The familistic concept of the state[3] was conceived by the Meiji government leaders in order to counteract the more liberal theory of popular sovereignty based on equality and freedom of the people.[4] After the overthrow of the Tokugawa government in 1868, the Meiji elites perceived that the affective manipulation of the people was the most effective way to unify the country (then divided into about 270 feudal domains) and to enhance nationalism. This was achieved by adopting familism or the analogy of the state (nation) as family.

In an official commentary on the *Imperial Rescript on Education* (1890), Confucian scholar Inoue Tetsujirō attempted to clarify the concept of the family-state (*kazoku kokka*) with the help of many other prominent scholars. Drawing an analogy between the family and the state and using the two fundamental Confucian moral principles, Inoue maintained that loyalty (*chū*) to the emperor (*tennō*) was identical with filial piety (*kō*), as the emperor was the head of the state as family. It was then explained that there should be only one principle of unification, because the state was an organism consisting of individual families as its cells. Kawashima Takeyoshi (1957: 44) argues that the ideology of the family-state was formulated through the combination of the two types of familism, namely, the Confucian ethics of familism confined to the samurai in the Tokugawa period and the aforementioned indigenous family institution prevalent among the common people. The samurai type was oriented primarily towards 'normative consciousness' and the common people type towards 'emotive reactions'.

The state of Japan, the foundation of which was the emperor system, was firmly grounded in familism, which was supplemented by State Shinto. (A clear distinction must be made between folk Shinto, which was an indigenous animistic worship of one's ancestors among the common people, and State Shinto, which was a modern and politicised nationalist ideology based on emperor worship.[5]) *The Imperial Rescript on Education* issued in 1890 taught that the emperor was divine because of the unbroken imperial lineage from time immemorial (from the Sun Goddess). The emperor presided as the head of the main family, from which all Japanese families have subsequently branched out.[6]

The state had firm control over moral education in schools. The Ministry of Education instructed elementary school authorities that the familism expounded in the *Imperial Rescript on Education* (1890) should be the basis of moral education. Also, textbooks used after 1903 were compiled directly by the ministry. The notion of the

family-state was stressed by the government from that time forward
and was especially emphasised in the period prior to and during the
Second World War. In 1937, the Ministry of Education published
Kokutai no Hongi (The Principles of the National Polity) and declared
that education must be founded on *The Principles*. The following
passages from *The Principles* are indicative of the importance of
dōzoku-type kinship and Shinto in the emperor system.

> Our country is one great family nation, and the Imperial House-
> hold is the head family of the subjects and the nucleus of national
> life. The subjects revere the Imperial Household, which is the
> head family, with the tender esteem [they have] for their ancestors;
> and the Emperor loves his subjects as his very own.
> (Translated by Gauntlett and compiled in Hall 1949: 89–90)

> The unbroken line of Emperors, receiving the Oracle of the
> Founder of the Nation, reign eternally over the Japanese Empire.
> This is our eternal and immutable national entity. Thus, founded
> on this great principle, all the people, united as one great family
> nation in heart and obeying the Imperial Will, enhance indeed the
> beautiful virtues of loyalty and filial piety. This is the glory of our
> national entity. This national entity is the eternal and unchanging
> basis of our nation and shines resplendent throughout our history.
> (ibid.: 59)

'Familistic enterprise'

The company is one institution at the intermediate group level
where familism is firmly established. By 'familism' I do not mean
simply a small family business (*kagyō*), but rather the notion of
company-as-family which has been deliberately applied to large
modern companies. Unlike that of the family-state, the notion of
company-as-family is alive and well today. Since the development
of familistic enterprise has been extensively discussed by numerous
scholars, it will suffice to relate briefly only the background here.[7]

For about two decades following the Meiji Restoration in 1868,
Japan was essentially an agrarian society. Although a large textile
industry developed, production was done mainly in small family
workshops with not more than forty workers, most of whom were
young, subservient women recruited from the countryside. But with
the growth of the metal-working and engineering industries from

about the turn of the century, in which the employees were men, and with chronic shortages in skilled labour and increases in labour mobility, employers were forced to offer incentives for workers to stay, such as the prospects of a better career, better jobs and higher pay after a certain length of service, welfare schemes and bonuses. Along with these demands of the labour market, the rise of the labour union movement and the controversy over labour legislation provoked reactions from among industrialists and challenged them to develop a coherent employment policy. A common reaction was to have recourse to the metaphor of the family. It was asserted that in Japan, unlike in the West, the relations between employers and employees were harmonious, characterised by sentiments of mutual warmth as in a family; the former maintaining the traditionally benevolent attitudes towards the latter, who, in response, worked loyally for the former (see Clark 1979: 37–41; Marshall 1967: 57–64). Fukutake describes the sentiment attached to familism:

> For a Japanese, brought up in a familistic atmosphere, the world beyond the family was a turbulent world, an *ukiyo*. . . . The only way to achieve security in that *ukiyo* was to forge relationships outside the family which were also of a *familistic* kind. The parent –child relationship, which was the axial relationship within the family itself, was strongly colored with accents of subordination, and it was this which caused such relationships to proliferate in Japanese society as a whole.
>
> (Fukutake 1982: 49–50)

Fukutake then remarks that dependence on the fictive family relationship between *oyabun* (literally, 'player of the father role') and *kobun* ('player of the child role') enabled Japanese workers to survive the harsh realities of the world. As in the family, relations between management and employees in factories and workshops were supported by affective ties rather than rational contract. Furthermore, the *zaibatsu* (the large industrial and financial combines) sought to create a sentiment of the whole enterprise as one big family by treating the employees with benevolent paternalism, providing welfare measures, bonuses and so on. The notion of familistic management developed from the end of the Meiji period (1868–1911) throughout the Taishō period (1912–26), when Japan's economy was rapidly growing (Odaka 1984: 58–9), and this tendency accelerated in the 1920s. Rodney Clark (1979: 35) points out that the period in which these developments took place (from 1886 to the early 1920s) was the time when the Japanese elites began to have second thoughts about Westernisation and to re-evaluate Japan's traditional customs. Clark (ibid.: 41) makes an interesting point that it was the first generation of bureaucratic managers recruited straight from universities, not the owner–entrepreneurs of traditional family businesses, who adopted the tradition-oriented theme of familism as a means of controlling labour:

> The best trained men, and those who might have been expected to be the most receptive towards Western ideas of individualism, preferred instead a traditional-looking thesis which served their interests better. It is even possible that the graduate managers were indispensable to the general acceptance of familism. . . . [T]he new generation of business leaders could justly present themselves as company servants, more privileged, certainly, than their subordinates, but part of the same community of endeavour.
>
> (Clark 1979: 41)

But the slogans promoting 'enterprise-as-family' became particularly prominent in the second half of the 1930s and during the war due to the organisation created in each enterprise out of the earlier trade unions, i.e. the 'Movement for Service to the Nation through Industry' (Fukutake 1982: 51; Hazama 1963: 206ff.).

Unlike the outmoded idea of the family-state, the notion of familistic management exists even today. In fact, Japan's well-known employment practices – lifetime employment and pay-by-age – often cited as essential elements of familism, were only firmly institutionalised in the post-war period, but only among male employees of large companies (Clark 1979: 45–7; Taira 1970: 153–60). Scholars and business elites have often employed the notion of familism to explain the uniqueness of Japan's employment practices.

THE VILLAGE COMMUNITY AS A PROTOTYPE OF MODERN SOCIETY: PEASANT TRADITIONS

Tokugawa Japan (1600–1867) was a feudal society organised according to a strict hierarchy of four estates: samurai, peasants, artisans and merchants. Each group had its own patterns of social organisation, norms and values. Towards the end of the Tokugawa period, the samurai constituted only 6 to 7 per cent of the total population; peasants 80 to 85 per cent.[8] After the Meiji Restoration, the samurai institution was officially abolished, but it was the former samurai who, as the ruling elite, took the lead in state-building and industrialisation, by which process many samurai institutions were adapted to the models of the modern nation-state. It is particularly important that, along with the samurai culture, traditional peasant culture also persisted and expanded its sphere in the process of industrialisation. This development has led to a perspective on the characteristic features of modern Japanese society which is widely held among Japanese scholars. According to this perspective, former samurai and merchants may have led in the development of modern political and economic institutions, but it is former peasants that have been responsible for the social patterns which appeared in these institutions. In this context we should understand the lasting influence of Yanagita Kunio (1875–1962), a founding father of Japan's folklore studies. Being critical of the then prevalent academic style, which depended heavily on Western-derived concepts and theories, Yanagita, by collecting a vast amount of data from throughout Japan (particularly from agrarian regions) sought to establish an indigenous scholarship based on the life experiences of the common people. Yanagita's work has had a continued impact on those interested in the study of society and social history. Inspired by Yanagita's folklore studies, Aruga Kizaemon developed a rural sociology. Aruga's influence is particularly evident in the area of the family institution and familistic loyalty. The notion of Japanese society being vertically structured rather than horizontally structured, which Nakane (1967, 1970) has popularised, originates with Aruga (1943: 33).

The village community in pre-industrial Japan

The village community or hamlet (*mura*) as discussed here refers to that community which existed before the beginning of the Meiji period (1868–1911). Yanagita calls such a village the 'natural village' and distinguishes it clearly from the 'administrative village' which was superimposed by the Meiji government as one of its centralisation measures. The 'natural village' was the indigenous unit of self-rule in the Tokugawa period, with twenty to fifty households as constituent units (Yanagita 1971: 178).

Many scholars, including Yanagita, have emphasised the absolute necessity of communal solidarity among village members for the survival of the community. Solidarity was required for the management of an elaborate irrigation system, which alone could ensure the constant supply of water for rice cultivation in Japan. Also, Kamishima Jirō (1961: 41) indicates that cohesive patterns of behaviour developed among villagers in order to prevent the fragmentation of villagers' sentiment in the face of external threats such as natural disasters and heavy taxes (imposed by samurai administrators), as well as internal threats and dangers such as over-population and economic inequalities.

In the following discussion of the characteristic features of solidarity in the village community and the diffusion of such features throughout modern Japanese society, I shall rely primarily on Kamishima's influential work, *The Mental Structure of Modern Japan* (1961), in which the view on the reproduction of peasant traditions in modern Japanese society is most articulately formulated. (I do not wish to be taken as implying that Kamishima is promoting nationalism through this work, which, on the contrary, is intended to examine the social basis of fascism in pre-war and wartime Japan in a critical manner.)

Kamishima describes social order in the 'natural village' in the religious, economic, social and political realms. Shinto (in the sense of folk beliefs) was based on an animistic belief in the fusion of gods and people as well as on ancestor worship. This belief was reinforced through the experience of the cyclical rhythm of *hare* (fine weather, meaning festivals) and *ke* (cloudy weather, meaning ordinary working days). Festivals worked towards the affective integration of community members and played a primary role in maintaining order in the village. These religious features penetrated into the other spheres of village life, economic, social and political.

The economic sphere was governed by the principle that hard work was reciprocated by rewards. The natural village was based on a self-sufficient economy, in which the results of labour could be experienced directly by anyone. Rewards for labour and perseverance in routine work were demonstrated through the collective experience of abundance and liberation at festivals. Labour thus came to be regarded not merely as a means of survival but more as the true source of values in life. The social sphere was characterised by the belief that docility earns protection. The basic units of the natural village were families. Since economic inequality among families was inevitable, one might naturally expect a conflict between the rich and the poor as a result. But this did not often take place because harmony was ensured by a principle under which rich families aided the poor in cases of famine. Such protection of the poor was considered a source of pride for high-status families (especially landlords) and the responsibility of 'main families' (*honke*). This 'familistic *Pietät*' ensured docility on the part of villagers of lower social ranks. Docility ensured protection. The greater the risk of famine, the easier it was for such familistic protection to elicit docile endurance in everyday work. The political sphere was characterised by the principle of unanimous consent in decision-making. This principle originated in village festivals where the individual mind transformed into the collective mind through the affective chain reactions among community members who together concentrated their minds on 'communion' with the village gods. Those who did not join the collective consent were subject to negative social sanctions (Kamishima 1961: 24–8, 41–58).

Familism was another important feature related to various other features of the community. There were two types of familism in the village. One was kinship relations or *ie* (family system), which have already been discussed. The other was a quasi-parent–child relationship. It was customary for villagers to have several quasi-parents as patrons in addition to their natural parents. The relationship between *nedo-oya* and *nedo-ko* is one such example. (*Oya* means a parent/parents, *ko* a child/children.) Young villagers gathered at a *nedo* (a lodging place) after a day's work and experienced group living. The *nedo-oya*, who was the host of the place, played a role in the *nedo-ko*'s social training, which was undertaken to become full-fledged village members. The *nedo-oya* looked after the *nedo-ko* with fatherly care, which made the *nedo-ko* feel obliged to repay. In addition, a *nedo-oya* normally acted as a *nakōdo-oya* (a go-between) at a *nedo-ko*'s wedding. In this way, the relationship between the two became even closer than that between real parents and children. This relationship continued throughout their life. The quasi-parent–child relationship played an important role in other social spheres of the village community.[9] Yanagita Kunio (1963a: 337–88) once counted thirty-one varieties of quasi-parents in villages all over Japan.[10] Sakurai Tokutarō argues that the quasi-parent–child relationship supplemented the relatively unstable and weak ties of blood in the Japanese villages (1974: 194–207). This relationship also constituted an important hierarchical relationship. Yanagita Kunio remarks:

The fact that *oya* was not confined to one's own parents can be seen by the way the word *oyakata* (parent-like patron) is used today. . . . In the old days, labour organisations of a size larger than what we now call a family unit required a leader to whom their followers looked up to as *oyakata*.

(Yanagita 1963b: 246)

In addition to the quasi-parent–child relationship, hierarchy in the village was based on age groups. The village community comprised several age groups, such as *kodomo-gumi* (children's group), *wakamono-gumi* (young men's group), *chūrōgumi* (middle-aged men's group) and *toshiyori-gumi* (aged-men's group). Each age group was further divided into sub-age groups.[11] The hierarchical order based on age distinction can be clearly seen in the fact that those who entered *wakamono-gumi* on the same occasion were called *tsure* (literally, one who accompanies) and that group members were distinguished according to their time of entry. The members of the same age group (or sub-age group) formed co-equal relationships; those of different ages formed hierarchical relationships. These relationships mutually strengthened the overall solidarity of the village community.[12]

Diffusion of the village social organisation and belief system throughout modern Japanese society

No explicit ideologies comparable to the family-state and familistic enterprise were formed in the case of village social culture. But it is a widely-held view that the basic elements of order characteristic of the natural village diffused throughout society in the process of industrialisation and urbanisation.

When villagers migrated to the city, they brought with them village-style social organisation and belief systems and formed what Kamishima calls the 'secondary village' or 'quasi-village' within cities. Thus, even after 'natural villages' gradually disintegrated as a result of a series of centralisation measures imposed by the Meiji government, the traditional patterns of order persisted in the quasi-village. Consequently, it is argued, village-style communal order has become a characteristic feature found throughout modern industrial Japanese society in general and in the company in particular.

In what ways, then, is the type of social order characteristic of the natural village explained as having reproduced itself and expanded its sphere in the process of industrialisation and urbanisation?

Kamishima answers this by attributing it to the inability of the Japanese city to produce any alternative form of order.

> The mere expansion of cities by absorbing unlimited numbers of the peasant population did not guarantee the operation of laws of history according to which *Gesellschaft* replaces *Gemeinschaft*.
>
> (Kamishima 1961: 36)

The rapid development of industry following the Meiji Restoration required a swift mobilisation of labour, which was supplied by the rural areas. Considering that no social group can operate without shared norms and patterns of interaction and that there was not enough time to develop new ones, the former villagers adapted their agrarian and communal patterns of behaviour to their city life. Modern Japanese society thus lost an opportunity to produce its own principles of social integration and had thus to resort to 'regression to *Gemeinschaft*' as a way of securing order (ibid.). This situation was then accelerated by the development of mass society and the atomisation of social relations. Kamishima writes:

> The city 'turned into a mere gathering of people' and could not provide the prototype of [new] order [in modern Japan], which was found in the natural village ('primary village'). The 'crowd-like' phenomenon spread from cities to agricultural and fishing villages. . . . The destruction of the natural village, together with the 'crowd-like' development of the city, stimulated the formation of the quasi-village ('secondary village'), by which process the patterns of order characteristic of the natural village expanded nation-wide.
>
> (Kamishima 1961: 167)

In order to consider the diffusion of village-style order, it is also necessary to pay attention to the process by which such patterns of order were transmitted between generations. In the traditional village community, *wakamono-gumi* (young men's group) and *musume-gumi* (young women's group) were important indigenous agencies of socialisation. These were peer groups which young villagers were required to join from the age of about fifteen and in which they remained until they married. Communal living at a *nedo* (a lodging place), as discussed earlier, was an important part of socialisation whereby young villagers acquired the roles expected of adult village members (Yanagita 1963c; Nakayama 1958). Even after modern institutions replaced traditional ones, peer group socialisation remained important and continued to exist in peer groups within modern schools such as boarding schools, training camps of secondary schools, teacher-training schools and military schools (Kamishima 1961: 28–9).[13] In schools, students learnt principles of order quite akin to those of the natural village: the enhancement of solidarity through boarding school festivals and inter-school competitions; observance of age hierarchy; dependence on fatherly and brotherly figures as well as nostalgia for the family; justification of privilege and hierarchy on the basis of academic performance; and closed attitudes towards out-groups (ibid.: 29–30). When they left school to join an enterprise, they brought with them these norms, which contributed to the reproduction of this type of order.

The company is frequently regarded as the epitome of the quasi-village. The view that the village community is the prototype of the modern company organisation has been constantly reiterated by Japanese scholars and, in particular, scholars of Japanese-style management.[14] The modern company consists of two related but distinct aspects: formal organisation, in which members are organised in rational and bureaucratic ways for the effective fulfilment of specific company goals, and the informal group, in which members have personal contacts with one another. It is in the informal social relations that the social principles characteristic of the traditional village community are considered to have reproduced themselves. Such an informal group is not necessarily a primary group that develops of itself after a certain period of interaction, but is rather deliberately built in within the formal structure of the modern Japanese company.

The affective ties which exist in a company are viewed as having roots in the village. Although religious Shinto festivals are not relevant to the company setting, the function of the festival to maintain and enhance communal solidarity is fulfilled by various company activities such as after-work drinking sessions with fellow office workers, sporting events, company outings and so on. The so-called 'life-time employment system' and the 'enterprise unions' reflect familism. The seniority or 'pay-by-age' system, which is part of this employment style, may be understood as being grounded in age-group consciousness. (It should be noted that these systems are now threatened by an alternative system that stresses the need for innovative talent.) The list also includes communal decision-making and consultation style such as *nemawashi* and *ringi*.[15]

As another important feature, vertical relationships formed between age groups in the company correspond to quasi-parent–child relationships. A senior member of a company, who is a parent-role player, takes personal care of his subordinates and often acts as a *nakōdo-oya* (go-between) at their weddings. Vertical relationships are also formed between sub-age groups, each group of which is constituted by those who have entered the company in the same year. This is reminiscent of the *tsure* consciousness in the *wakamono gumi* (young men's group) in the village community. Horizontal relationships are formed simultaneously, consisting of the members of the same age group or sub-age group. Informal groups with such characteristics 'inherited from peasants' are popularly believed to provide a sense of collective solidarity that not only promotes the effective attainment of goals set by the organisation but also benefits individual members by providing psychological security.[16]

CONCLUSIONS: FOLKLORISM AND A THEORY OF IDEALISED PEASANT SOCIAL CULTURE

What I call the 'reproductionist' (or 'extensionist') theory of modern society depicts modern industrial society as a coherent and uniform whole and explores the cultural ethos believed to underlie differentiated modern institutions. The family system (*ie*) and village community (*mura*) as real entities may have disintegrated in the process of industrialisation and urbanisation,[17] but modern Japanese society is characterised by idealised familial and communal culture. For some, it is an expression of regret over a change from *Gemeinschaft* to *Gesellschaft*. Or, rather, it is an affirmation: 'modern' Japan is not characterised negatively and passively in terms of its retained medieval structures but positively and actively in terms of enlivened traditional structures and culture.

This chapter also suggests a point that concerns the time and space orientations in the formulation of ideas of national distinctiveness by intellectuals. In much of the popularised *nihonjinron*, a concern to understand the behavioural differences of the contemporary Japanese from non-Japanese predominates over historicist concerns to discover the uniqueness of ancestral culture and to emphasise a shared history. This chapter has seen that a historicist perspective is not absent in post-war holistic theories of Japanese society, especially theories viewing the traditional village community as the prototype of the modern company organisation. Scholars look back to pre-modern

Japan to affirm a vision of historical continuity. We are reminded here of a number of scholars in the age of Romanticism who also looked to the Middle Ages for a source of national identity. H.D. Harootunian, using the language of Michel Foucault (1972: 12), remarks on modern Japanese scholars' concern with national uniqueness:

> The promise of *nihonjinron* as it self-consciously recycled the nativist vision through folklorism, was to restore everything that had 'eluded' the Japanese in a reconstituted unity, 'to make sure that time, especially, modern time, disperses nothing without being returned back in some whole and integrated form.
>
> (Harootunian 1988: 437)

(Note that in this quotation the term *nihonjinron* is used in a much broader sense than our usage, to include both popularised ideas and more serious theories such as some of those discussed in this chapter.) Considering that some of the theories discussed in this chapter (such as those of Yanagita and Kamishima) are often important sources of ideas in the popularised *nihonjinron*, it may be said that historicist concerns have not lost their relevance in the contemporary discussions of Japanese uniqueness, even though such concerns may not be so evident as in the case of primary nationalism. Also, a difference should be noted between the approach of the Romantic-age writers (as well as Japanese *kokugaku* scholars of the eighteenth century) and the approach discussed in this chapter. Whereas artistic and literary culture dominated the mind of the Romantic thinkers, *social* culture is a predominant concern in those Japanese theories to which contemporary Japanese thinkers have looked for a source of national identity.

Particularly relevant for the present study is the type of theory on social culture that views the village community as the prototype of modern Japanese society. The focus on peasant culture as the tradition of Japan suggests a number of important things. This subject will be discussed in chapter 8, but a point or two may be made here. The choice of peasant social culture, not the 'high' culture of the upper social strata, as the tradition of Japan assumes an ideological character when social patterns in the modern company, which tends to be regarded as a quasi-village, are associated with Japan's post-war economic success and when the communal features of the company, which are reminiscent of the pre-industrial village community, are celebrated as a cause of Japan's industrial strength. The social theory, which regards the pre-industrial village community as the prototype of modern Japanese society, thus idealises 'our' past (what we were) and 'our' present (what we are), and also the continuity between the two. This inclination towards peasant tradition is closely related to the question of which social group has become the main social bearers of cultural nationalism in contemporary Japan, as will be discussed in chapter 8.

Lastly, we return to where we began our discussion in this chapter, holism and functionalism. Regarding historicism as the intellectual basis of nationalism, Breuilly (1982: 338) remarks that, for historicists history is the only way to understand the wholeness of a society. But he goes on to point out the emergence of functionalism as a new approach to understand society as a whole:

> In more modern times an ahistorical approach has been added to these forms of understanding. Certain types of social anthropology insist on the need to understand the whole community, and in its own terms. However, this understanding has little histori- cal dimension. The notion of wholeness tends to be expressed through the idea of every activity having a function within the community.
>
> (Breuilly 1982: 338)

This chapter has introduced another holistic perspective on modern society that combines both a holistic view and a historicist vision.

Chapter 6

Perceptions of Japanese uniqueness among educators and businessmen

RESEARCH DESIGN

The discussion in preceding chapters focused on the ideas of the professional thinking elites. In this and the next two chapters the focus will be shifted to the ways in which the thinking elites' ideas of Japanese uniqueness become integrated – or do not become integrated – into the traditions of the broader sections of society. The main line of enquiry will examine what has occurred between thinking elites and the rest of the population as regards the dissemination of the *nihonjinron*. As a research strategy, I have limited the scope to the educated sections of the population and concentrated on educators and businessmen because they both have a profound influence on the members of modern Japanese society. The former by way of formal socialisation of the youth at school, the latter by virtue of the fact that large numbers of the population are employed by companies, and thus their ideas are expected to be widely disseminated among the public.

Methods of collecting data

I selected a fairly large provincial city of several hundred thousand inhabitants in central Japan, which I shall call Nakasato, as the site of my research[1] and contacted thirty-five educators and thirty-six businessmen there. Almost all of the respondents had university education or an equivalent. The main part of the research was conducted between October 1986 and September 1988,[2] though frequent visits to and extended stays in Nakasato were also made before and after this period. The reason for choosing Nakasato was that it is representative of the nation as a whole. Nakasato is typical in some of the basic demographic, social and economic characteristics such as the distribution by industry of gainfully employed residents, the age structure of the population, the average size of family, the proportion of students advancing to high school and university, and the average level of income. In the case of each of these characteristics, Nakasato is close to the national average. All of the respondents regarded Nakasato as an ordinary Japanese city.

The research techniques employed were mainly qualitative, although some statistical evidence was obtained as an outcome of the research. Intensive face-to-face interviews were the chief method of investigation.[3] Supplementary methods such as questionnaires, telephone interviews and letters were also employed. Attempts were also made, wherever possible, to understand the respondents' role, profile and ideas in the context of the school or the company and community through talks with other residents of the city. The main objective was a qualitative exploration of some of the factors involved in the educators' and businessmen's perceptions of Japanese uniqueness and their response to the ideas of Japanese uniqueness as formulated by intellectuals. Primary emphasis was therefore given to selecting respondents prepared to participate in long sessions of 'in-depth' interviews. It is for this reason that I refrained from random sampling.

My original plan was to concentrate on educators – in particular, high school headmasters – supposing that, because their role was to relate the family, the school and the community to society at large, they would be highly sensitive to developments in ideas concerning national culture and society. Moreover, I was predisposed to accept the conventional view that educators play a central role in cultural nationalism. I thus assumed that an intensive study of headmasters alone would yield sufficient data on various aspects of the role of the educated Japanese in cultural nationalism. In the course of my interviews with educators, however, it became increasingly apparent that the experience of working in a company could significantly promote one's interest in Japanese uniqueness and encourage one's orientation to the *nihonjinron* and to cultural nationalism. This suggested the possibility that a study of businessmen would point to some of the important variables as regards the diffusion of the ideas of national distinctiveness. It was against this background that I decided to compare educators and businessmen.

By educators, I mean those occupationally engaged in formal

education. Considering that nearly 95 per cent of young people (aged 15) go on to high school for three-year, upper-secondary education and that high school serves as a transition phase between school life and the real working world (for 70 per cent of school leavers), I concentrated on educators at high schools. I contacted all the high schools in Nakasato except one with a foreign headmaster. In all I contacted thirty-five high school educators, of whom there were eighteen headmasters and one headmistress, and fourteen ordinary teachers.[4] Two headmasters from a middle school (for pupils aged between 12 and 15) and a primary school (for pupils aged between 6 and 12) were also included as suggestive cases.

By businessmen I mean, first, managerial and non-managerial members of relatively large companies.[5] They are usually university graduates who have joined companies and have become something like 'company men'. Another type of businessmen are those who run their own firms, most of which are relatively small and maintain the basic characteristics of family firms with the board of directors drawn from relatives and their personal acquaintances.[6] In reality, a line between the two types of companies is hard to draw partly because many family firms grow into larger and more bureaucratic companies and partly because big companies are not so prominent in Nakasato. About half the businessmen contacted are from each of the two types of company. Twelve of our businessmen are from manufacturing companies, eight from finance, twelve from retailing, three from trading and one from services. Unlike in the case of high schools, the number of which is limited, companies in Nakasato are too many and varied to study comprehensively. Most of the businessmen were therefore selected on a case-by-case basis through personal contacts.

Of all the characteristics of the respondents, age is a particularly important factor in a study of Japan's nationalism. The respondents' age distribution is shown in Table 6.1. (For a detailed discussion of age distribution, see chapter 10.)

Main theoretical points of interest

In the following chapters I shall be particularly interested in:

1 an examination of the process that occurs between thinking elites and other educated sections of the population (educators and businessmen) in relation to the ideas of national distinctiveness;

Table 6.1 Respondents' age distribution

Age cohort	Educators	Businessmen	Total
55 and above	22	20	42
48 to 54	3	4	7
under 48	10	12	22
Total	35	36	71

2 a reassessment of the view which regards educators as playing the major role in transmitting and diffusing ideas of national distinctiveness and an assessment of the role of businessmen in cultural nationalism;

3 an exploration of the characteristics of 'secondary' nationalism in comparison with those of 'primary' nationalism as observed in the areas stated in 1 and 2.

Before examining these questions concerning the place of educators and businessmen in cultural nationalism, it is essential to enquire into their own perceptions of Japanese uniqueness, which is the primary task of this chapter. Emphasis will be given to the following two enquiries. The first is an analysis of the content of Japanese culture to which respondents refer in expressing their ideas of Japanese uniqueness and an explanation of the ways chosen to express those ideas. It is also important not simply to limit the analysis to culture as such but to examine the relationship between culture and race in the respondents' perceptions of national identity, which is the second task of this chapter. Although it is an error to confuse nationalism and racism (or race thinking), I will maintain that it is important in some instances, such as the Japanese case, to examine the role of race thinking in nationalism.[7]

CULTURE AND NATIONAL IDENTITY

A general discussion of the different expressions of national cultural identity will first be given in order to facilitate the discussion of the Japanese case. The intellectuals' different manners of expression of national distinctiveness such as the holistic and institutional approaches have already been discussed in the preceding chapters, but, since the present chapter is concerned with the perceptions of 'ordinary' people, it will be useful to reformulate them with illustrations drawn from a more contemporary context.

General discussion

At the most abstract level, culture refers to all learned aspects of human activity, embracing the ideas, practices, and material and symbolic artefacts that are products of group life and transmitted from one generation to the next. As such, culture is an obvious and important source of ethnic and national identity. The relationship of culture to national identity can, and indeed does, take different forms, of which two in particular concern this study.

First, national identity may or may not be objectified (or 'externalised'). National identity may be expressed in terms of abstract, amorphous cultural ethos or characters, described variously as *Volksgeist*, national character, patterns of behaviour, modes of thinking and so on. Or it may be objectified (or 'externalised'), or expressed in terms of objectified cultural items such as artistic and literary products, institutions, customs and practices, rituals and ceremonies, and some forms of material culture. Objectified culture and abstract (non-objectified) culture are not mutually exclusive: the former is quite often the embodiment of the latter. For example, whereas Victorian architecture (objectified culture) embodies the Victorian values of practicality and simplicity (abstract culture), Georgian architecture expresses dignity and restraint. Second, national identity may or may not be institutionalised. This classification deals with the question of whether national culture is perceived and expressed in terms of differentiated parts of society or in terms of a monolithic whole. Institutional culture refers to the culture of an institution (or a part of society) such as the pub, the club, the countryside, the House of Commons and so on. Holistic culture, on the other hand, refers to cultural characteristics diffused throughout national society. The two classifications – objectifying/abstract and institutional/holistic – are closely interrelated, as will be seen later.

For illustration, examples may be drawn from the English context. English identity may be expressed in a holistic and abstract manner, or in terms of ideals, values and patterns of behaviour and thought considered to be shared by the members of the nation. Indeed, there is a large body of literature on the English national character, in which the English are often described as being self-restrained, aloof and shy, preferring understatement, having a sense of humour, respecting privacy, distrusting intellectualism and so on. The English themselves refer to these qualities from time to time.

But there is another way in which English people often express their ideas of Englishness: they objectify it. If asked to describe their ideas of Englishness, English people would probably refer to a whole range of concrete cultural traits, thereby objectifying their ideas of Englishness. They would probably mention everyday objects and activities such as fish and chips, high tea, pub drinks, Sunday lunch, cricket, queuing and so on. The educated English might also cite peculiarly English (or British) institutions such as the monarchy, the City, parliament, public school, the BBC, the National Trust and so on.[8] They might mention Turner and Constable, Wordsworth and Byron, and Elgar.

Another important source of Englishness may also be found in various rituals and ceremonies such as the state opening of parliament, the Queen's Christmas broadcast and Remembrance Day rituals. Englishness is often expressed by the manner in which customs and practices are related to institutions; for example, the manner in which a Bill is passed in parliament, and the manner in which tutorials are given at Oxbridge. Also, English people often express their ideas of Englishness by suggesting abstract cultural characteristics in the context of objectified cultural objects and practices. For example, they might speak of cricket as something to embody the English values of fair play, sportsmanship and, perhaps, a leisurely pace of life. They may also use the example of the seating plan of the House of Commons as something to embody the English tradition of debate and parliamentary democracy, symbolised by adversary politics. This is also to suggest that English people tend to express their ideas of Englishness in terms of institutional culture. They might mention a variety of institutions such as the aristocracy, the City, Oxbridge, the working class, the East End and the countryside to touch upon certain English values embodied in these institutions.[9]

The general discussion of the different expressions of national distinctiveness using English examples now opens the way for an enquiry into the ways in which our respondents express their ideas of Japanese cultural distinctiveness.

Japanese cultural uniqueness as perceived by respondents

The object and limits of this section should clearly be stated at the outset. My intention is not to furnish my own ideas of Japanese uniqueness. My purpose is confined to describing the respondents' reference to the aspects of Japanese uniqueness they chose to discuss and to explaining their choice of such aspects and their manner of expressing them. It should be emphasised that one's ideas of Japanese uniqueness are expected to vary depending on one's occupation, age, sex, level of education and so on. One's expressions of Japanese uniqueness are also expected to vary depending on the circumstance in which one discusses it – for instance, whether one discusses it at work, in a pub or at an interview is expected to make some difference. Furthermore, it should be made clear what we can know and what we cannot know on the basis of the type of data obtained from the interviews. What we cannot know is the 'overall' content of the respondents' national identity, although we attempt, wherever possible, to explore it. What we can know is how respondents, when asked, express their ideas of Japanese cultural uniqueness. It is unlikely that 'ordinary' people – who are not professional thinkers – should concern themselves with the question of ethnic/national identity except under unusual circumstances such as war or intense ethnic relations. Bearing in mind the object and limits of this research, I shall now examine the content of Japanese uniqueness as expressed by the respondents and the characteristic manners in which they expressed it.

For the purpose of discussion, culture may be classified as: artistic and literary culture, everyday-life culture, institutional culture and 'underlying culture' (or abstract and holistic culture). Needless to say, these types are not mutually exclusive. Nor is this classification submitted as exhaustive. I am concerned only with the types of culture which, in my judgement, are useful for the purpose of this study.

Artistic–literary culture

Artistic–literary culture (such as literature, visual arts, music, and artistic artefacts and rituals) is an important source of national cultural identity in many countries. Japan, too, has a rich variety of distinctively Japanese artistic–literary culture, which is generally associated with tradition and referred to as *dentō geijutsu* (traditional art), *dentō geinō* (traditional entertainment) or *dentō bunka* (traditional culture). It is possible to cite an endless list of various types of pottery and porcelain, lacquer ware, paintings, wood-block prints, calligraphy, dolls, folding fans, flower arrangement, tea ceremony, dance, music played on Japanese instruments, songs with a distinctly Japanese tempo and rhythm, theatrical arts such as *noh*, *bunraku* (puppet theatre), *kabuki*, lyric poetry such as *tanka* and *haiku*, and so on.

Most respondents did not express their ideas of Japanese uniqueness in terms of this type of culture. If asked, however, whether traditional arts were an important element of Japanese cultural uniqueness, all answered in the affirmative. Some of the items of artistic–literary culture mentioned are Buddhist and Zen art, *kabuki* plays, *haiku* poetry, martial arts (jūdō, kendō, karate) and seasonal festivals. The following remark of a company manager shows the background of the respondents' initial neglect of this culture:

> People in Europe go to art galleries and theatres as part of their regular activity. How many of us Japanese regularly go to art galleries to see Japanese paintings of great historical value? No one denies that the *Noh* play is an important cultural heritage of ours, but how many of us really enjoy it as an entertainment? Arts for the majority of Japanese are little more than something they study in the school history textbook.

Care should be taken not to overgeneralise about Europeans' attitudes towards 'high culture', which varies, of course, depending on class, social group and individual. Nor should the impression be given that the Japanese are not conscious of their traditional artistic heritage, which again depends on social group and varies from one individual to another. But this remark illustrates something about the place of traditional artistic culture in contemporary Japan. There is no doubt that, objectively, traditional artistic–literary culture is a very important aspect of Japan's cultural heritage, but its role as an active reminder of Japanese cultural identity is limited to a relatively small number of art lovers. There is a sense of the divorce of traditional art of high aesthetic value from the largely Westernised contemporary cultural environment.[10] The majority of the Japanese lack the sense of living in an environment linked to the 'high culture' of earlier times, as is suggested in the following remark by a high school headmaster:

Europe has 'stone culture' and Japan has 'wood culture'. Just as stone buildings in Europe have remained there for centuries – and this is why you can have the comforting sense of living in history when walking in their streets – Europeans take a long time in building up solid cultural structures. By contrast, one rarely gets a sense of history in our streets. Wooden houses in Japan are easily knocked down by typhoons and replaced by new ones. Too bad that we scrap old things without trying to restore them and replace them with new ones. But it is part of our culture to value novelty and flexibility.

One should not forget, of course, that there are also more popularised forms of traditional Japanese culture such as *rakugo* (comic story-telling) and *manzai* (comic dialogue), which most respondents do actually enjoy.

Everyday-life culture

Respondents tended not to express Japanese uniqueness in terms of their everyday-life culture, either; possibly because it was so much part of their everyday life that it lay outside their consciousness. But the apparent inattention of the majority of the respondents to everyday-life culture does not deny its importance to them. The everyday lifestyle of ordinary Japanese is distinctively Japanese in many ways and an essential source of Japanese identity, as is illustrated in the following remark made by a businessman who often travelled abroad:

Nothing makes me feel happier to be Japanese than when I get into the *furo* (Japanese-style bath) and relax, sit on the *tatami* floor and eat Japanese food.

The everyday lifestyle of the ordinary Japanese, especially in the private sphere, is still distinctively Japanese in many ways.[11] For example, even a house which is Western in appearance normally has at least one *tatami* mat room, and many people wear Japanese clothes when they relax at home. Japanese food is a particularly important source of Japanese identity. So are *sake* (rice wine) and drinking habits. There are also very Japanese leisure activities such as taking holidays at hot spring resorts, watching *sumō* on television, playing *shōgi* and *go* (Japanese equivalents to Western chess and checkers) and so on.

What is important, however, is that respondents referred to these items only after their attention was deliberately drawn to the everyday sphere. Some even suggested that it was meaningless to discuss these everyday characteristics. Rather, 'it is more important', one businessman remarked, 'to approach this subject of Japaneseness from a more philosophical point of view', suggesting the importance of systematising ideas of Japanese cultural distinctiveness in a more abstract or non-objectifying manner: that is, to explore the cultural ethos behind objectified customs and practices. Although he stood out by being explicit on this point, his inclination towards abstraction was shared by the majority of the respondents.

Institutional culture

This refers to the culture embodied in social institutions, an aggregate of which makes up society. Just as an Englishman might point out institutions, such as the pub, trade unions and the royal family as symbols of Englishness, institutional culture can be an important source of national identity. But the only major institution touched upon by respondents was the company, and the uniqueness of the Japanese company was discussed more in the context of holistic, behavioural culture, or what I call 'underlying culture'.

Underlying culture (abstract and holistic culture)

The term 'underlying culture' refers to the more intangible aspects of culture, referring to cultural ethos, national character or modes of thinking and behaving that exist and are believed to exist behind objectified institutions and practices. It corresponds to abstract (non-objectified) and holistic culture. The concept of underlying culture resembles what Hoetink calls 'anthropological culture'. Making a morphological distinction between 'anthropological' and 'sociological' culture, Hoetink employs the concept of 'anthropological culture' to refer to the distinctiveness and recognisability of complex behavioural and organisational patterns as opposed to sociological culture, which deals with the set of value orientations, norms and expectations as a correlate or result of the position of a social group. 'Anthropological culture' warrants consensus on the identification of such behavioural and organisational patterns, thereby creating ascriptive loyalties (Hoetink 1975: 16–25).

The majority of the respondents tended to express Japanese uniqueness in terms of underlying culture. More businessmen than educators showed an interest in this type of culture. There are two main areas on which respondents' attention focused: 'linguistic and communicative culture' and 'social culture'. As was discussed in chapter 2, the first deals mainly with the non-logical, non-verbal and emotive mode of interpersonal communication of the Japanese, the second with their so-called group orientation.

In addition to the 'linguistic and communicative culture' and 'social culture', respondents also gave considerable weight to the following two characteristics. Although these characteristics do not necessarily deal with the content of Japanese culture, the fact that they were remarked on in the context of culture itself is worth paying attention to. First, more than half the respondents touched upon the 'homogeneity' of the Japanese, meaning both 'racial' and social homogeneity. This is a particularly important aspect of the respondents' Japanese identity, as will be discussed later. Second, nearly half the respondents remarked on the active receptivity of the Japanese towards foreign cultures, as well as their ability to blend them with Japanese culture to create a distinctive form of culture, as another example of Japanese uniqueness. This theme can be discussed more fruitfully in another context later in this chapter.

The findings show rather clearly that the majority of the respondents tended *not* to objectify Japanese cultural uniqueness in terms of either 'high' culture or 'low' culture. The following remark made by the president of an electrical appliance company is typical of such an abstract (non-objectifying) manner of presentation:

> For the Japanese, sentiment and intuition are more important than logic. We are expected to avoid a black-or-white decision and to reach a conclusion that doesn't make anyone unhappy. We value *haragei* or tacit understanding.

Even in the following example, in which a high school headmaster discusses a concrete item, the Japanese garden, his first and foremost concern lies in what is symbolically behind this objectified item:

> The western garden has a fountain; the Japanese garden has a waterfall. This suggests an important difference between the cultures of the West and Japan. Western culture challenges nature: the idea behind the fountain is to go against the natural law of gravity. The waterfall, on the other hand, symbolises the nature of our culture: we accept nature as it is.

The primary concern of this respondent is to infer the cultural ethos of the Japanese from the objectified cultural item. Japanese cultural uniqueness is expressed in a holistic and non-objectifying manner.

It is important to note here the two different levels of cultural identity: the actively conscious and the less conscious (or subconscious) levels. Earlier, we discussed the objectifying approach with reference to the English example. We have observed the abstract (non-objectifying) and holistic approach among the majority of the respondents. It should not be concluded hastily, however, that this illustrates the difference between the Japanese and English contents of national identity. Such a conclusion would neglect the different levels of national identity. Whereas what may provisionally be called the 'English approach' deals with the more passively conscious level of identity, the 'Japanese approach' – again provisionally called as such – concerns the more actively conscious level. The characteristic ways in which our respondents expressed Japanese cultural identity may be regarded as a reflection of their active consciousness concerning this subject, as will be discussed fully later.

Although, quantitatively, the majority referred to the abstract, underlying culture, we should not overlook the presence of those respondents who expressed their ideas of Japanese uniqueness in terms of more objectified traits such as artistic–literary and everyday culture. This group is composed mostly of educators, especially older educators. In the process of investigating the reasons for this, a number of important points have emerged, but this theme belongs to the following chapter. In this chapter, I shall stick to the representative trend among the respondents.

'RACE' AND CULTURE IN PERCEPTIONS OF JAPANESE UNIQUENESS

Respondents expressed in one way or another that the Japanese are 'intrinsically different' from other peoples. This phrase carries the connotation of 'that which cannot be shared by non-Japanese'. The following remark made by a company president was typical:

> Unlike in America where any people – Italians, Japanese, Hispanics, blacks – could become Americans and appreciate the American way of life, you have to be born a Japanese in order to understand *nihonjin no kokoro* (the Japanese heart).

This remark suggests that the notion of a unique Japanese culture is closely associated with that of 'race' (or 'quasi-race', to be more precise). The concept of race, as was stressed in chapter 2, has no real biological foundation and is used here to refer to a *socially constructed* difference.

The argument in chapter 2 was that, although an association of race and culture usually suggests genetic determinism, the Japanese 'race thinking' should not be equated simplistically with it.[12] A distinction was thus made between two types of relationships with regard to race and culture: first, genetic determinism and second, racially exclusive possession of a particular culture. Genetic determinism has been the more widely-held doctrine as well as a habit of thinking among 'ordinary' people. In his discussion of what the everyday person in the street means by race, Charles Husband (1982: 18) maintains that biological determination of behaviour is at the core of race thinking. By contrast, the notion of 'racially exclusive possession of particular cultural characteristics', which I have proposed, postulates that particular cultural characteristics belong exclusively to a particular 'race'. It is fundamentally this type that characterises the 'race thinking' ('quasi-race thinking') in Japan with which the present study is concerned. The usefulness of this concept will now be examined on the basis of the interview findings.

Respondents' perceptions of the relationship between 'race' and culture may be approached through an exploration of their views as to the extent to which foreigners could acquire Japanese culture or, to be more precise, the Japanese way of thinking and behaving. All the respondents, both educators and businessmen, considered it impossible for foreigners to learn to 'behave and think like the Japanese'. Of course some things can be learnt, but some cannot, and most respondents thus qualified their response. An exploration of the respondents' initial reaction towards the ability of non-Japanese to acquire Japanese culture leads to the subject of 'race'. Since race consists of two related yet separate aspects (phenotypical and genotypical), attention will first be given to differences in the respondents' reactions depending on different phenotypical types. For the purpose of contrast, two types of foreigners – phenotypically different foreigners (Westerners) and phenotypically similar foreigners (Koreans and Chinese, and Japanese-Americans) – are considered.

Let us first enquire into the respondents' explanations as to why it is impossible for phenotypically different foreigners (Westerners) to learn to think and behave like the Japanese. Respondents' explanations centred around what they regarded as the obstacles that foreigners would be likely to face in their attempt to acquire Japanese culture.

The first conceived obstacle concerns the nature of Japanese culture characterised by its subtlety and implicitness. As one high school teacher remarked, 'You have to be born a Japanese to appreciate the subtlety of Japanese thinking'. Michael Banton's 'stranger hypothesis' deals with more or less the same aspect of inter-racial interaction. Contrasting England and the United States in the 1960s, Banton pointed out that in England dependence upon implicit norms and tacit modes of instruction was so high that it was very hard for a foreigner to become English, whereas in the USA, where social norms were explicitly stated, people were used to the idea of 'turn[ing] various groups of immigrants into patriotic American citizens' (1967: 371). What Banton wrote about English society in the 1960s also applies to Japanese society, except that the degree of such a tendency is considerably greater in Japan.[13]

The second obstacle concerns the relationship between culture and 'race'. Supposing that foreigners have somehow overcome the difficulty of mastering the subtlety of Japanese patterns of behaviour, it was pointed out that they would still not be regarded as having acquired Japaneseness in their behaviour – a tautological reasoning among respondents. As one headmaster put it, 'there is something strange about the type of person who speaks and behaves like us but does not look like us'. In other words, the Japanese perceive what may be called 'role inconsistency' for such a non-Japanese person. The following remark made by a headmaster is illustrative:

Japanese-speaking foreigners have increased in number both on television and even in our town. I have met an American woman teaching in one of our schools, and her Japanese is 'so good as to make us feel uneasy' (*kimi ga warui hodo umai*).

A company manager remarked on a related point:

We have always been accustomed to the idea that those who speak Japanese should look like the Japanese.

Some respondents also suggested that it would make little difference if the foreigners were born and raised in Japan as long as their parents were foreigners. The same would apply to the third or fourth generation because, as the same company manager remarked, 'their different appearance will remind themselves and us of their difference, thereby making it difficult for them to feel and think like the Japanese and for us to accept them as those who have acquired Japaneseness'. This remark shows the respondent's 'uni-racial consciousness', which assumes, first, the unchanging 'racial' homogeneity of Japan and, second, cultural homogeneity – culture in the sense of behaviour and ideas – shared by the Japanese. In fact, many respondents referred to the 'racial' homogeneity of the Japanese in the context of Japanese cultural uniqueness, as is typified by the remark of a high school teacher: 'The Japanese have always been homogeneous, and this is part of our uniqueness'. The perceived 'role inconsistency' results in a defence mechanism to preserve the 'racial' and cultural homogeneity of the Japanese.

This point can be explored further by considering the case of phenotypically similar foreigners. Second and third generation Japanese-Americans are of particular interest here. Did respondents also foresee any obstacles for such foreigners – US citizens born and raised in the States – in integrating culturally in Japan? All of the respondents suggested that Japanese-Americans could 'become like us' because they are 'of Japanese origin'. A headmaster said:

> Yes, that would be very possible because they are Japanese anyway concerning blood. Those who have just returned from America might take some time and effort, but their children will certainly become perfectly like us.

Many respondents used the phrase *nihonjin no chi* (Japanese blood) to refer to what they considered to be the immutable aspects of Japanese identity, suggesting that because Japanese-Americans 'have Japanese blood' they can acquire Japanese culture. Does this imply genetic determinism? Here, Koreans and Chinese serve as good suggestive cases, because, by definition, they 'do not have Japanese blood' and, as such, they are supposed not to be able to 'become Japanese' culturally. They may be phenotypically indistinguishable, but are imagined as 'genotypically' different. Respondents' first reactions to the Korean and Chinese cases were, on the whole, very negative, as the following remarks by a high school headmaster and a businessman suggest:

> Although Chinese and Japanese look alike, we have very different customs and mentalities. Unlike the Continentals who are *ōzappa*

(relaxed enough not to be concerned about small points), we Japanese have more delicate feelings. It is important to know our differences for the sake of better mutual understanding.

No matter how long they live here, I think they will remain Chinese or Koreans. After all, we are different *minzoku* (ethnic/ racial groups).

But, when their attention was drawn to a number of those former Koreans and Chinese who had become naturalised and who passed as Japanese, including some well-known sports players and enter- tainers, most respondents agreed that Koreans and Chinese could 'become Japanese' (*nihonjin ni nareru*). The following remark by the same businessman typifies this attitude:

As long as we are not informed of their former origins, it is true that they can become Japanese.

This seems to contradict the previous point that one has to have 'Japanese blood' to possess Japanese culture. Now, Koreans and Chinese, who 'do not have Japanese blood' but who look like the Japanese could 'become Japanese' unless reminders of their foreignness such as names and other signs of their origins are presented.

This rather quick 'change of mind' suggests that the respondents' explanation of the relationship between culture and 'race' lacks coherence and logic. This is normal, as a lack of systematic thinking usually characterises race thinking. Husband remarks that 'people experience "race" as a highly complex body of emotive ideas' (1982: 18–19) and endorses Barzun's ([1937] 1965) point that it is very important to focus on 'the ease with which people flow from one proposition to another in sustaining their race-thinking'. 'After all', he continues, 'race-thinking usually occurs in the context of off-the- top-of-the-head, spontaneous utterance' (Husband 1982: 19).

'Race', just like culture, can be an important symbol of Japanese- ness. This is illustrated by the notion of 'Japanese blood' as applied to Japanese-Americans (who are imagined to be 'racially' Japanese but culturally American) and to the Korean minority in Japan (who are imagined to be 'racially' different from the Japanese but have culturally integrated into Japan). The two contrasting cases show the importance of this notion in defining Japanese identity. 'Race', as a significant symbol of Japanese national identity, elicits significant psychological responses which are, in turn, closely associated with the psychological responses elicited by other factors. Percy S. Cohen's remark is suggestive on this point:

> The degree of emphasis on racial difference which may activate the most powerful psychological responses will depend on a host of cultural and social factors which mould and channel such responses and even, to some extent, not only elicit but *even create them.*

> (Cohen 1976: 26, emphasis added)

Indeed, the symbol of 'Japanese blood' is socially invented *not* to point to genetic traits as such *but* to mould and channel psychological responses as regards 'we'-ness and 'them'-ness. This is why it is so easy for respondents to change their mind as regards the cultural integration of Koreans and Chinese. The 'quasi-racial' symbol of 'Japanese blood' strengthens ethnic identity by focusing upon, and exaggerating, one aspect of ethnicity, namely kinship and kin lineage. It promotes, and is promoted by, the image that 'we' constitute kinship (again imagined) whose members have interacted among themselves to perpetuate its lineage in isolation from other peoples. (This represents the assumption of breeding isolation, characteristic of race thinking.) The promoted sense of great psychological distance between 'us' and 'them' coupled with the assumption of 'our' continuing homogeneity facilitates the habit of thinking that only 'we' – members of the in-group with this special collective experience – can share with one another 'our' special modes of thinking and behaving.

Respondents are accustomed to using the fictive, 'quasi-racial' notion of 'Japanese blood' to define membership of the Japanese nation. Considering this point and also that the characteristics of the Japanese nation are defined in cultural (or culturalistic) terms, we may understand why 'race' and culture are closely associated in respondents' perceptions of Japaneseness. This type of race thinking may best be characterised as 'perceptual association'. A deterministic relationship between race and culture – in the sense of genetic determinism – cannot be established as regards our respondents' perception of Japanese identity. Throughout the interviews not a single suggestion was made to indicate a belief in genetic determinism with regard to perceptions of Japan's unique culture. The Japanese mode of thinking and behaving is habitually associated with the 'Japanese race', itself an imaginary notion, in perceptions of Japanese identity. This perceived relationship itself, in turn, depends upon the 'uni-racial assumption' of respondents, according to which the racial homogeneity of the Japanese is unchanging.

Before concluding this section, I will clarify my remark that genetic deterministic thinking is not absent among respondents. There is an area in which genetic determinism is evident: a belief that one's blood type is a cause of one's personality and temperament (see chapter 2). Most respondents were interested in the subject of blood types, remarking that they often brought up this subject in daily conversation with friends and colleagues; for example, when discussing congeniality between sexes, the types of jobs and leisure activities suitable for persons with different blood types and so on. But none of our respondents associated blood type composition with ethnic/national character. This is clearly shown by the fact that only a few knew that blood-type composition could vary from one ethnic/national group to another. It is my contention that the notion of what I call the 'racially exclusive possession of particular cultural characteristics', which best characterises our respondents' perceptions of Japanese uniqueness, should not be conflated with another type of thinking that suggests genetic determinism.

Finally, it would be fair to point out that our respondents had ambivalent feelings about the adaptation of foreigners to the Japanese way of life. Despite their 'race thinking', many respondents encouraged the current tendency of foreigners to attempt to adapt to the Japanese way of thinking because, as many remarked, this promotes the 'internationalisation' of Japan and helps to broaden the minds of the Japanese. On the other hand, however, they assumed that 'racial' and cultural homogeneity is at the core of Japanese uniqueness.

JAPANESE CULTURE AS THE EXCLUSIVE PROPERTY OF THE JAPANESE: ITS CONTENT

It is now in order to examine what actually constitutes the Japanese culture which is perceived to be the exclusive property of the Japanese. The following two remarks made by the same respondent, a company executive, are suggestive:

> Of course, we cannot expect foreigners to understand such expressions as *kareta bunshō* and *ikina niisan*.[14] Only the Japanese can get a feel of such notions.

There are an increasing number of foreigners now who can appreciate things Japanese. I heard there are a lot of Japanese restaurants opening in New York nowadays. Japanese management style is being adopted in America, too. Things Japanese are being internationalised.

The two statements are seemingly contradictory. In the first, non-Japanese are not expected to acquire Japanese culture. In the second statement, this is expected of them. What this discrepancy suggests is that while there are some aspects of Japanese culture accessible to non-Japanese, there is also a realm perceived to be the 'exclusive property' of the Japanese.

Symbolic boundary process and 'our own realm'

Before enquiring further into the core content of the 'exclusive' property of the Japanese, I shall offer a conceptual view of what has made the Japanese *possessive* of certain aspects of their culture. This question may be approached from the point of view of the boundary marking process of ethnicity (see chapter 4). Ethnicity may be viewed as a symbolic boundary process of selecting and organising significant differences between 'us' and 'them' (Wallman 1978, 1979). The boundary perspective is useful because we are concerned here with the actively conscious aspects of ethnic identity: that is, how respondents express their ideas of the uniqueness of the Japanese *vis-à-vis* non-Japanese. The process of defining Japanese uniqueness (or at least part of the process) may be viewed as the process of marking the symbolic boundary of 'us' (the Japanese) against 'them'. 'Them' does not merely refer to other countries (in particular, the countries of the West), in opposition to which difference is stressed, but also exogenous elements present in Japan. The process of marking the symbolic boundary of 'us' for the Japanese is, therefore, the process of delineating 'our own realm' within 'our' nation.

What is characteristic about the Japanese attitude towards (some of) the foreign cultures is their active absorption of them. Generally speaking, exogenous elements may enter into a society in a forced manner (such as in the case of military invasion and colonisation) or be introduced in a voluntary manner. Japanese elites have historically developed a pattern of voluntarily, selectively and actively introducing exogenous elements – mainly those of, first, Chinese civilisation from the sixth century, then Western civilisation from the second half of the nineteenth century – into Japan, and the consciousness of this process has helped Japan to develop its technologies, institutions, philosophies, arts and so on, while at the same time remaining a separate cultural and political entity. Thus, the process of strengthening ethnic sentiment in Japan has, on the whole, not been the process of rejecting the very presence of 'them' within Japan, but rather of delineating 'our own realm' within Japan while simultaneously allowing exogenous elements (e.g. institutions, technologies, philosophies, religions and arts) to perform their own active roles within 'our' nation.[15] In order for 'our own realm' to be marked, significant differences have been selected and organised not merely to differentiate between 'us' (the Japanese) and 'them' (other countries from which cultural elements are borrowed), but, more importantly, to emphasise the existence of 'our own realm' and therefore to demonstrate the uninterrupted continuation of 'our' nation as a cultural entity. In this way, the sense of historical continuity can also be maintained. It is this cultural realm of 'ours' to which the Japanese claim exclusive ownership.

Actively conscious absorption of foreign elements requires an actively conscious marking of the boundary, which in turn makes it possible to continue to absorb actively further foreign elements. As long as the Japanese know that 'we' have 'our own realm' as an exclusive source of Japanese identity, 'our' identity is secured and the presence of exogenous elements within 'our' nation is felt to be no threat to that identity. As about half the respondents pointed out, the ability of the Japanese to take foreign cultures and to blend them not only with Japan's indigenous culture but with other foreign cultures ('Japan as a bridge between the Eastern and Western civilisations') is a uniquely Japanese quality. Thus, two seemingly contradictory features, their actively conscious absorption of things foreign and their actively conscious sense of uniqueness, are the inseparable aspects of the same process. An active awareness of 'our own realm' is essential to the Japanese sense of uniqueness (and also to the continuing active absorption of foreign cultures).

What aspects of Japanese culture, then, do respondents regard as the exclusive property of the Japanese or as 'our own realm'? As has been already suggested, much of what I call the 'underlying culture' (or abstract and holistic culture) corresponds to this realm. To give a rather obvious example, non-Japanese can master the formal rules of the Japanese language but not the subtle meaning system behind the use of the language, as it involves implicit and tacit modes of communication on which the fundamental principles of Japanese culture are believed to depend. Non-Japanese in general are not expected to share what symbolically underlies objectified institutions and customs. In fact, most of the cultural traits or objects which respondents considered accessible to non-Japanese are objectifiable. The list includes various aspects of traditional artistic–literary culture and everyday-life culture: martial arts such as karate and jūdō;[16] theatrical arts such as *kabuki* and *noh* plays; other artistic products such as pottery, paintings, *ukiyoe* or other wood-block prints; architecture and gardens; and daily items such as Japanese food and drinks, Japanese-style bathing, Japanese-style bedding and so forth. These objectified aspects of culture cannot replace the underlying culture as boundary items to constitute 'our own realm'.

Two reasons may be pointed out as to why the underlying culture is suitable for this purpose. First, the underlying culture is, by definition, free of exogenous influences. Although everyday-life and artistic types of culture are, without doubt, distinctively Japanese in many respects, unravelling of the indigenous and foreign elements in these types of culture is on the whole extremely difficult and requires a conscious effort. By contrast, conscious delineation of the underlying culture as a source of Japaneseness is unnecessary because it is by definition 'our own Japanese realm'. It is this taken-for-grantedness of the underlying culture that marks it off from the other types of culture. It is a convenient means of indicating the presence of 'our own realm', as many respondents remarked: 'Japan may look Westernised on the surface, but our modes of behaving and thinking have not changed all that much'.

Second, the underlying culture is the type of culture of which the majority of the respondents were actively conscious. As already observed, traditional artistic–literary culture is so far removed from everyday reality and everyday-life culture is so closely part of it that our respondents were not actively conscious of these two types of culture. This is understandable and certainly not peculiar to the Japanese. The 'ordinary' members of society, who are not professional thinkers, are not expected to be actively conscious of their distinctiveness except under extraordinary circumstances such as war, when the sense of 'us' against 'them' is heightened. But, even so, is it not more natural that 'ordinary' people should be more interested in everyday customs and objects rather than 'theories' of society? One reason why this is not the case for the Japanese may be that most of the 'ordinary' Japanese do not experience regular face-to-face contact with people of different ethnic and national groups, so that they do not perceive cultural differences in terms of everyday lifestyle. Japan's geography allows no cross-border contacts with different national groups, and the presence of ethnic groups within Japan is relatively inconspicuous compared to multi-ethnic societies.

This means that the majority of our respondents' active interest in the abstract theories of Japanese culture and society reflected a special circumstance. But what special circumstance? To answer this question requires an examination of the respondents' orientation to the thinking elites' ideas of Japanese uniqueness (which is a theme I shall return to in the next chapter). For the moment, let us continue our enquiry into the content of the 'exclusive property of the Japanese'.

The changing perceptions of Japanese identity and the persisting core of Japanese uniqueness

Let us enquire further into the core content of the underlying culture as the exclusive property of the Japanese as perceived by the respondents. The context in which this question may appropriately be discussed is that of *kokusaika* (internationalisation) of Japanese culture, a theme frequently mentioned by the educated Japanese in contemporary Japan. One aspect of this concerns the 'exportability' of Japanese culture.

So far national identity has been discussed more or less as a static phenomenon, but the Japanese sense of uniqueness has been undergoing some change since the late 1970s. From around the early 1980s the emphasis of thinking elites began to shift gradually from the 'particularistic' aspects of Japanese culture to the transferable or 'universalisable' aspects.[17] There has been discussion to the effect that some traditional characteristics of Japanese society are more congruent to modern industrial values than those of the early industrialisers and that, therefore, Japanese culture can be diffused to other countries as an alternative model of industrial society. This occurred at a time when the other aspects of Japanese culture, such as Japanese food, design and film came increasingly to be known in other countries.

A large number of our respondents, especially businessmen, were well aware of this shift of emphasis in national identity. The following remark by a company manager illustrated his changing perceptions of Japanese uniqueness: 'It's wonderful that the so-called Japanese management practices are being adapted abroad and are contributing to economic development in other societies'. He felt that *some* aspects of what had previously been regarded as being 'uniquely Japanese' might not be so exclusively 'ours'. What aspects, then, were perceived as 'transplantable' to other national settings?

The majority of the respondents, as seen above, perceived Japanese uniqueness in terms of social and linguistic/communicative culture. Pursuing our enquiry further, we find that respondents had an ambivalent attitude towards the so-called group orientation as a main feature of Japan's unique social culture. On the one hand, they regarded it as an 'intrinsic' quality of the Japanese; on the other, they encouraged diffusion of it, or some aspects of it, to other countries. The following remark by a company president was illustrative of this ambivalence:

> Our business and management style is part and parcel of our unique spiritual culture. It's nice to think that it is being adopted in foreign countries, too.

Group orientation as perceived by the respondents actually consists of the two closely related yet distinguishable aspects. On the one hand, emphasis is given to the aspect of the group as a 'framework' in which individuals are enclosed. This may be further divided into two notions. The first is the notion of a group – typically a company – as an institutional framework with various group-oriented practices such as participatory decision-making, teamwork systems, 'quality control' circles, length-of-service systems, recreational activities with office mates, a type of canteen at work where class barriers are removed and so on. These institutional aspects of group orientation can be diffused to other countries and, as such, are not an inevitable property of the Japanese. In fact, when respondents discussed the 'internationalisation' of Japanese culture, they concentrated on these objectified company practices.

Second, the notion of 'a group as a framework' depicts the group and the individual as dichotomies, thereby suggesting that one precedes the other in importance. (See chapter 2 for a discussion on methodological holism and individualism.) The relative importance of the group suggests a lack of self-autonomy, a submergence of individuality in the group, a preference to act in the group in order to obtain psychological security and so on. When many of our respondents discussed group orientation in this sense, they

interpreted this feature negatively. Although, on the whole, educators and businessmen shared a negative view of this aspect of
group orientation, educators tended to be more explicit in their
criticism, perhaps in part because the importance of enriching
one's individuality (*kosei*) was a theme of debate in education at
the time of the interviews. Since group orientation in this sense
tends to be viewed in a negative light, it cannot be an inevitable
source of Japanese identity.

The other aspect of the so-called group orientation does not
deal with the group as a framework within which individuals are
contained, but emphasises interpersonal relations, which are characterised by an emphasis on interactional sensitivity. The distinction
between 'groupism' and 'interpersonalism' (or 'contextualism') proposed by Hamaguchi (see chapter 2) is of analytical use here. From
this perspective, lack of individualism implies a consideration and
sensitivity expressed towards other persons. Sensitivity shown in
social interaction requires the ability to understand the subtlety
of the Japanese mind, and this constitutes an important aspect
of the exclusive sense of Japanese uniqueness. When respondents
suggested that behind the so-called group-oriented institutions and
practices was a mentality peculiar to the Japanese, they were most
likely to be referring to this aspect of social culture.

Furthermore, this aspect of social culture is closely related to the
other feature of Japanese uniqueness, the linguistic and communicative culture, which may be summarised as the Japanese celebration
of reticence as a valued mode of communication, as opposed to
the Westerners' rhetorical means of communication, as well as
the highly valued use of sentiment and intuition in interpersonal
communication among the Japanese in contrast to the heavy reliance
on reason and dichotomous logic in Western-style communication.
The following remark of a company manager was typical:

> We are not so assertive as Westerners. Our homogeneous society
> is less conflict-ridden than Western society. Sensitivity to other
> people and flexibility in human relations are the virtues of the
> Japanese.

To sum up, the respondents' sense of Japanese uniqueness was essentially *social*. Even when reference was made to the use of language,
such reference was actually about interpersonal communication and
social interaction. In other words, what may be called the cultural
ethos of the Japanese is expressed in terms of the above-mentioned

social characteristics considered to underlie Japanese interpersonal relations rather than the artistic and poetic tastes of the Japanese. Related to this is the fact that most respondents' perceptions of Japanese uniqueness tended to be *a*historical in the sense that they were not concerned to express Japanese cultural uniqueness in terms of historical memory (i.e. a glorious past, the greatness of their ancestral culture). Their interest in Japanese uniqueness centred around the question of how the contemporary Japanese behave differently from non-Japanese or of where the symbolic boundary may be drawn between 'us' Japanese and 'them' foreigners.

We have somehow located the core element of 'our own Japanese realm' perceived by the respondents as the exclusive property of the Japanese, but care should be taken not to be overly simplistic. The analysis has tended to concentrate on the ways in which the respondents *expressed* their ideas of Japanese uniqueness, even though an attempt has been made, wherever possible, to go deeper into the more subconscious aspects of the respondents' national identity. The respondents' sense of Japanese uniqueness, if considered at all its levels, is, without question, much more complex. But this is not to underestimate the usefulness of this study because we are particularly interested in the question of why the respondents expressed Japanese uniqueness in the way they did.

Furthermore, it is important to point out that Japanese perceptions of their uniqueness are now undergoing gradual but significant changes in response to a set of new phenomena surrounding the Japanese. I shall briefly mention two types of change that have not yet been covered – both being brought about by the new types of ethnic relations. First, the increasing numbers of migrant labourers from South-East Asia and other developing regions are serving as a catalyst for the Japanese to reconsider the homogeneous nature of Japanese society. The Japanese are for the first time witnessing the presence of a sizeable number of visible foreigners labouring as fellow workers in the workplace and living as neighbours in the community. Second, the type of race thinking which I have called 'racially exclusive possession of Japanese culture' is being challenged, on the one hand, by the increasingly evident presence of foreigners (Westerners and others) whose use of Japanese is as natural as that of the native Japanese and, on the other, the increasing number of Japanese returnees from abroad (*kikokushijo*) whose behaviour and use of the Japanese language are perceived as 'different' from those of the 'normal' Japanese. *Kikokushijo* are school-age children who have received an important part of their education abroad, usually on account of their father's overseas business posting. Wallman's (1978: 212) concept of 'boundary dissonance', which means a lack of fit between lines of difference (real or imaginary), is useful here. These cases of 'Japanese-like' foreigners and 'un-Japanese' Japanese give rise to a misfit between cultural and 'racial' lines of difference, thereby causing an inconsistency in and inefficacy of the symbolic boundary system that defines Japanese identity. The assumption that those who speak and behave like the Japanese should be 'racially' Japanese and vice versa is gradually but profoundly being challenged through the experience of such 'boundary dissonance'.

CONCLUDING REMARKS: VARIATIONS AMONG RESPONDENTS

The discussion in this chapter has centred around the representative tendency among the respondents. However, it is also necessary to look into the variations among the respondents and investigate carefully the meaning of such variations. Differences exist between educators and businessmen in the ways they chose to express Japanese uniqueness. There are also age differences, especially among educators. Most businessmen tended to express their ideas of Japanese uniqueness in terms of (abstract and holistic) underlying culture. The majority of the educators shared this tendency, but an appreciable number of educators, especially older educators, objectified their ideas of Japanese uniqueness in terms of arts and everyday customs. Younger teachers were more uniform in their expressions and in this sense more closely resembled businessmen. The response of older educators, on the other hand, tended to vary considerably. What do these differences mean? Why are the businessmen's responses rather more uniform and better organised? Why are there more variations among educators than among businessmen, and among older educators than younger ones? These questions will be examined in more depth in the following chapters, but a few suggestions may be made in closing this chapter.

The preceding discussion has suggested that many respondents were accustomed to expressing their ideas of Japanese uniqueness in terms of abstract 'theories'. It would appear that the dissemination of the *nihonjinron* is an important explanatory factor here. The *nihonjinron* may have stimulated, if not created, some of our respondents' active consciousness of Japanese identity as well as their perceptions and expressions of it. One way of examining whether the *nihonjinron* affected our respondents' own perceptions and expressions of Japanese uniqueness is to investigate whether there is any significant relationship between those respondents who had been actively exposed to the *nihonjinron* and those who, in expressing Japanese uniqueness, did not objectify it. We found that the degree to which respondents did not objectify this uniqueness is strongly and positively correlated with their level of exposure to the *nihonjinron*: that is, the more exposure, the less 'objectification (the more abstraction)' (see Tables 6.2 and 6.3). This applied both to educators and businessmen. This finding endorses my hypothesis that a reason why the majority of the respondents expressed Japanese identity in terms of well-formulated theories even though they were not professional thinkers is that their perception of Japanese uniqueness or, at least, their expression of it, was conditioned in this particular manner under the influence of the *nihonjinron*. But one should not seek to rely exclusively on the quantitative data, which should rather be regarded as supplementary to qualitative analysis.

In the next chapter I shall examine more closely the nature and extent of the influence of the *nihonjinron* on our respondents. In doing so, I shall compare educators and businessmen and examine which social group was more significantly affected by the *nihonjinron*, and why and how. This is a very important question in view of the fact that the *nihonjinron* is an important intellectual source of cultural nationalism in contemporary Japan.

Table 6.2 Level of exposure to the *nihonjinron* and degree of abstraction in expression of Japanese uniqueness: educators

Percentage of abstract cultural features referred to by respondents	Active exposure to** the nihonjinron		Passive exposure to the nihonjinron		No exposure to the nihonjinron		Total	
	X*	Y*	X	Y	X	Y	X	Y
A 100–75	9	(96.0)	8	(79.8)	0	(0.0)	17	(88.3)
B 74–50	1	(74.0)	3	(73.3)	0	(0.0)	4	(73.5)
C 49–25	0	(0.0)	4	(45.2)	2	(39.0)	6	(43.1)
D 24–0	0	(0.0)	4	(19.8)	4	(20.3)	8	(20.1)
Total	10	(93.8)	19	(58.9)	6	(26.5)	35	(54.9)

Notes
* X = no. of respondents; Y = the average of the percentage of abstract cultural characteristics among all the traits of Japanese uniqueness referred to by the respondents.
** 'Active exposure to the *nihonjinron*' means that the respondent had approached and read some of the *nihonjinron* literature with an active interest; 'passive exposure' that the respondent had been exposed to the *nihonjinron* in one way or another but had had no active motivation to do so; 'no exposure' that the respondent had not read the *nihonjinron* (as far as the respondent remembered).

Table 6.3 Level of exposure to the *nihonjinron* and degree of abstraction in expression of Japanese uniqueness: businessmen

Percentage of abstract cultural features referred to by respondents	Active exposure to** the nihonjinron		Passive exposure to the nihonjinron		No exposure to the nihonjinron		Total	
	X*	Y*	X	Y	X	Y	X	Y
A 100–75	26	(95.1)	8	(75.0)	0	(0.0)	34	(90.4)
B 74–50	1	(71.0)	0	(0.0)	0	(0.0)	1	(71.0)
C 49–25	0	(0.0)	0	(0.0)	0	(0.0)	0	(0.0)
D 24–0	0	(0.0)	0	(0.0)	1	(20.0)	1	(20.0)
Total	27	(94.2)	8	(75.0)	1	(20.0)	36	(87.9)

Notes

* X = no. of respondents; Y = the average of the percentage of abstract cultural characteristics among all the traits of Japanese uniqueness referred to by the respondents.

** 'Active exposure to the *nihonjinron*' means that the respondent had approached and read some of the *nihonjinron* literature with an active interest; 'passive exposure' that the respondent had been exposed to the *nihonjinron* in one way or another but had had no active motivation to do so; 'no exposure' that the respondent had not read the *nihonjinron* (as far as the respondent remembered).

Chapter 7

The diffusion of ideas of Japanese uniqueness: the response of educators and businessmen to the *nihonjinron*

Cultural nationalism normally involves the dual process by which intellectuals (or thinking elites) formulate ideas of national distinctiveness and by which the intelligentsia respond to such ideas, thereby diffusing ideas of national distinctiveness. This chapter investigates which sections of a population have responded favourably and actively to the thinking elites' ideas of Japanese uniqueness (the *nihonjinron*), and why and how. Specifically concerned with two types of intelligentsia, educators and businessmen, I shall examine the nature of the social process that has occurred between thinking elites and educators and businessmen as regards the diffusion of the *nihonjinron*.[1] Such a sociological perspective of 'what occurs, by whom, and to whom' within Japanese society is absent in the existing literature concerning the phenomenon of the *nihonjinron*. Furthermore, I shall critically assess some of the conventional propositions and assumptions concerning cultural nationalism on the basis of our findings on the diffusion of the *nihonjinron* in Japanese society.

This chapter consists of two sections. The first half of the chapter presents the findings concerning the respondents' reaction to the *nihonjinron* in the form of generalised statements. The second half, headed 'Case studies', focuses on some individual cases and examines more closely the background against which some respondents became interested in the *nihonjinron*, paying attention to the respondents' personal profile.

EDUCATORS' AND BUSINESSMEN'S RESPONSE TO THE *NIHONJINRON*: A COMPARISON

Our findings show that educators and businessmen differ significantly in their response to the *nihonjinron*. A significantly larger number of businessmen than educators showed an active concern with the *nihonjinron*. (Table 7.1 shows that the difference between the two groups is statistically significant [$X^2(2df) = 15.847, p<0.001$].)[2] Since one should not seek to rely too much on statistical data, it is important to enquire analytically into this difference between educators and businessmen. What does this difference mean? What explains the difference between educators and businessmen? Why and how did our respondents concern themselves with the theories of their own society despite the fact that they were not men of ideas for ideas' sake?

Table 7.1 A comparison of educators' and businessmen's exposure to the *nihonjinron* (no. and percentage of respondents)

	Active exposure to the nihonjinron	Passive exposure to the nihonjinron	No exposure to the nihonjinron	Total
Educators	10 (28.6)	19 (54.3)	6 (17.1)	35 (100)
Businessmen	27 (75.0)	8 (22.2)	1 (2.8)	36 (100)

Chi square = 15.847; 2 degrees of freedom, $p<0.001$.
Note: 'Active exposure to the *nihonjinron*' means that the respondent had approached and read some of the *nihonjinron* literature with an active interest; 'passive exposure' that the respondent had been exposed to some ideas of the *nihonjinron* in one way or another but had had no active motivation to do so; 'no exposure' that the respondent had not read the *nihonjinron* (as far as the respondent remembered).

Educators and the *nihonjinron*

Only 28.6 per cent of the educators actively responded to the *nihonjinron*, compared with 75.0 per cent of the businessmen. In order to examine why the *nihonjinron* attracted relatively fewer educators than businessmen, one can turn the question around and explore why and how some educators were attracted to it. Five major reasons for the educators' interest in the *nihonjinron* have been identified: moral, academic, cross-cultural, educational and occupational (organisational).[3] Since all respondents were motivated differently, only careful case studies of their life histories would do justice to them. This will be attempted in the second half of this chapter (see pp. 143–56). Here, the five types of educators' concern with the *nihonjinron* will briefly be pointed out.

First, the *nihonjinron* was used as a source of reflecting morally upon the Japanese character. Moralistic discussions of the Japanese character were prevalent among post-war opinion leaders. The majority of our educators, too, remarked that they had once reflected upon Japanese behavioural characteristics morally and critically during the two decades following Japan's defeat in 1945 but were no longer interested in such self-criticism. Our research set contained only one educator still morally interested in the peculiarities of Japanese society. It is not possible to generalise as to why some people retained their moral concern with the Japanese character and why others did not, since it depends on the unique experience of each individual (see the section on case studies).

It is especially important to recognise that the other educators actively receptive to the thinking elites' ideas of Japanese uniqueness had more specific – often practical – interests: academic, cross-cultural, educational and occupational (organisational).

Two of our educators exhibited the second type of interest in the *nihonjinron* – academic. Both were social studies teachers and had studied sociology or other social sciences at university, which is an understandable background. But not all social science graduates and not all social studies teachers are interested in 'theories' of Japanese society. Again, the motivation for and extent of each individual's interest depends on his personal background. The third type of interest is cross-cultural. Four of our educators' active interest in the *nihonjinron* grew out of their first-hand experience of cross-cultural contacts with non-Japanese and of their interest in shedding light on problems of intercultural communication and in their own cultural identity. This is an understandable and important motivation considering that one becomes sensitised by cross-cultural contacts to cultural differences and to the distinctiveness of one's culture and that the *nihonjinron* provides supposedly useful ideas on cultural differences. But only a minority of educators in Nakasato were regularly exposed to intercultural contacts. Fourthly, four educators had shown an interest in the *nihonjinron* in order to gain insights for an educational purpose. Educators occasionally gave talks to their pupils on Japan's role in international society within which context they touched upon Japanese peculiarities. Since educators in this category also had other types of interests in the *nihonjinron* (i.e. moral, academic and cross-cultural), it may be supposed that they first acquired a taste for the *nihonjinron* in some other circumstances and subsequently used some of the ideas obtained from the *nihonjinron* in education. In other words, their other types of concern preceded their educational concern with the *nihonjinron*.

Finally, but very importantly, there was one headmaster whose interest in the *nihonjinron* had been motivated by his occupational concern with human relations at work and his concern to increase morale among teachers with the aim of their more active participation in committee work and administrative activities. This headmaster had read some of the literature on Japan's business culture in the hope of obtaining useful insights on organisational matters. (A great deal of the *nihonjinron* discusses Japan's distinctiveness in the context of business culture, as will be discussed in chapter 8.) This suggests that the popularity of the *nihonjinron* may be related to a person's organisational concern with human relations at work. In this connection, attention may be drawn to the case of another headmaster (called Mr J in the case study), who had the experience of working in a private company, a rare experience for school educators. Of particular importance is the fact that his business experience had led to his interest in the *nihonjinron*. His systematic ideas of Japanese and other cultures derived largely from his reading of the *nihonjinron* literature written by leading members of the Japanese business elite. As he remarked:

> Businessmen write more convincingly than academics because they actually do business with foreigners and thus learn the hard way what it means to be Japanese in international society.

Asked why he was interested in the *nihonjinron*, he said that the so-called *nihonjinron* had direct bearing on businessmen's everyday working lives because much of its content dealt with Japanese behaviour in the context of company organisation.

This educator's observation suggests an important point regarding one's concern with the *nihonjinron*: one's occupational concern with business and management practices and active work organisation can be an important reason for one's interest in the *nihonjinron*. Leading members of the business elite tend, by writing books, to systematise their ideas of cultural differences as manifested in business practices and organisation, to which they have become sensitised in their experience of dealing with foreign business and management practices. Businessmen, in general, respond favourably to such literature because its content directly concerns daily practices in their working life. This headmaster is one of many such men who acquired a taste for the *nihonjinron* during their career in a company.

It is precisely for this reason that I decided to examine business-men as a comparative case and to examine whether the experience of working in a Japanese company significantly affects one's response to the *nihonjinron* and whether in turn one is significantly affected by it, and if so, why and how.

To sum up our findings on the educators' orientation to the *nihonjinron*: First, educators tended to be less interested in the thinking elites' theories of Japanese uniqueness than I had originally expected. I originally supposed that educators would be one of the social types most likely to be interested in ideas regarding their society and culture, because the nature of their work is to transmit the knowledge and values of the society and the development of culture. Second, educators' relative lack of interest in the *nihonjinron* can be understood if one considers that most of the educators' concerns with the *nihonjinron* were not intrinsically associated with the social role of the educator.

Businessmen and the *nihonjinron*

In contrast to educators, most of our businessmen were actively responsive to the *nihonjinron*. They were also ready to discuss this subject and better informed of the content of the *nihonjinron* as well as developments in the 'theories' of Japanese uniqueness.[4] Both educators and businessmen first displayed modesty by stating that this was not an easy topic for them to discuss because they were not professional thinkers. But the difference between the two groups became conspicuous as the interviews progressed. The majority of the businessmen's understanding of the content of the *nihonjinron* was clearly in evidence, and the educators' relative lack of knowledge of, or indifference to, this topic became noticeable.

The two main types of businessmen's interest in the *nihonjinron* were cross-cultural and occupational (or organisational). There were also other types of concern, but they were much less common or significant.[5]

It is particularly important to point out that the majority of our businessmen shared one common concern: an occupational (or organisational) concern. The *nihonjinron* interested them because it provided them with ideas and insights useful for their organisational concerns at work. The following remark of a bank employee illustrates this point very well:

> It is natural that we in business should show some interest in this
> sort of discussion (on Japanese uniqueness) because it is basically
> about our own business practices and human relations.

Indeed, the social culture portrayed in the *nihonjinron* has much to do with Japanese management and business practices. For example, Japanese group orientation is often discussed in the context of Japanese-style employment practices, industrial relations and decision-making processes. Aspects of the Japanese linguistic culture (e.g. the lack of emphasis on the explicit use of language and logic) are also discussed in the context of human relations among businessmen. In other words, the company is often regarded in the *nihonjinron* as a typical social context in which the Japanese cultural ethos or underlying culture is 'externalised'.

The exceptions were businessmen in small family businesses, the employers and core employees of which were members of the extended family and their personal acquaintances. It was understandable that, because of the familial atmosphere that already existed, there should be no reason for them to be consciously concerned with the ways of creating and maintaining affective ties and that there was little room for the thinking elites' ideas to play any significant role. But there were also some businessmen in this group who were very knowledgeable about the *nihonjinron*. They were the relatively young businessmen who had worked in a big company before succeeding to a relative's family business. (It is customary for prospective owners of family businesses to gain practical experience in large companies upon graduation from university.)

The everyday working environment in the large, bureaucratic company motivates businessmen to read the *nihonjinron* either at their own will or as a result of someone else's recommendation. Understandably, senior members of companies in managerial positions tend to be more voluntary in their approach to the *nihonjinron*. A company president said:

> It's not easy to maintain good human relations in the company.
> Reading literature on Japanese social characteristics written by
> distinguished business leaders gives us a sense of direction.

Younger businessmen's approach to the *nihonjinron* may be either voluntary or involuntary depending on the context and the individual. Sometimes, the company provides its newly-recruited employees with a list of recommended books. A 35-year-old company employee remembered that 'the list included a number of books on the so-called *nihonjinron*'. This may make it appear that younger company employees are directly manipulated by their superiors in such a manner as to be exposed to the particular ideology of Japanese business culture, or by management ideology emphasising the managers' ideas of harmony within the organisation. Although such an inter pretation is possible, another example suggests that it is not so manipulative as it seems. A 34-year-old bank employee made an interesting remark:

> I try to read literature on Japan's business culture out of an instinct to defend myself in the organisation. Our managers study organisational theory very well. So, I feel we have also to supply ourselves with the same kind of knowledge they have.

In this example, the respondent finds himself in the situation where he feels that it is to his advantage to be informed of the theories of Japanese business culture to which managers often refer. Businessmen's approach to the *nihonjinron* may be manipulated or 'voluntary'. But, of course, one can act voluntarily, while at the same time being manipulated.

A comparison

We have found that businessmen tended to be more concerned with the *nihonjinron* than educators. This is an interesting finding because we normally think that educators are more concerned with ideas about society and culture and that businessmen are more concerned with mundane, material matters. The opposite has been found to be the case. There are two main explanations for this. First, businessmen – especially, business elites – are more likely to have cross-cultural contacts than educators during the course of their work and, therefore, to have more practical opportunities to be interested in the peculiarities of Japanese behaviour. In reality, only a small proportion of our businessmen made regular contacts with non-Japanese on business, but we cannot ignore the fact that many businessmen engage in 'anticipatory socialisation' to be a *kokusai-jin* ('an international person').[6] Many of our businessmen stressed that the so-called 'internationalisation' of Japan was already taking place even in a provincial city like Nakasato and that it had become a reality that they themselves might have to do business with foreigners, to employ foreigners or to work in a foreign country some day. Second, their interest in the *nihonjinron* was caused by or coincided with their occupational concern with management and business practices and human relations in organisation. Since productive organisation is not so much a preoccupation of educators as it is of businessmen, fewer educators were interested in the *nihonjinron*. Unlike businessmen, educators as a social category had no uniform reason to be attracted by the *nihonjinron* in this organisational sense. It is for this reason that we found more differing reasons for the educators' concern with the *nihonjinron*. This does not mean, however, that varying reasons did not exist among businessmen. Rather, the variety of businessmen's reasons were overshadowed by their stronger and more uniform interest: their work-related interest in obtaining useful knowledge.

Another difference between educators and businessmen was that, whereas businessmen had actively been exposed to the *nihonjinron* regardless of age, significant variations with age were found in the case of educators. Younger educators tended to be more informed of the *nihonjinron* than older educators. Whereas most younger teachers, especially those in their thirties, had been exposed to the *nihonjinron* in the 1970s as students and were therefore knowledgeable concerning the 'theories' of Japanese uniqueness and tended to express their ideas using language characteristic of the *nihonjinron*, older educators in general had no uniform opportunity to familiarise themselves with the *nihonjinron*. By contrast, businessmen had constantly been exposed to situations in which the way of life portrayed in the *nihonjinron* was part and parcel of their real working life, and their interest in the *nihonjinron* had thus been reinforced. It is this difference in their everyday working environment that explains the presence and absence of age differences for educators and businessmen, respectively. An interesting case in point was that of the 74-year-old headmaster (Mr J) discussed earlier, who, despite his old age, became attracted to the *nihonjinron* precisely because of his experience of working in a private company. This was a strong example in support of the proposition that the nature of work in the company promotes one's positive orientation to the *nihonjinron*.

THE IMPLICATIONS OF OUR FINDINGS FOR THEORIES OF CULTURAL NATIONALISM

Our findings will now be related to a more general theory of cultural nationalism. Two points will be raised in relation to the conventional views of cultural nationalism. It is widely assumed that in cultural nationalism:

1 elites *mobilise* the ordinary sections of the population by 'giving' them their ideas of the identity of the nation;
2 educators play the major role in receiving and diffusing the ideas of national distinctiveness formulated by intellectuals.

In fact, these are two inseparable aspects of the same question, as will be seen later.

Let us start with the point about mobilisation. This represents an elitist view of society in that it is based on the notion of 'haves' and 'have-nots' of knowledge and of the uni-directional transmission of knowledge from the former to the latter. Such a view is implicitly assumed in much of the existing literature on nationalism through emphasis on historical art culture as the major source of national identity and educators as the major disseminators of ideas of national distinctiveness.

In an attempt to assess the mobilisation assumption, I enquired into the respondents' own evaluation of the *nihonjinron*, asking them what they had acquired from it. Most of those respondents who had been exposed to the *nihonjinron* in one way or another did not consider it a source of new information about Japanese society and culture. In other words, they did not respond to the *nihonjinron* in order to be taught about their own society uni-directionally by the elite, but rather to *endorse* what they had already known and felt about their own society and culture. This was typically shown by the following remark of a president of an electrical appliance company:

> They [writers of the *nihonjinron*] discuss what I already know. In this sense, there is nothing new to learn from them. But they are so good at expressing what we normally feel about the Japanese by using carefully selected words that it helps us to organise our thought and express it.

A similar remark was given by a high school headmistress with regular intercultural experiences:

> Reading such literature is useful in the sense that it helps me to organise my thought on the Japanese. Although they simply write about what we already feel about our society, the fact that they can discuss it so systematically means that they are indeed professional thinkers. We are so busy with school administration and what not that we have no time left to ponder over important issues like these.

This finding may be presented to modify a conventional theory of cultural nationalism which is based on the experience of primary or original nationalism. As was discussed earlier, primary nationalism is basically the realm of historians, artists and art scholars who explore the nation's historical culture, particularly historical art culture. In secondary nationalism, or at least in the contemporary Japanese version of secondary nationalism, present-day social culture increases its relative importance over historical art culture. Whereas the knowledge of historical art culture has, in a sense, to be taught rather unilaterally to 'ordinary' people through the medium of formal education because ordinary people cannot obtain the historical knowledge without the help of intellectuals (historians and artists) – and this may be why mobilisation is assumed in much of the existing literature – the realm of social culture is already directly known to, and experienced by, ordinary people. The task of intellectuals in the case of social culture is to provide ordinary people with new perspectives from which to think more systematically about their society and behaviour. The shift of emphasis from historical/artistic culture to social culture is reflected in the way ideas of national distinctiveness are diffused in society. Intellectuals' mobilisation of ordinary people is less likely to occur in secondary nationalism.

If we take into account this point about what the *nihonjinron* does and does not do to the ordinary educated members of society, then we may also understand why businessmen – and not educators – have a more central role in receiving and diffusing the elites' ideas of national uniqueness in Japan's secondary nationalism, which leads to our second point.

Businessmen find the *nihonjinron* useful. What they find useful is *not* new information concerning their own society – which, in fact, the *nihonjinron* does not provide – but theoretical, conceptual and comparative perspectives on what they already feel about their own society in one way or another. Such perspectives as are given in the *nihonjinron*, especially those on the patterns of interpersonal communication and group-oriented business practices in the Japanese company, help businessmen to organise, express and endorse their ideas about their behaviour in their everyday working environment and with cross-cultural business contacts. By contrast, theoretical perspectives given in the *nihonjinron* are of less practical use in the context of the school as an educational institution and as a working environment for teachers. It is, therefore, understandable that businessmen should have played a more active role in receiving and diffusing the theories of Japanese uniqueness formulated by thinking elites in the *nihonjinron*.

CASE STUDIES

Having presented our findings in the form of generalised statements, I shall now examine more closely the respondents' interest in the *nihonjinron* in some case studies, taking note of their personal backgrounds. I have selected high school headmasters for case studies in order to show the diverse factors involved in one's concern with the *nihonjinron* in view of the fact that the headmaster's role is to relate the family, the school and the community to national society. In fact, unlike businessmen who appeared to be rather uniformly oriented to the *nihonjinron* due to the nature of their work, more varied orientations were readily found among headmasters. The five major reasons for headmasters' active interest in the *nihonjinron* were moral, academic, occupational, cross-cultural and educational. We are not concerned here with whether our cases were representative of others. Our concern is to explore qualitatively some of the variables that explain why and how educated Japanese 'consumed' works on Japanese uniqueness produced by the thinking elites.

The *nihonjinron* as a source of moral reflection on the Japanese character

There was one headmaster (hereafter called Mr I) who regarded the *nihonjinron* as a source of moral reflection upon Japan and the Japanese.   Born in 1928, Mr I belonged to the *senchū-ha* (war generation). Many of our other headmasters were more or less of the same generation, but Mr I was the only one who emphasised this generational factor. In a telephone call to make an appointment for the interview, he said:

> Being part of the war generation, I have not quite organised my thought on the Japanese yet, but I'm happy to have a chat on this question.

At the interview, he voluntarily discussed his life history and even supplied a copy of his article in a school journal which looked back to his childhood. Such readiness to discuss one's own personal history was not so common among the respondents.

He was born and raised as the sixth of eleven children in a farming family in a poor mountain village in southern Kyūshū. Japan was at war then. His dream as a child was to become a sailor or a military officer, but as he grew up he began to be attracted to the teaching profession. Although Mr I's youth coincided with the war years, he did not go off to war himself since at the end of the war he was still two years too young to be conscripted. He experienced the war at home, working at a radar construction site.

He was the only headmaster who explicitly stated that the wartime experience was still an issue of moral importance that had to be discussed on every possible occasion in education. Supposing that the war had equally affected other headmasters, one wonders why and how Mr I had retained an exceptionally strong interest in his wartime experience. As a clue to this question, Mr I recollected some events of his youth which, he thought, had been pivotal in forming his political attitude in general and his critical perception of war-related phenomena in particular. Of one such event, he recalled the actions of a teacher in his secondary school days who had no principles and 'made a 180° -turn in his attitudes' at the time of Japan's defeat in 1945:

> During the war this art teacher was the embodiment of militarism. He was an ardent supporter of the war. He often took us to where the spirits of the school's former pupils, who killed themselves in *kamikaze* attacks, were enshrined, glorifying the young men's courage in serving the emperor. When the war was over, he quite easily and remorselessly switched over to belief in democracy and, this time, became an enthusiastic advocate of the new creed. Seeing his overnight change, I told myself that I could never change my belief so easily as he did.

Moreover, Mr I gave his own interpretation according to which the way he related to the war explained his continued concern with the war as well as the wartime mentality of the Japanese people:

> Perhaps it's because I experienced the war indirectly that I could keep thinking of it all these years.

An indirect involvement in an event often helps to retain an objective interest in it, but one might also argue that those who actually fought as soldiers may equally find the subject of the war interesting in retrospect. Moreover, most of the other respondents belonged to the same generation and therefore experienced the war in more or less the same way as Mr I; nevertheless they did not respond to this subject in the same way. We might also indicate that one's explanation of his present action or action of the immediate past in terms of his earlier experience should be treated with scepticism because respondents often try to see themselves, retrospectively, as having the right values. Various objections such as these may be raised against Mr I's own interpretation of his experience; but whether or not his interpretation has general explanatory value does not matter much. What is important for us to notice is the fact that Mr I was highly retrospective and moralistic in thinking about Japan and the Japanese.

In 1946 he entered the Faculty of Education of the university and studied world history. One of the momentous events he experienced as a student in the late 1940s was his encounter with Ruth Benedict's *The Chrysanthemum and the Sword*. Written with an intent to understand the patterns of behaviour of the Japanese during the Second World War, this was one of the first major publications on the Japanese national character in post-war Japan. Many other respondents also read this book during this period when the mood of the nation was extremely introspective. Mr I described his sense of shock upon reading this book by saying, 'It was as if this American scholar had seen through me'. Benedict's book left him with so much thought and so many insights that he acquired a taste for literature on the Japanese national character.

The next series of literature he read on Japan and the Japanese dealt with the experiences of Japanese prisoners of war. Between the late 1950s and the early 1960s, he read Takasugi Ichirō's *In the Shadows of Auroras* (1950) and the famous work by Aida Yūji, *The Ahlone Concentration Camp* (1962). (Both authors are university professors. Aida is also known for his *The Structure of Japanese Consciousness* [1972], one of the representative books of the *nihonjinron*, which was mentioned in chapter 2 and which Mr I also read.) These are the memoirs of the Japanese prisoners of war taken by the Russians and by the British in Burma, respectively. They deal less with the Japanese character than with the British or the Russian character, and both can even be read as a critique of Western civilisation, but Mr I regarded these works as rare sources of information on how the people of the defeated country had thought and behaved, and interacted with people of the victorious countries. He remarked:

> One sees there a microcosm of defeated Japan. These are important materials in reminding us of that war and Japan's defeat in it.

Just about the time when Mr I's interest in the identity of the Japanese was enhanced by reading literature on Japanese prisoners of war, an increasing number of books on the uniqueness of the Japanese character began to emerge, leading to the *nihonjinron* boom of the 1970s. The boom is often said to have been triggered by Isaiah BenDasan's *The Japanese and the Jews* (1970). Immensely impressed by this work, Mr I read one book after another on the subject of the Japanese character published during this period, including *The Japanese and the Chinese* (1978) by writer Chin Shun Shin, *The Japanese and the Germans* (1977) by sociologist Shinoda Yūjirō, *Thoughts from Europe* (1978) by historian Kimura Shōzaburō, and *Japan, the Strange Country* (1975) by Paul Bonet, a self-proclaimed French businessman. These books share the approach of discussing the Japanese character in contrast to the national character of other peoples. He also read Nakane Chie's *Human Relations in Vertical Society* (1967).

The case study so far suggests how Mr I gradually acquired a taste for literature on the Japanese national character written from a comparative – or, rather, contrastive – perspective. His ideas of the distinctiveness of the Japanese character clearly reflected ideas presented in these works. In discussing what he considered to be the unique features of Japanese society, he gave what seemed like a model summary of the *nihonjinron*, listing such traits as group-oriented behaviour, various modes of maintaining and enhancing harmonious human relations, dependent mentality, lack of emphasis on logic, emphasis on affectivity, and flexibility obtained as a result of these features.

Interestingly, he said that these ideas stemmed from his own experience. However, one has to know about other peoples in order to say that certain features are unique to Japan, and Mr I had had no personal contact with foreign cultures. When this was pointed out to him, he said, 'I suppose I have to admit that my thinking about the Japanese has been influenced by those books I had read'. This suggests that Mr I had an ambivalent attitude towards the influence of the *nihonjinron* on him. Despite his perception of the *nihonjinron* as an interesting subject, he said that it had not provided him with much new information concerning the facts of Japanese culture and society. This caused him to think that the *nihonjinron* had not seriously influenced him. However, as Mr I himself suggested, the *nihonjinron* had significantly influenced him in the sense that it provided him with perspectives on the Japanese and with the language through which to express his ideas on Japanese culture systematically. (We have discussed this point in the general criticism of the 'mobilisation' assumption.)

In conclusion, Mr I's interest in the *nihonjinron* had been motivated and maintained by his moral concern with the national character of the Japanese. Being moralistic, he was one of the few headmasters in the research set who were still critical, or said that they were critical, of the Japanese character. He stated:

> The critical attitude we have had towards the Japanese character in the post-war period is now being reconsidered. But we should not regard this change as something to boast of. Throughout the history of Japan, what was the cause for rejoicings was also the cause of the destruction of the country in each period. In the Tokugawa period, what seemed like a stable system of estates was self-destructive in the end. In the Meiji and after, Japan boasted of her military power which turned out to be the cause of Japan's self-destruction. Today, we take pride in our economic power and our national character which supports it . . .

Those of the other respondents actively concerned with the *nihonjinron* had more specific interests in it.

The *nihonjinron* as a source of academic interest

There was only one headmaster (hereafter called Mr S) whose concern with the *nihonjinron* was academic.

Born in 1931 (age 55), he was the youngest headmaster interviewed, but only a few years younger than most of the others. What made Mr S remarkably different from the others was his academic background. At university he read management and industrial relations and graduated with a sociology degree in 1955. Considering that sociology was not such a popular university subject then, one can see that he had a highly favourable orientation towards theories of society. He said:

> In those days when Taylor's theory of scientific management was in vogue, there were only a handful of students of sociology. I, myself, was keenly interested in studying people's behaviour in society.

Upon graduation he chose to become a high school teacher of social studies instead of going into business.

The *nihonjinron* had long excited his attention. Asked why, he remarked that he had a personal and educational interest in it. By personal he meant 'academic' in that he had an intellectual bent to study and think about Japanese society and that such study gave him intrinsic pleasure.

Like many other respondents, he read *The Chrysanthemum and the Sword* as a student in the early 1950s. Since then, he kept abreast of developments in theories concerning the Japanese patterns of thought and behaviour, and read widely on this theme during the *nihonjinron* boom in the 1970s. In response to my request to mention some of the books he had read of this genre, he quickly responded with a long list of books including BenDasan's *The Japanese and the Jews* (1970), Nakane's *Human Relations in Vertical Society* (1967), Gregory Clark's *The Japanese Tribe: The Origins of Its Uniqueness* (1977), Tsunoda Tadanobu's *The Japanese Brain* (1978) and so forth. As to his ideas of the unique characteristics of the Japanese, he gave a very systematic summary of the features of Japanese society and culture typically dealt with in the *nihonjinron*: first, the homogeneous composition of society; second, a sense of cohesion among members of a social group modelled upon clan and kinship; and third, the priority of emotions and sentiment to reason and logic in human relations. He added that the three features were interrelated to produce the unique society of Japan.

One wonders why he had retained an academic interest in 'sociology' for so long after graduation when there are many who lose interest in the subjects they studied as students. Regarding this point, we may take note of a curious correspondence between theoretical developments in management studies, which he studied as a student, and developments in the perceptions of the nation's industrial culture in post-war Japan. This is understood to have helped him to maintain his interest in sociological ideas. In industrial sociology there was a shift of emphasis away from the scientific management view of employees as isolated individuals maximising material gains, to the human relations approach of regarding employees as oriented towards groups, requiring peer groups at work, and giving priority to group interests. In the perception of Japan's industrial culture, too, there was a shift away from the emphasis of the importance of rational and individuated society, which Japan was not, to the re-evaluation of group orientation, group consensus and cohesive informal groups within modern organisations. The latter features are commonly cited in the *nihonjinron* literature. Mr S said that it had been right for him to have studied sociology because it was very useful for thinking about the development of post-war Japanese society.

Although it is quite understandable for a sociologically-minded person like Mr S to take an academic interest in the intellectuals' ideas of the distinctiveness of Japanese society, such a case is more of an exception than a rule.

The *nihonjinron* as a source of useful perspectives on work organisation

There were two headmasters (hereafter called Mr M and Mr J) whose interest in the *nihonjinron* had been motivated by their occupational concern with human relations at work. Although they both shared the same motivation, Mr M and Mr J differed in the occupational background that had sparked this motivation. Whereas Mr M had always been a high school teacher since his graduation, Mr J had other occupations before becoming a headmaster. Mr J's interest in the *nihonjinron* had originated in his business career in a private company.

Mr M was born in 1930. During his school years he was attracted to natural science and eventually read physics at university. Upon graduation, he became a physics teacher at high school. He had always been a student of, and subsequently a teacher of, natural science. Unlike Mr S (discussed in the previous case study) who has always been sociologically minded, Mr M had not originally taken much interest in the study of society. As a way of emphasising his inclination towards natural science, he stated in his self-introduction that, because he was a typical 'science person', he was not sure if he could discuss an 'arts' topic like this one satisfactorily.

In the mid-1970s he became involved in a study group formed to work out ways to build up morale among teachers, whose passive attitudes towards education and school administration was causing some concern. In the hope of obtaining useful insights, Mr M and other members of the study group studied the literature on human relations in the organisation, and were in the end attracted to some of the *nihonjinron* literature. He remarked:

> In particular, those written by Japanese business leaders are useful and convincing because they are based on their first-hand experience of the Japanese company organisation which was the driving force of Japan's economic performance.

Among the books he had read, he stressed the usefulness of *Reviving Organisation* by Kobayashi Shigeru, a former factory superintendent of Sony Corporation. This paperback, published in 1971, was one of the earlier works to enlighten general readers about Japanese-style management. The book begins with the theme entitled 'Rediscovering the Japanese ways', refers to remarks made in BenDasan's *The Japanese and the Jews* and P.F. Drucker's 'What can we learn from Japanese management?' (1971), and discusses on the basis of his practical experience as a manager of Sony how distinctive features of Japanese social culture can enliven the organisation.

Although Mr M himself did not clearly remember reading the widely-read *nihonjinron* literature written by scholars, he was quite knowledgeable about theories such as Nakane's vertical society thesis and Doi's *amae* (dependence) thesis, because these theories were frequently quoted and referred to in the literature written by business executives, which Mr M enjoyed reading. This shows something about the process by which theories formulated in the *nihonjinron* diffuse within society, a point which will be elaborated further in the following chapter.

The case of Mr J, too, can usefully be discussed in this connection. Born in 1912, he was the oldest among our headmasters. What is interesting about his career is that he had worked in a private company before being invited to take up his present position of headmaster. Mr J had studied at a teacher training college and spent most of his working career in the Prefectural Board of Education. Upon retirement from the civil service, he joined a private food manufacturing company and worked as head of department including being head of the personnel department. Although there were several other headmasters who, like Mr J had worked as civil servants in the Prefectural Board of Education, Mr J was the only one with business experience in a private enterprise. This experience deserves particular attention from the point of view of this study.

Mr J articulately discussed his ideas of the distinctive characteristics of Japanese society and culture. He had his own term to characterise the Japanese: *sangaku minzoku* (a mountain people) or a people whose culture is shaped to fit to a lifestyle in a mountain village. But, his ideas incorporated some of the important points made in the *nihonjinron*, such as the communal and familistic features of society, and vertical society. As to the sources of his ideas on Japanese and other cultures and societies, he said:

> You academics do not seem to contribute much to this field. I read books written by leading businessmen because their books are more interesting. Businessmen write more convincingly than academics because they actually do business with foreigners and thus learn the hard way what it means to be Japanese.

Mr J, like many other headmasters, regarded leading members of the business elite in top companies as one social type of intellectual. A question was then asked why he was himself concerned with a comparison of national characteristics because it was apparent that, unlike such business elites, Mr J had no direct contact with foreign cultures. On this point he said:

> I don't know how you scholars regard it, but doesn't the so-called *nihonjinron* deal with business society, how people relate to one another in an organisation? I haven't read that famous book on Japanese society, but isn't it about 'society in a company'? I was also in business and so like anyone else I read what concerned our daily working life.

Mr J's observation suggests some of the important points concerning businessmen's interest in the *nihonjinron*. Businessmen are both 'producers' and 'consumers' of the *nihonjinron*. Because of their frequent contacts with foreign cultures, leading business elites are sensitised to the cultural differences between Japan and other countries as typically manifested in business practices and tend, by writing, to systematise their ideas and to share their perceptions of Japanese business culture with other businessmen. Businessmen in general react favourably to such literature because it directly concerns their everyday working life. Mr J was one such company man who had shown an interest in the *nihonjinron* during his career in a private company.

The interviews with Mr M and Mr J thus helped to draw attention to the possibility that a work-related interest to create and maintain active human relations in the organisation is an important factor behind concerns with the *nihonjinron*. This is the background against which I decided to examine the case of businessmen as a comparative case, and to explore whether the experience of working in the company could significantly promote an interest in the *nihonjinron*.

The *nihonjinron* as a source of useful perspectives on cross-cultural experience

There were one headmaster and one headmistress of the cross-cultural type (hereafter called Mr H and Miss I). They both had regular contacts with people of different nationalities, which was rather exceptional for educators in Nakasato.

Miss I was a headmistress at a private mission school for girls. Miss I was born into a middle-class family in Tokyo in the late 1920s. While she was still a child, many of her relatives went to live abroad, and she had kept in touch with them since childhood and was strongly influenced by them. She said that her interest in foreign civilisations had originated in this childhood experience. She chose this occupation as a way of realising her wish to work as a bridge between the Japanese and people of foreign countries. In fact, she had made regular visits to countries in Europe and Asia to exchange views with Catholic teachers in those countries.

In the course of intercultural interactions, Miss I was compelled to think more objectively about Japanese patterns of thought and behaviour. In France she was amazed at the French way of stating even the obvious to express themselves; in Malaysia she was struck by the self-assertiveness of English-educated Malaysians. (She added that native Malays were different and less individualistic, just like the Japanese.) Miss I remarked that she had developed her sensitivity to and curiosity about cultural differences in thought and behaviour as a result of these cross-cultural experiences. She read extensively popular literature on the peculiarities of Japanese patterns of behaviour including the works of scholars such as Kimura Shōzaburō's *Thoughts from Europe* (1978) and Watanabe Shōichi's *Japan and the Japanese* (1980) as well as the works of writers such as Inukai

Michiko's *My Europe* (1972) which dealt with cultural differences in child-rearing practices between Europe and Japan on the basis of the writer's personal experience. The book she considered to be the most educative and useful was Araki Hiroyuki's *Japanese Patterns of Behaviour* (1973), a typical book of the *nihonjinron* which systematically discusses the various aspects of the group-oriented behaviour of the Japanese. Miss I said that such literature provided useful knowledge for solving problems of communication with non-Japanese. Her interest in the *nihonjinron* was therefore attributed to her personal concern with intercultural communication.

It should be noted that her concern was not merely restricted to the behavioural aspects of intercultural communication, but was also extended to what she called her 'life-long concern' with the relationship of Japanese culture to the Christian civilisation. On the one hand she was aware of the necessity of recognising fully the distinctiveness of Japanese culture as she herself had learnt through her cross-cultural experiences; on the other hand she knew that as a Christian this was not enough. She once remarked to European Catholic sisters that the unique culture of Japan impeded the dissemination of Christian beliefs in Japan. This remark evoked criticism from the sisters who said that such cultural narrow-mindedness was itself a problem. As a result of this and some other related events, Miss I came to view Japanese culture in a more universal light.

When Christianity came into Japan, Japan lacked philosophy that corresponded to Christianity. Japan has always lacked ideas with universal meanings for human beings. By studying more about the Japanese, I wish to discover ideas that originate in Japan but have universal meanings. For this purpose I find the *nihonjinron* very interesting and useful, but the way it is useful to me may have changed over a period of time.

Mr H's case was one in which the influence of the *nihonjinron* was most conspicuous. Several factors may be pointed out to explain the active role of the *nihonjinron* in his perceptions of Japanese culture and society, but the one that deserves special attention was his experience of closely interacting with Americans. Born in 1928, he belonged to the same generation as most of the other headmasters. But, what made Mr H remarkably different from the others was his command of spoken English and his experience of living abroad. During the American occupation following Japan's defeat in the

Second World War, he acted as an interpreter for the occupation forces. In 1960 he went to an American university for a six-month university programme of study and research on the retraining of teachers. He later became the headteacher of a high school which had an exchange programme with its sister school in America, and in this capacity he maintained regular contact with Americans.

When asked to give his ideas of Japanese uniqueness, Mr H gave a model summary of the *nihonjinron*. He first discussed the general features of the group orientation such as the individual's loss of identity in a group and the importance of maintaining harmony among group members, followed by a description of the harmony-maintaining social skills such as *haragei* (or the non-verbal art of reading the other's mind and avoiding confrontation) and *nemawashi* (or making adjustments of individual opinions before formal meetings take place as a means of avoiding possible conflicts). He then went on to discuss the problem of so-called 'democratic' education in post-war Japan, remarking that, unlike British democracy which emphasised individual excellence, 'democratic' education in Japan was designed to produce people of the ordinary standard who fitted into control-oriented society. At the same time, he indicated the difficulty of introducing a drastic change into the present educational system. Mr H also assessed the strengths and weaknesses of groupism:

> Whereas it has worked favourably towards building a stable society and successful economy, it has also formed a society in which its members have lost the spirit of challenge and rely too much upon others.

Regarding how he became so interested in the characteristics of Japanese behaviour, he said that his experience of working for the occupation forces had much to do with it. He recalled:

> I often enjoyed reading comic strips and paperbacks American officers left behind in their lockers. One day I found a textbook for a correspondence course on anthropological geography, and I was so impressed by the fact that Americans were studying about the cultures of their enemies. Impressed because Japan went to war against America with no knowledge of the American way of life.

Mr H's interest in comparing the Japanese and American patterns of behaviour originated in this and other cross-cultural experiences with American officers. Even more important in this regard was his encounter with Ruth Benedict's *The Chrysanthemum and the Sword*, which, he said, had been monumental:

> It was in 1949 that I heard of this work by Benedict, managed to obtain a copy from an American scholar who was visiting this city then, and read it with great excitement even before its Japanese translation was available. The book was so enlightening that I felt as if the scales had suddenly fallen from my eyes.

He felt through this intellectual 'enlightenment' that the problems of culture and identity could be put into perspective by acquiring an 'anthropological' understanding of cultures. Following this experience, he acquired a taste for books on Japanese characteristics and kept up with current publications. Among the many books he read on the *nihonjinron* were: BenDasan's *The Japanese and the Jews* (1970), Nakane's *Human Relations in a Vertical Society* (1967), Doi's *The Anatomy of Dependence* (1971), Reischauer's *The Japanese* (1978) and Vogel's *Japan as Number One* (1979).

He suggested that literature on the distinctiveness of Japanese patterns of behaviour had helped him considerably to reaffirm the existence of something to fall back upon when interacting with Americans and thus emphasised the importance of having a cultural niche when participating in international society. In order to stress this point still further, he mentioned the names of three Japanese intellectuals in history whom he considered ideal in this respect: Okakura Tenshin (1862–1913), a leading scholar of Japanese art and author of *The Book of Tea* (written in English) (1906); Nitobe Inazō (1862–1933), an intellectual seriously interested in the exchange of Western and Japanese civilisations and author of *Bushido: The Soul of Japan* (written in English) (1899); and Uchimura Kanzō (1861–1930), a leading Christian who dedicated his life to 'the two J's', namely, Jesus and Japan. What they had in common, he said, was

> the coexistence of their remarkable command of English and their extraordinary Japaneseness. Intellectuals today have much to learn from them in this respect. Intellectual discussions today often lack the national perspective without which one can't really discuss international relations. One must be a Japanese first, an international person second.

In summary, both Miss I and Mr H developed their favourable orientation towards the thinking elites' discussions of the distinctiveness of Japanese behaviour as a result of their first-hand, cross-cultural experiences and with a view to shed light upon the problems of intercultural communication and identity.

The *nihonjinron* as useful materials for education

Four headmasters showed an interest in the *nihonjinron* from an educational point of view, but all of them (Mr H, Miss I, Mr S and Mr I) have appeared already in the discussion and have other types of concern with the *nihonjinron* (i.e. cross-cultural, academic, moral) in addition to an educational one. In other words, they first acquired a taste for the *nihonjinron* under the varied circumstances discussed and subsequently used the ideas derived from the *nihonjinron* in education, by touching upon such concerns in public speeches at school ceremonies or including them in their written articles in school journals.

CONCLUDING REMARKS

The aim of this chapter has been to identify the process of diffusion of the *nihonjinron*. Although the *nihonjinron* is an important base of cultural nationalism in contemporary Japan, it does not follow that one's response to the thinking elites' ideas of Japanese distinctiveness will necessarily make one a social bearer of cultural nationalism. Whether or not a person becomes a social bearer of cultural nationalism depends on the absence or presence of a consciously critical attitude towards such ideas of Japanese uniqueness. As the case studies have shown, respondents reacted to the *nihonjinron* for diverse reasons and in diverse manners. Some reacted to it actively but critically, and one respondent even tried consciously to go beyond a cultural nationalistic understanding of the Japanese towards a more universalistic one.

The limitations and validity of the data

The limitations of our data should be clarified here. One main problem, as pointed out in chapter 6, is that interviews sensitise respondents to particular issues and that, therefore, we cannot know the extent to which the respondents' remarks reflect their feelings of national identity, whether conscious, subconscious or unconscious. I employed interview methods despite these limitations because they were the only methods available if the aim of the research was to investigate the educators' and businessmen's perceptions of Japanese uniqueness and to examine the nature and extent of their exposure to the *nihonjinron*. As long as an awareness exists of such limitations, interviews are valid methods of investigation. It was found, for example, that many of our respondents were interested in discussions of Japanese uniqueness in the absence of the interviewer because there was an extensive literature they had read or sampled, whose contents they were to a greater or lesser extent familiar with. Furthermore, despite the fact that both educators and businessmen were equally sensitised in interviews, we found a significant difference between the two groups in the degree of concern with the *nihonjinron*.

Second, the limitations of finance and resources restricted our sample to one fairly large provincial city. One can hypothesise, however, that our findings have some relevance for Japanese society as a whole in view of the fact that Nakasato, as pointed out in chapter 6, is a highly representative Japanese city in terms of its main social and economic characteristics. Moreover, we may conjecture that what our educators and businessmen read (e.g. *nihonjinron* written by business elites) was also read by comparable social groups in other parts of Japan, not only because these books sold well nationwide but also because we found that none of the reasons for the respondents' concern with the *nihonjinron* were intrinsic to Nakasato, but rather were highly generalisable for the Japanese population as a whole.

The two points made here on the data also apply to most of the findings in the remaining three chapters.

Chapter 8

Leading business elites, nationalism and cultural nationalism

In the last chapter we saw that businessmen have been actively receptive to the *nihonjinron* because much of the *nihonjinron* deals with Japanese social culture as manifested in management, employment practices and industrial relations, and thus provides useful insights for 'organisation men'. Furthermore, the subject of cultural differences is useful for internationally active businessmen.[1] Here 'businessmen' means 'organisation men' or 'company men' of relatively large bureaucratic companies rather than the owners and managers of relatively small family enterprises. The owners of family enterprises are less likely to concern themselves with such issues as the uniqueness of Japanese-style management and business practices.

In this chapter I shall expand on the role of businessmen in cultural nationalism and focus on leading members of the Japanese business elite. I shall argue that leading business elites have themselves been active in formulating and diffusing ideas of Japanese uniqueness and that they may even be called thinking elites.

Although my argument in this chapter is that leading members of the business elite have played a significant role in the development of the discourse of *cultural* nationalism in the 1970s and 1980s, it is necessary to recognise that in modern Japanese history influential figures in Japanese business circles have from time to time been closely associated with nationalism in general, if not *cultural* nationalism in particular.[2] In fact, one cannot discuss the development of modern Japanese business without reference to its close relationship with nationalism. It is therefore appropriate to begin this chapter with a historical account of the place of business leaders in modern Japanese nationalism in order to put businessmen's *cultural* nationalism in contemporary Japan into perspective.

BUSINESS LEADERS AND NATIONALISM IN MODERN JAPANESE HISTORY

What concerned Japan's leaders first and foremost at the dawn of the modern era in the late nineteenth century was defence against foreign intrusion. Industrialisation was perceived as a necessary means of strengthening the country, but the psychological obstacles to industrialisation, derived from the Tokugawa tradition, were significant.

The development of an altruistic business creed in early modern Japan

Business and commerce were viewed strictly in negative terms in the Tokugawa period (1600–1867). Tokugawa society was organised according to a rigid hierarchy of basically four estates, with Confucianism providing the ruling stratum with a justification of the social hierarchy and extolling the virtue of loyalty on the part of the ruled. The samurai or warriors were the highest order because they governed the country and provided the source of moral virtues; the peasants and artisans were allotted the intermediate rungs because they produced national wealth; and the merchants were the most inferior because they merely traded what others produced.

The Meiji Restoration of 1868 marked a turning point. Recognising the necessity to reshape the country's basic structures, the Meiji leaders engaged initially in political efforts to strengthen the new government and to unify the nation, but became increasingly aware of the economic tasks which lay before them. Under the new national agenda, if the country was to become rich and powerful, the previous view of business would have to change.

The first signs of a nationalistic business creed can be traced to the beginning of the Meiji period (1868–1911) when the effects of the opening of foreign trade became increasingly evident. The Meiji leaders became aware that the economic challenge posed by the West was as urgent as the military threat (Hazama 1980: 65;

Marshall 1967: 14). When Bōeki Shōsha (The Trading Company) was founded by government initiative in 1869, its aim was to restore commercial rights and to reclaim markets that had fallen into the hands of Western traders. The government called upon merchants to cooperate with one another in order to guard against the foreign threat in trade, to enhance national solidarity through selfless service on the part of merchants, and thereby to secure the independence of the Imperial state (Hazama 1972: 85–91). Such a view of business activity as the benefactor of the national interests was reflected not only in the policies of such semi-governmental companies as Bōeki Shōsha, but also in companies started by private entrepreneurs. The following are the words of the founder of the trading company Maruya Shōsha (presently, Maruzen) at the time of its foundation in 1869: 'I would be neglecting my duty as a Japanese if I just sat [and did nothing] and saw trading and commercial activities being monopolised by foreigners' (quoted in Hazama 1972: 94). The basis of the modern Japanese business creed was thus formed as part and parcel of the reactive nationalism of the early Meiji period.

   The most explicit repudiation of economic individualism can be found in the writings of Shibusawa Eiichi (1840–1931), the son of a farmer, who was educated in the Confucian tradition and who joined the plot to overthrow the Tokugawa Shogunate for a nationalistic cause. Shibusawa's career in the banking industry and skills in writing and public speaking made him one of the most influential opinion leaders among Meiji businessmen. His main idea was that business activity should be undertaken with the right motives. As he put it: 'My object does not lie in the increase of wealth, but from the nature of the business it so happens. That is all. Never for a moment did I aim at my own profit' (quoted in Marshall 1967: 40). The Confucian-derived notion of self-sacrificial devotion of the samurai towards their lord was now replaced by a similar idea that businessmen should devote themselves to the Imperial state and put national interests first. Godai Tomoatsu (1835–1885), a prominent Osaka promoter, remarked similarly: 'The wealth of the Empire must never be considered a private thing. . . . My hopes will be fulfilled when the happiness of the nation is secured . . .' (quoted in Marshall 1967: 36). Business activity was regarded as a service to the state and businessmen as benefactors of the nation.

   In their search for social respectability, Meiji business leaders dissociated themselves from the image of Tokugawa merchants and compared themselves to the samurai. What made the 'men of affairs' (*jitsugyōka*) distinct from the 'immoral' Tokugawa merchants, who made profits for their own sake, was that the new businessmen were portrayed as possessing the virtues practised by the followers of the 'way of the samurai' and the Confucian ethic. The following description succinctly summarises the Meiji business ideology:

> The claim of the Meiji business leader was that he had demonstrated his sincere concern for the defense of the nation by undertaking the arduous task of developing an economic base for national greatness, thereby proving himself as worthy a successor to the mantle of leadership of the Tokugawa samurai as those who served in the military or government. Thus the feudal warrior remained the ideal cultural type even in the ideology of the Meiji business elite.
>
> (Marshall 1967: 50)

A major change thus took place in the public perceptions of business and its practitioners in the early years of the Meiji period. Of course, such an altruistic business creed does not necessarily show the true intentions of Meiji businessmen, and we may suppose that businessmen were under pressure to morally justify their business activities. The themes of altruism and patriotic devotion and a favourable analogy linking the new businessmen and the traditional samurai put Meiji businessmen in full accord with the nationalism of the period (Marshall 1967: ch. 3).

The main difference between the classic British and American business creed and the Meiji business ideology lay in the manner in which the two explained the importance of businessmen in society. In the West, industry was the realm of private enterprise. The businessman pursued self-interests, but the businesses he created benefited society as a whole not merely through the commodities produced but also by bringing about a natural harmony of interests. Self-oriented activity was considered to turn eventually to the public good under an 'invisible hand'. It is understandable that such straightforward economic individualism, which hardly received unanimous sanction even in the West, should not have entered easily into the Japanese business creed, although some literate Japanese were not slow to grasp this Western doctrine. For example, Fukuzawa Yukichi, the founder of Keiō University, attributed Japan's backwardness to the Confucian contempt for commerce and advocated business for its own sake, but, as Rodney Clark remarks, the fact that Fukuzawa was an academic rather than a businessman is significant in that 'avarice in the public interest is more comfortably extolled by unacquisitive savants than by the people who are actually making money' (1979: 28). The dominant trend was to be found in the views of entrepreneurs such as Shibusawa Eiichi who rationalised their motives for engaging in business by means of high principle of a Confucian sort and nationalism.

Following the Russo-Japanese War (1904–5), the independence of Japan as a modern nation became secured and the foundation of Japanese industry increasingly established. Under these circumstances reactive nationalism, intended to protect the country from foreign threats, became less relevant and the nationalistic cause of business activity less emphasised.[3] The *zaibatsu*, the large industrial and financial combines, not only enjoyed governmental protection but began to influence the decisions of the government in their favour in the 1910s and 1920s. Such a worldly and profit-oriented posture of the *zaibatsu* invited attack both from the political left and the right. The attack from the left was made on the grounds of labour relations, and in response the ideal of familistic and communalistic interdependence of management and labour was emphasised (see chapter 5). In the 1930s right-wing groups began to excoriate the *zaibatsu* for their pursuit of egoistic interests to the neglect of national defence. In response, business leaders were forced to place national interests before those of the *zaibatsu*, at least outwardly, and to attempt to justify private enterprise along nationalistic lines. Business leaders expounded upon economic competition as a prerequisite to economic efficiency and stressed the role of modern industry and commerce. Material progress was claimed as a necessary condition of national greatness rather than as a value in itself (Hazama 1980: 67–8; Hirschmeier and Yui 1975: 152, 211–12, 218).

Economic nationalism in the 1950s and 1960s

Some of the ideas about business established during the early decades of modern Japan have persisted to the present: among them, the precept that the businessman should be motivated by high, altruistic principles rather than profit. I shall argue that, although altruism has on the whole remained an important feature of Japanese business creed, there has been a shift of emphasis in the content of the creed of business altruism. Before going on to discuss the scene in the

1970s and 1980s, it is necessary to touch upon the developments from 1945 to the 1960s.

Post-war Japan experienced a state of spiritual vacuum with the demise of the basic national values symbolised by the imperial institution and, therefore, the loss of national pride and purpose. The turning point came with the signing of the San Francisco Peace Treaty in 1951 and the occurrence of the Korean War (1950–3). Now that Japan had regained independence and that signs of an economic recovery were in sight, a sense of national re-awakening spread among the people. Under these circumstances, business leaders developed an attitude reminiscent of the one formed in the early years of the Meiji period, an attitude which explains business activity as a service to the reconstruction of the nation. Such an attitude was reflected in business leaders' resolutions to engage in concerted efforts to reconstruct the economy and to make economic growth a new national goal. Business leaders' organisations made a joint appeal for businessmen to be aware of and to reaffirm their moral responsibility to the nation (Nihon Seisansei Honbu 1965: 690). From around 1954 the pursuit of economic growth became the highest national goal, and it is appropriate to characterise this orientation as *economic* nationalism. Hirschmeier and Yui describe the mood of this highly economically oriented period as follows:

> It is this basic, and all strata embracing, consensus concerning the GNP as focus and symbol of a new national self-confidence, and even self-identity, which made such growth possible . . .
>
> (Hirschmeier and Yui 1975: 294)

Towards the end of the 1960s, however, the disenchantment with and criticism of the identification of production as a national goal became noticeable. The nickname 'economic animal' was widely used to caricature the excessive emphasis placed on GNP growth as a national goal of the Japanese. This resulted in a shift of emphasis among the country's elite from GNP as a symbol of restored national confidence and regained international status to the rediscovery of national identity in cultural terms. Closely related to this shift of emphasis was the belief that Japan's economic success was caused largely by 'Japanese-style' management and business, which elites emphasised as being the product of Japan's cultural tradition. It is this background against which leading sections of the business elite have become key spokesmen for the uniqueness of Japan's business (and social) culture and have come to play an important part in formulating and diffusing the ideas of national distinctiveness.

Business elites and cultural nationalism in the 1970s and 1980s

The nationalistic business creed in pre-war and early post-war Japan was chiefly characterised by its claim to pursue national interests through the concrete, *material* activities of building and expanding the nation's industry. In this sense it was a case of *economic* nationalism. By contrast, business nationalism in the 1970s and 1980s is characterised by the fact that business elites have played an important role in advancing a cultural thesis and is in this sense a manifestation of *cultural* nationalism. Of course, such an attempt by leading business elites to speak for Japanese culture does not necessarily reflect their true intentions, and we may suppose that businessmen were under pressure to rationalise their business activities in terms of what they regard as a higher principle than profit.

It is therefore necessary to clarify the circumstances in which business elites have come to play an important role in cultural nationalism in the 1980s. All the more so because it seems rather unusual that business executives, who are supposed to be preoccupied with mundane economic affairs, should play an important role in cultural matters.

In the late 1960s or early 1970s many were surprised at Japan's sudden emergence as a world-class industrial power. The Japanese experience was unique in history in that Japan achieved its 'centrality' in the international community without military prowess, but mainly with industrial skills. Japanese-made manufactured goods flooded world markets, and it was through these products that the centrality of the Japanese came to be felt and with which the Japanese came to be largely identified. The other image of Japan widely held abroad is the image of traditional and exotic Japan. Japan's artistic and exotic culture is on the whole well known in the West (e.g. Mishima's novels, Kurosawa's films, Hiroshige's wood-block prints, Arita porcelain, Noh plays, *haiku* poems). In other words, there is a gap in the Westerners' image of Japan: on the one hand, there is a popular image of Japan as a manufacturer of electronic goods, cars and cameras; on the other, there is an Orientalist image of exotic Japan. This paradoxical image of Japan has been reiterated in the Western media and rather firmly established in the

West. Japanese thinking elites were themselves first perplexed about Japan's centrality in the world but gradually became dissatisfied with such a simplistically dualistic image of Japan held by the West.

These circumstances have provided leading members of the business elite with an opportunity to act as spokesmen for the majority of ordinary Japanese, for whom 'high culture', although important, is not really part of their everyday life. It has thus been pointed out as important for non-Japanese to understand the more 'down-to-earth' culture of the ordinary Japanese and for the Japanese to be able to explain this culture systematically to non-Japanese. Culture here does not mean artistic and literary culture removed from the everyday life of ordinary Japanese, but the social culture or modes of behaving and thinking of ordinary white-collar 'company men'. Focus on the social culture of 'ordinary' Japanese is regarded as a key factor in a more balanced understanding of the Japanese. This is because it is not only considered a background factor of Japan's economic performance, but also because it concerns how 'ordinary' Japanese behave and think in ordinary interpersonal interactions, a clear understanding of which is considered indispensable for anyone interacting with the Japanese. Leading business elites are well aware through their frequent contacts with non-Japanese that the Japanese – businessmen in particular – are the subject of conversation and a source of wonder in the world, and they generally know how to present themselves to the rest of the world. Other educated groups such as school teachers have less part in the discussions of Japan's culture because, unlike business elites, they hardly attract attention abroad.

One important image being projected through the social culture of ordinary 'company men' is the image of Japan as a community of ordinary folks. Japanese businessmen today are still placed in a superficial analogy with the samurai of feudal Japan in that the men's loyalty towards their company is compared to the samurai's loyalty towards their lords. The actual content of their social culture, however, is more reminiscent of the traditional village community of peasants. I have already discussed this view in chapter 5, a view that regards the pre-industrial village community as the prototype of the modern Japanese company. One might wonder whether the behavioural culture of peasants, which lacks grandeur, can become a cultural symbol of a nation, but it is an appropriate cultural symbol in contemporary Japan because, first, although the image associated with the samurai may be more elevated, the image of ordinary communal people working cooperatively is more appropriate than that of fighting warriors as an image of the industrious Japanese in the post-war period. Second, communal or group-oriented features of the company, which are reminiscent of the pre-industrial village community, are often celebrated as a source of Japan's industrial strength. Many leading business elites stress national identity and pride in terms of the 'uniqueness' of Japanese business culture of which they are part.[4] Business elites have participated in the *nihonjinron* themselves by formulating and diffusing ideas concerning the distinctiveness of Japanese business culture. Business elites differ from other thinking elites in that they are explicit in pointing out the strengths of Japan's social culture.

Business elites rarely discuss explicitly their peasant traditions and tend more to confine themselves to describing the social behaviour of contemporary Japanese. But, since educated Japanese are often already exposed to academic literature indicating the continuity between the pre-industrial village community and the modern business institution, it is usually enough merely for business elites to mention in passing the communal aspects of business culture to remind the reading audience of the village tradition.

It is important to recognise that the subjects of discussion of leading business elites are not confined merely to Japanese-style management but include broader themes relating to Japanese patterns of behaviour and thought. The promotion of cultural understanding of Japan may be aimed towards an overseas audience (e.g. Morita 1986), but is, more importantly, intended for the Japanese themselves, who are aware of, or assume, a lack of understanding in the West of the Japanese but do not know how to explain their own modes of behaving and thinking in a way that effectively communicates to non-Japanese. This is why much of the literature by leading business executives takes the form of the *nihonjinron* intended for Japanese readers.

In the following discussion I shall first clarify what I mean by 'business elites as thinking elites' and then examine the activities of Japanese business elites and companies concerning the perpetuation of the *nihonjinron*.

LEADING BUSINESS ELITES AS THINKING ELITES

Edward Shils (1972: 22) divides the types of intellectuals into 'productive intellectuals' (who produce intellectual works), 'reproductive intellectuals' (who engage in the interpretation and transmission of intellectual works) and 'consumer intellectuals' (who read and concern themselves receptively with such works). Contemporary Japanese businessmen interested in the subject of Japanese uniqueness may be characterised according to these three types of 'intellectuals' in varying combinations. Businessmen who concern themselves with the *nihonjinron* are almost always 'consumer' intellectuals, but some are not merely 'receptive' but also 'productive' and 'reproductive'. When leading members of the business elite publish their ideas of Japanese management and business culture on the basis of their own experiences, they are 'productive intellectuals'. Probably the more important type of 'businessman-intellectual' in relation to the *nihonjinron* is the 'reproductive' intellectual, who interprets academics' theories of Japanese society with reference to his own first-hand experience, rephrases them with his own words and transmits them to the rest of the population. This is one of the important channels through which the academics' *nihonjinron* are diffused to a wider audience, that is, through interpretation and transmission by business elites. In fact, as we found, many of our respondents, both educators and businessmen, have familiarised themselves with the theories of the *nihonjinron* (such as Nakane's 'vertical society' theory) through leading business elites' writings, public lectures and television interviews in which such theories were referred to. In reality, it is not usually possible to draw a clear line between their reproductive and productive activities or to identify where business elites have reproduced ideas borrowed from academics and where they have produced their own original ideas. Either way, business elites play an important role in promoting an interest in ideas concerning Japanese uniqueness in contemporary Japan.

S.N. Eisenstadt points out the importance of analysing the role of 'reproductive' intellectuals in the social construction and transmission of traditions. 'Reproductive' intellectuals – or what Eisenstadt calls secondary intellectuals – may be defined either in terms of the quality of their intellectual work or in terms of their occupational roles as teachers, civil servants, journalists or those engaged in popular entertainment (1972: 18). 'It may well be', Eisenstadt remarks, 'that it is they, through their activities in teaching, entertainment, and communications, who serve as channels of institutionalization, and even as possible creators of new types of symbols of cultural orientations, of traditions, and of collective and cultural identity' (ibid.). He also points out that with regard to the different types of secondary intellectuals in the construction of tradition we have few systematic studies. The role of business elites as secondary intellectuals has rarely, if at all, been mentioned, much less studied. I therefore hope that the present study is a worthwhile contribution in this direction.

It is worth pointing out that many respondents, both businessmen and educators, classified leading members of the business elite as thinking elites, given that thinking elites are defined as those elite members of a society who have influence over others by virtue of thinking. (See Table 8.1 for the respondents' perceptions of who constitute thinking elites.) There are two main reasons why leading business elites are included in the category of thinking elites. The first concerns the validity of their 'theories' of Japan's social (and business) culture. Respondents tended to regard businessmen's theories as the more accurate reflections of the empirical world. Whereas business elites' ideas are well grounded in the real working world, the academics' theories are bound to suffer a gap between what the theory has to say about Japan's social (or business) culture and what it actually feels to be part of it. The following remark of a high school headmaster was illustrative:

Table 8.1 Educators' and businessmen's ideas of who constitute thinking elites[a]

	Educators	Businessmen
University professors/lecturers (academics)	33	30
Business elites	16	13
Journalists[b]	15	10
Critics	11	17
Top career bureaucrats in government ministries and offices[c]	7	6
Researchers affiliated to companies	6	3
Writers	4	10
School teachers/educators	3	7
Others (lawyers, doctors, etc.)	8	8
Did not specify occupational groups	3	4

Notes
[a] The total number of respondents was 35 educators and 36 businessmen. (More than one occupational type was given by most respondents.)
[b] Journalists are sometimes classified as critics; hence there is overlap between the two occupational types.
[c] Top career bureaucrats in government ministries and offices enjoy prestige in Japanese society. The elite of career officials comprises those who have passed the special higher examination.

Business leaders are well-read and very learned. We [teachers] are so busy with everyday routine that we have no time to study and think about society and the world. Or maybe we are just lazy, because business people are probably busier. . . . I am not saying that you academics are no good. It's just that armchair theories do not offer very much to direct our society in this fast-moving world. [In this sense] business elites are ideal as thinkers in today's Japan because they are both highly knowledgeable and practically experienced.

Interestingly, the majority of our respondents regarded business elites to be more 'value-free' in their discussion of Japanese society than academics, and this is the second reason why business elites are thought of highly as thinking elites. The other types of thinkers (academics, journalists and critics), they believed, are affected by a particular value orientation: that is, to be still constrained by the post-war self-restraints on the expressions of national pride. (In reality, many academics and critics today are no longer so much constrained by the post-war restraints on the expressions of national pride as many of our respondents surmised.) Business elites are therefore regarded as more qualified thinking elites and as having a more useful influence on society. A high school headmaster remarked, 'Whereas the so-called *shimpoteki bunkajin* (liberal-minded opinion leaders) are unrealistic in their critique of Japanese society, businessmen are more responsible and have a more useful impact on the rest of our society'.

It is an interesting finding that businessmen, who are usually categorised as those concerned with mundane money matters, are regarded as one of the most qualified group of commentators on society and culture and also as creators of new types of collective and cultural identity.

ACTIVITIES OF BUSINESS ELITES AS THINKING ELITES

What have we to say about the activity of leading members of the business establishment as 'productive' intellectuals and their ideas of Japanese social culture? What can we say about business elites as possible creators of new types of collective and cultural identity? We are also interested in the process whereby intellectual works, conceptualised and elaborated by 'productive' intellectuals, become integrated into broader social traditions in contemporary Japan. What materials have we to offer about the role of business elites in this reproductive process?

Leading members of the business elite

There is a fairly large publishing market for successful company chairmen, top managers and internationally active businessmen who publish books on their own experiences. (Successful presidents of big-business companies often publish their autobiographies after they have become company chairmen finding they have more free time to look back at their achievements.[5]) Such literature quite often includes subjects such as Japanese-style management, employment practices, industrial relations and cross-cultural business negotiations. There is such an abundance of this type of literature that a comprehensive discussion of it would require a separate study. It will suffice for the purpose of illustration to select one representative best seller by a powerful figure in Japanese business circles who has succeeded both in management and international business. Morita Akio's *Made in Japan* (1986, 1987) seems an epitome of this type of literature.

Morita, Chairman of the Sony Corporation, recounts how he and his partners founded the world-famous electronics company and made this company what it is. Although this book is written in the style of an autobiography, it is so full of comparisons between Japanese and American business and management practices that it may also be read as a work on comparative culture and management. Several chapters are devoted to the more explicit discussion of the distinctiveness of Japanese modes of thinking and behaving manifested in Japanese-style business and employment practices, and industrial relations, with insight gained through his experience in America. Let us see in his own words how one of the most successful entrepreneurs in post-war Japan summarises Japan's business culture. Among others, he evaluates the principle of familistic management:

> The most important mission for a Japanese manager is to develop a healthy relationship with his employees, to create a familylike relationship within the corporation, a feeling that employees and managers share the same fate.

(Morita 1986: 144)

As to how the sense of unity between managers and employees is achieved, he remarks on group-oriented decision-making practices:

As an idea progresses through the Sony system, the original presenter continues to have the responsibility of selling his idea to technical, design, production, and marketing staffs and seeing it to its logical conclusion. . . . That way the family spirit continues to prevail and the group or those within the group can feel they are not only a part of the team but entrepreneurs as well, contributing profitably and creatively to the welfare of all of us in the family.

(ibid.: 189)

Also, on group consensus and group decision-making:

The concept of consensus is natural to the Japanese, but it does not necessarily mean that every decision comes out of a spontaneous group impulse. Gaining consensus in a Japanese company often means spending time preparing the groundwork for it, and very often the consensus is formed from the top down, not from the bottom up, as some observers of Japan have written.

(ibid.: 220)

The following passage sums up Morita's attitude towards management, namely, the importance of informal human relations in the familistic organisation, and the de-emphasis of logic and rationality in informal human relations:

Americans pride themselves on being rational in their business judgments: the total logic of the American business schools seems to be cold, deemphasizing the human element. We in Japan see the bases for success in business and industry differently. We believe that if you want high efficiency and productivity, a close cordial relationship with your employees, which leads to high morale, is necessary. . . . [S]ometimes you must make decisions that are, technically, irrational. You can be totally rational with a machine. But if you work with people, sometimes logic has to take a backseat to understanding.

(ibid.: 224)

Morita's conclusions resemble those of the academics' *nihonjinron* except that his are an insider's account of Japanese business. In fact, Morita provides a number of concrete examples concerning problems and difficulties that he has actually experienced and overcome in management and international negotiations.

Similar autobiographies are written by a number of company

chairmen such as Shindō Sadakazu (1987), former chairman of Mitsubishi Electric Corporation, and Shintō Hisashi (1988), former president of Ishikawajima Harima Heavy Industries Co. Ltd. and later Chairman of Nippon Telegraph and Telecommunications Corporation, just to mention only a couple from recent publications. The interest of the late Matsushita Kōnosuke, one of the leading industrial entrepreneurs of post-war Japan, in writing about Japan and the Japanese (e.g. 1982) is also well known.

In addition to leading members of the business establishment, company managers in general, too, often publish their ideas on Japanese management. *Reviving Organisation*, which Kobayashi Shigeru (1971) wrote on the basis of his practical experience as a manager and factory superintendent of Sony, is one of the earlier works to enlighten general readers about the strength of Japanese-style management. (See chapter 7 for the way in which this book was read by one of our respondents and promoted his interest in the *nihonjinron*.) Also, magazines for business executives provide opportunities for top company managers to express their ideas on business management. To give a few examples, the journal *President* (January 1978) published discussions held among managers from various industries on diverse aspects of the 'uniqueness' of Japanese management and company organisation. Also, the same magazine (July 1977) carried an interview article in which Kobayashi Kōji, Chairman of the NEC Corporation, talks with social anthropologist Nakane Chie on the latter's theory of 'vertical society' with reference to the former's actual business experience.

The direct involvement of Japanese companies in the diffusion of the *nihonjinron*

The type of literature that deserves our special attention is that written and edited directly by the staff of big business companies and designed mainly for businessmen and students. This clearly shows the direct role Japanese companies play in disseminating the *nihonjinron*. Such literature, edited in the form of textbooks, handbooks and glossaries, deals in one way or another with the peculiarities of Japanese culture and society manifested, for example, in 'untranslatable' Japanese expressions, business and management practices, and company men's everyday lifestyle. Such literature popularises the *nihonjinron* in such a way that it may be applied to practical use.

A dual-language handbook, *Nippon: The Land and Its People* by Nippon Steel Corporation, personnel development division (1984) is an epitome of this type of literature. It contains a wide range of subjects on Japan and the Japanese including their national character, various aspects of linguistic/communicative and social culture (i.e. the non-assertive mode of communication, 'interpersonalism', various aspects of group behaviour, communal mentality), and business, management, decision-making processes, employment practices, and industrial relations. That this book is essentially a businessmen's interpretation of the academics' *nihonjinron* and *nihonteki keieiron* (literature on Japanese-style management) is shown by the fact that its reference materials cover the vast extent of *nihonjinron* literature written by Nakane Chie, Doi Takeo, Edwin Reischauer and so on. Taiyō Kōbe Bank Ltd (1988) also produced a dual-language cultural handbook entitled *The Scrutable Japanese*, which carries articles on various aspects of the lifestyle of Japanese company men. The president of the bank explains the background of, and reactions to, this book:

> When we decided to place a serialized ad. in the JEJ [Japan Economic Journal] we considered that the journal's readership might be interested in Japanese salarymen's daily life through which they might glean something of Japanese culture, society and the economy.
>
> (Taiyō Kōbe Bank 1988: 2)

> Foreigners were interested in the topics taken up, while Japanese students were anxious to know how customs and practices unique to the Japanese were described in English.
>
> (ibid.)

Similarly, Mitsubishi Corporation (1983) produced a dual-language *Japanese Business Glossary*. According to the general manager of the corporate communications office of the company, the book is intended to introduce 'unique Japanese business practices and expressions in a light but informative form' (1983: 4). What is characteristic about such literature is that the ideas of Japanese uniqueness are popularised in such a manner as to be used in a practical context of cross-cultural interactions in which the Japanese are expected to explain things Japanese to the non-Japanese.

More illustrative of this point is the type of spoken English textbooks, designed mainly for businessmen, in which the *nihonjinron* are summarised and edited in the form of dialogues so that the reader can use model sentences in explaining Japanese culture in English. The following dialogue illustrate the point (note that Mr J stands for Mr Jones, an American, Mr S for Mr Suzuki, a Japanese businessman):

> Mr S: Most Japanese tend to avoid doing anything that sets them off from others. They worry about what others think and change their behavior accordingly.
>
> Mr J: That's probably one of the reasons why people talk about Japanese groupism.
>
> Mr S: It's a factor. It's also why Japanese are poor at asserting themselves. We tend to speak and act only after considering the other person's feelings and point of view.
>
> Mr J: You can't say that about most Westerners. In America, we try to teach our children to be independent, take individual responsibility, develop their imaginations and creativity. . . . We also try to train them to think logically, and learn how to express their thoughts and opinions.
>
> Mr S: Yes, I know . . . Foreigners often criticize us Japanese for not giving clear-cut yes or no answers. This is probably connected to our being basically a homogeneous society and our traditional tendency to try to avoid conflicts . . .
>
> (Nippon Steel Human Resources
> Development Co. Ltd 1987: 405)

In the 'age of internationalisation' – as so called by the Japanese – in which a knowledge of cultural differences is considered essential in addition to a spoken command of English, this type of learning material which combines both language study and discussions on cultural differences is increasing. What is particularly important about this type of English textbook is that it can condition the way one expresses one's ideas of Japanese characteristics by providing the language (vocabulary, catch-phrases, etc.) one uses. (Foreign language students often memorise model sentences and use them in actual conversations.) We might even suppose that the particular cultural values can be subconsciously implanted into the person in this way.

All these examples suggest that Japanese companies play an active part in popularising and transmitting the *nihonjinron*. While many of such publications by companies tend to look to the academics' *nihonjinron* for sources of their ideas, some are more original, drawing

their materials from their own sources. For example, another major
trading company, Nisshō Iwai Corporation (1987), produced a
book entitled *Skills in Cross-cultural Negotiation*. The book discusses
the manner in which Japanese businessmen cope with cultural
differences in intercultural business contacts. The following passage
by the editor illustrates a way in which businessmen participate in
the *nihonjinron*, that is, on the basis of their practical experience:

> Some [of the social skills and episodes discussed in this book] deal
> with superficial differences in customs; others, differences deeply
> rooted in national characters. Anyhow, *these are the differences
> that company men have actually experienced through their trials and
> errors. . . . We are businessmen and not specialists on the discussions of
> 'culture'*. Nonetheless, we thought that, by publishing the stories
> of our practical experiences as regards 'skills in negotiation' [with
> foreign businessmen], we might be able to provide some hints
> for reducing the 'cultural frictions' that the Japanese are now
> undergoing [with non-Japanese].
>
> (Nisshō Iwai Corporation 1987: 4–5, emphasis added)

Top Japanese companies play a direct role in socialising businessmen
and students (prospective businessmen) to be aware of the distinctiveness of Japanese patterns of behaviour. (It is noteworthy that the
personnel department is quite often in charge of such publications.)
Companies' publications on Japanese culture are quite often originally intended for their own employees and prospective employees.
For example, the articles compiled in the cultural handbook by Taiyō
Kōbe Bank were originally serialised in the *Japan Economic Journal*
from 1983 to 1985, and were then compiled into the company's
public relations booklet distributed for prospective employees of
the company and then into the present book form. In addition, the
dual-language glossary by Mitsubishi Corporation, mentioned earlier, is also based on a series of short articles originally published in
the company's public relations booklet. Businessmen of any country
will learn about cultural differences anyway through their personal
experiences and by reading travelogues or handbooks on foreign
customs. In contemporary Japan, companies are an important agent
of socialisation concerning the cultural peculiarities of the Japanese.
The following paragraph, which explains the background against
which Nippon Steel Corporation produced a handbook on Japan
originally for its employees and later for a broader readership,
illustrates this point well:

Nippon: The Land and its People was originally compiled for the use of the employees of Nippon Steel Corporation.

Like many Japanese companies, Nippon Steel has been internationalizing its business operations very rapidly the past few years, with the result that the employees are now coming into increasingly frequent contact with foreigners, both in Japan and overseas.

At such times, the conversation often turns to subjects about Japan, and our employees are often asked about Japanese culture and other aspects of their country. Many of these questions are extremely difficult to answer accurately and to the satisfaction of the inquirer.

Two reasons for this are that the employee often does not know enough about the subject, and even when he does know the answer, he is often incapable of expressing it well in a foreign language.

(Nippon Steel Corporation 1984: 7)

The popularity of this book is shown by the fact that it sold 400,000 copies as of February 1989 (*Asahi Shimbun, 18 February 1989*). *There are a number of other similar publications by top Japanese companies such as Toshiba's Practical Cross-cultural Dialogs* by the personnel development department of Toshiba Co. (1985).

SOCIAL AND LINGUISTIC/COMMUNICATIVE CULTURE AS SOURCES OF CULTURAL NATIONALISM

Social and linguistic/communicative culture, as pointed out in chapter 2, are two of the main areas of concern in the academics' *nihonjinron*. These two types of culture also predominate in the business elites' discussions of Japanese uniqueness. In what ways, then, does the businessmen's concern with the uniqueness of Japan's social and linguistic/communicative culture promote their sense of cultural nationalism?

Social culture, as discussed by businessmen, refers largely to the distinctive characteristics of Japan's business culture covering such subjects as group-oriented management, decision-making and industrial relations. The distinctiveness of Japan's social culture tends to be associated with Japan's highly productive economic performance and, as such, widely recognised as a source of national greatness. Social culture is, therefore, an obvious source of cultural nationalism in contemporary Japan, and the business elites' emphasis on the strength of Japanese social culture is an obvious manifestation of cultural nationalism. Also, international diffusion of Japan's social culture as manifested in management and employment practices is now widely discussed. There has been a great deal of discussion among business executives (as well as academics) as to which aspects of Japanese-style management can and cannot be diffused to other countries. For example, Sakuma Masaru (1983), a research-oriented manager of Mitsubishi Heavy Industries Ltd, discusses the possibilities and limitations of the application of some aspects of the so-called Japanese-style management in other countries on the basis of case studies.

Whereas social culture can be a source of universalistic national sentiment, businessmen's concern with Japan's linguistic and communicative culture is more likely to enhance the particularistic sentiment that the Japanese are intrinsically different from non-Japanese.

Just as in the academic *nihonjinron*, the tacit, implicit, emotive and non-logical modes of Japanese communication are also pointed out in the businessmen's literature as those aspects which cannot be understood by non-Japanese. The following model dialogue from the English conversation textbook mentioned earlier is typical:

> Mr J [American]: . . . I don't think I could ever learn to make the subtle distinctions you need in Japanese.
> Mr S [Japanese]: It's so tied in with the whole culture. It's difficult to master for someone who grew up in another country. . . .
> (Nippon Steel Human Resources Development Co. Ltd. 1987: 405)

The linguistic and communicative culture tends to be discussed as an obstacle to communication between Japanese and foreign businessmen. Also, unlike in the case of social culture, there is no such shared recognition that the tacit, implicit and non-logical modes of Japanese communication are necessarily conducive to Japan's industrial success. The Japanese linguistic and communicative culture is, therefore, less obviously related to the promoted sense of cultural nationalism. How, then, does one's active concern with the linguistic and communicative culture promote the sense of cultural nationalism?

What is interesting about Japanese business elites' concern with the uniqueness of the Japanese patterns of communication is that it results from their stated concern to reduce cross-cultural misunderstandings that occur, or are expected to occur, between Japanese and non-Japanese. Their 'good intentions' are illustrated in the editorial comments in the literature published by various companies. For example, Mitsubishi Corporation intends their book to 'help smooth the way for better international communication' (1983: 6). Also, the Nippon Steel Corporation published their book 'in the hope of making some further contribution to mutual understanding between the people of Japan and the people of other countries throughout the world' (1984: 11). Similarly, the president of Taiyō Kōbe Bank explains the aim of their book, which is to

> make a contribution, if modest, to the promotion of an understanding of Japan and the Japanese people at a time when comprehension is badly needed to ease mounting trade tensions [and also to] help Japanese students who are destined to live in an era of internationalization, by providing hints about how things Japanese may be expressed in good English.
>
> (Taiyō Kōbe Bank 1988: 4)

Implicit in this statement are two characteristic ways of looking at the world: cultural reductionism and cultural relativism. By cultural reductionism I mean explanations of social, political and economic phenomena in terms of culture perceived to be characteristic of a nation. Here, conflicts resulting from trade imbalances between Japan and other countries are reduced to a cultural problem, that is, the failure of Westerners to understand, and the failure of Japanese to explain, the peculiarities of the Japanese patterns of behaviour. Furthermore, cross-cultural understanding is proclaimed through an extreme form of cultural relativism.[6]

In the following discussion I will show the curious parallels between anthropologists' views of world cultures several decades ago and the Japanese business elites' cultural views of today.

There are several varieties of cultural relativism in anthropology, of which three concern us here. The first is the 'relativity of ethics' according to which the standards of right and wrong or good and bad are relative to the cultural background of the person making the judgement. Second, the 'relativity of knowledge' has it that one's interpretation of events is relative to one's cultural background, since the concepts and theories one uses to understand the way the world works are conditioned by culture. Third, the term relativist often refers to a person who has the view that each culture is unique, that no generalisations can be derived from studying different cultures, and that each culture can only be understood in relation to the historical background of that culture. This may be called 'historical relativism' (Hatch 1983: 9–11).

Cultural relativism is a controversial theory and has evoked a series of criticisms and counter-criticisms, but we shall not concern ourselves with such a debate (see, for example, Geertz 1984; Hatch 1983). I am only interested in showing that cultural relativistic thinking permeates Japanese elites' perceptions of Japanese culture in relation to other cultures and, in particular, Western civilisation. For this purpose, it will be useful to know the background against which cultural relativism developed as a perspective on world cultures in order to show the interesting parallels between anthropologists' concerns several decades ago and Japanese business elites' concerns today.

The twin issues that engaged anthropologists after the turn of the century and favoured the development of cultural relativism were those of race and the place of the Western civilisation in the world. The nineteenth-century doctrine of racism held that races differ in moral and intellectual ability. This doctrine came into disrepute after the 1930s and was replaced by the theory of cultural relativism which explains differences among peoples in terms of cultural conditioning and social milieu. An equally important reason behind the popularity of cultural relativism was scepticism towards the Western-derived notion of progress and the equation of Western civilisation with civilisation *per se*. Non-Western cultures and values came to be re-evaluated without using the cultural values of the West as the standard in judging them. In this way cultural relativism emerged as a dominant perspective on the cultures of the world.

The concern of the Japanese business elite and, for that matter, the Japanese elite in general with cross-cultural understanding can be discussed within the framework of these themes of cultural relativism. First, the attempt of Japanese businessmen to improve cross-cultural understanding is made through the recognition and emphasis of cultural differences that exist and/or are believed to exist between Japan and other countries. Behind this attempt are the three propositions concerning cultural relativism: first, Japanese culture is unique and relative to Japanese history (historical relativism); second, because judgements of right and wrong are relative to the cultural background of the person making the judgement, Japanese patterns of behaviour and thought should be evaluated in their own light (ethical relativism); and third, because the ways in which we interpret events are conditioned by culture-bound concepts and theories, it is important for non-Japanese to recognise the uniqueness of the Japanese way of thinking and for the Japanese to point it out (relativity of knowledge).

The important issue to be considered from the point of view of cultural relativism concerns the perception of Japanese culture in relation to Western civilisation. Considering that the Japanese have almost always adapted themselves to the more 'central' or universal Western ways, cultural relativistic thinking as applied to the Japanese context is likely to result in the assertion of Japanese uniqueness because it involves the conscious attempt of the Japanese to challenge the assumption that the Western ways are the 'universal' ways and to emphasise that the Japanese ways should equally be respected in the community of world cultures. The following remark by the general manager of the personnel development division, Nippon Steel Corporation is typical of this line of thinking:

> The Japanese are not good at explaining themselves or expound-ing their opinions. Geographical and historical factors have long kept Japan an isolated nation and the people have felt no need to explain themselves to the 'outside world'.
>
> Even after the country was opened up, we still had very little to say about ourselves. Compared with the torrent of knowledge and information that poured into Japan, the amount that flowed out was negligible.
>
> Mutual understanding among the community of nations is based on the principles of self-expression and mutual tolerance.
>
> Japan has now earned a position among the advanced countries of the world and must begin reflecting its new status in its inter-national activities. . . . The likelihood of misunderstanding and friction arising between Japan and other countries will increase proportionally. From now on, it will be imperative for the Japanese to take every possible opportunity to assist people every-where to obtain a broader and deeper understanding of Japan.
>
> (Nippon Steel Corporation 1984: 11–12)

If the attempt at 'international understanding' is made through the actively conscious assertion of Japanese uniqueness or through the extreme version of cultural relativism, the unintended conse-quence of such an 'internationalising' attempt can ironically be the enhancement of cultural nationalism because it fails to stress the commonality shared by different peoples. It is in this sense that the businessmen's concern to improve intercultural communication and their cultural nationalism are often two sides of the same coin.

The other theme concerning cultural relativism is that, although cultural relativism developed as a reaction against racism, it had the ironic effect of promoting other types of race thinking.[7] The type of race thinking that concerns this study is what I called 'racially exclusive possession of particular cultural characteristics'. As discussed in chapters 2 and 6, strong emphasis on cultural differences between the 'particularistic' Japanese and the 'universal' others is likely to result in association of 'Japanese culture' with the 'Japanese race'. The linguistic and communicative modes of the Japanese in particular tend to be considered the exclusive property of the 'Japanese race'. In this sense, cultural relativism, which legitimates cultural differences, is inextricably associated with this form of 'race thinking' (or quasi-race thinking). It is in the association of 'race' (imagined) and culture that one of the main characteristics of Japanese cultural nationalism is to be found.

From the material presented in this chapter, two conclusions may be drawn. First, business elites in contemporary Japanese society play an active role in interpreting the academics' ideas of Japanese uniqueness and transmitting them to the broader sections of the population. Also, leading members of the business elite are themselves active creators of new types of collective and cultural identity.[8] In other words, business elites are both 'reproductive' and 'productive' intellectuals. Business elites may best be characterised as 'popular sociologists', whose main activity is to formulate and spread ideas of how the Japanese behave and think differently from Westerners. Second, and related to the first, business elites as 'popular sociologists' characterise Japanese society and social relations in predominantly 'spatial' terms rather than emphasising historicist concerns. Business elites reaffirm a sense of difference in a way that appeals to businessmen and other educated audiences. Other educated groups read the business elites' literature on Japanese uniqueness for the purpose of their practical activity as well as from intellectual curiosity.

BUSINESSMEN AS SOCIAL BEARERS OF CULTURAL NATIONALISM

In order to identify the characteristics of a specific case of cultural nationalism, it is useful to make a distinction between the two related yet distinct aspects of nationalism: the 'identity' and 'solidarity' aspects. The identity aspects are concerned with the exploration, formulation and emphasis of a nation's identity; the solidarity aspects with the creation, maintenance and enhancement of solidarity among members of a nation who share, or believe that they share, a distinctive culture.

Up to this point the discussion has concentrated on the ways in which leading members of the Japanese business elite participate in the formulation and diffusion of the ideas of Japanese uniqueness. It will be appropriate to conclude this chapter with some remarks on the solidarity aspects of the businessmen's cultural nationalism in contemporary Japan. That is, in what ways is the businessmen's experience of working in a Japanese company related to the creation, maintenance and enhancement of solidarity as members of the Japanese nation as a cultural community?

In 1951 political scientist Maruyama Masao made the following observation on the post-war situation regarding nationalism in Japan. Maruyama wrote that one conspicuous aspect of the post-war situation was

> what might be called the social decomposition of the former nationalist psychology. Constituted as it was by a systematic mobilization of traditional values and *mores*, such as regional sentiment and paternal loyalty, it was only natural that, once the cohesive power at the nation's centre weakened, national consciousness should quickly decompose and return automatically, as it were, to its old haunts in the family, village, and small local groups at the base of the social structure.
>
> (Maruyama 1963: 150, originally published in *Chūō Kōron* 1951)

Behind this remark is the view that pre-war Japanese national consciousness was an extension of the type of consciousness characteristic of the traditional family system (*ie*) and the village community (*mura*). Since the publication of this article in 1951, however, the traditional family system and village community, to which 'decomposed' national consciousness should have returned, have dissolved and disintegrated in the process of urbanisation to the extent that they can no longer be called the social units (see chapter 5). Considering such changes, one might question the validity of Maruyama's argument that national consciousness would decompose and return to its old haunts at the base of the social structure – the family (*ie*) and the village (*mura*). However, Maruyama's contention was that, with the weakening of the cohesive power at the nation's centre, the 'old nationalism', which embodied the traditional social structural principles and values, would be fragmented into some intermediate groups. In fact, Maruyama points to some other social groups such as gangs of hoodlums and mobsters and right-wing groups in the years following Japan's defeat in 1945:

> Organized along disciplinary lines similar to the military and offering the loyalty relations of *oyabun-kobun*, these 'anti-social groups' were well suited to fill the psychological void left when the central symbols collapsed.
>
> (Maruyama 1963: 150)

The 'old haunts' of pre-war nationalism, the traditional family system and village community as real social entities, may have disintegrated in the post-war period, but, as was discussed in chapter 5, the social and cultural features characteristic of them have remained largely in an idealised form and reproduced themselves in another institution, the company. We, therefore, have good grounds on which to argue that what Maruyama has referred to as a 'fragmentary form of nationalism' exists in the fictive family and village, that is, the company.

In what sense, then, are businessmen one of the main social bearers of cultural nationalism in contemporary Japan? The answer to this question is already provided in chapter 5 in our discussion on *Gemeinschaft*-type modern society. I pointed out that the modern Japanese company is often considered the embodiment of Japan's traditional and distinctive social culture. The Japanese company is regarded by businessmen and others as the microcosm of uniquely Japanese society, and businessmen (or, to be more precise, 'company men') as the typical bearers of the 'uniqueness' of Japanese social culture.

In the company Japanese uniqueness is not simply a matter of abstract theory but is given particular, concrete forms. There are three ways in which Japanese uniqueness is actually experienced in the company. First, through work practices and institutions (i.e. employment practices, industrial relations, decision-making processes) which embody the 'distinctly Japanese' social structure and values. Second, through out-of-office group rituals such as afterwork and seasonal informal drinking sessions and more formalised parties and 'recreational' events by which social solidarity among the members of the company is reaffirmed. Durkheim was quite right in arguing that the maintenance and enhancement of collective feelings 'cannot be achieved except by means of reunions, assemblies and meetings where the individuals, being closely united to one another, reaffirm in common with their common sentiments' ([1912] 1964: 427). In and out of the office, informal groups are given a particularly important part to perform in the company. In chapter 5 I discussed the view that it is in the informal group that the traditionally Japanese patterns of behaviour and thought are preserved and given an active role to play, and that such an informal group may be considered to be deliberately built into the formal company organisation so that the organisation can fulfil its goals effectively. In other words, proper *ningen kankei* (human relations) – a term frequently used in casual conversations of the Japanese, embracing the meanings of social norm, social etiquette, common sense and modes of behaving and thinking – are considered essential for an effective organisation in the Japanese company. This leads to the third point as to how 'uniquely Japanese' social culture is learnt by the members of the company. The Japanese company is a social institution in which one learns proper 'human relations' expected of a Japanese national. In this sense the role of the company can be compared to that of the army in pre-war and wartime Japan as an important agency of adult socialisation as regards national values.[9] That the company is an important agency of adult socialisation is endorsed by many respondents who remark to the effect that one should join a Japanese company in order to become full-fledged Japanese with common sense.

In summary, it is in the sense that 'company men' are the typical promoters and bearers of uniquely Japanese-style social solidarity that they are one of the loci of cultural nationalism in contemporary Japan. It does not necessarily follow, however, that such uniquely Japanese-style social solidarity among 'company men' will be linked to national solidarity at the societal level. In this sense, company men's cultural nationalism from the point of view of the solidarity aspects may best be characterised as 'fragmentary' cultural nationalism.

Chapter 9

Explanations of the *nihonjinron*

In this chapter I shall critically assess some of the explanations of the *nihonjinron* in general terms and on the basis of our findings with the aim of clarifying my position concerning explanations as to why the phenomenon of the *nihonjinron* has developed.

In an attempt to classify the explanations for the development of the *nihonjinron*, the two-fold classification made by M.S. Hickox (1984) of explanations of the development of 'classical' sociology as a school of thought in nineteenth-century continental Europe may usefully be applied. The first is the 'stimulus and response' approach which explains the emergence of 'classical' sociology in terms of its attempt to come to terms with the significant social transformation which affected European society in the nineteenth century. The second characterises 'classical' sociology as a kind of ideology, attributing the development of classical sociology to its role as bourgeois conservative ideology serving to maintain the existing social order. The conservatism of classical sociology is considered to be expressed in its lack of emphasis on class struggle and its utility as an ideological base to refute Marxist theory.

Explanations of the development of the *nihonjinron* as a mode of thought in Japan in the 1970s and 1980s may similarly be classified. First, there are attempts to see the central concern of the *nihonjinron* as an attempt to come to terms with significant changes that have affected post-war Japanese society. There are two sub-varieties of this type: an explanation that identifies the *nihonjinron* as a rescuer of Japanese identity threatened by Westernisation and an explanation that regards the *nihonjinron* as giving a cultural explanation to Japan's economic success. Second, there is an explanation that depicts the *nihonjinron* as a kind of ideology and explains its development by associating it with the interests of the ruling social class or stratum.

This explanation emphasises political conservatism inherent in the *nihonjinron* as expressed in its emphasis of such 'peculiar' char-acteristics of Japanese society as group orientation among the members of a company, 'vertical society' structured along company lines rather than class lines, enterprise unions and so on. In addition to these general explanations, there is a more particu-laristic view which explains the *nihonjinron* in terms of Japanese culture itself.

EXPLANATIONS OF THE *NIHONJINRON*: A REVIEW AND ASSESSMENT

The 'threatened identity' perspective

From this perspective the *nihonjinron* is viewed as an attempt to explore and reconstruct national identity threatened by Westerni-sation and rapid industrialisation. Such an activity is understood as the process of marking a symbolic boundary between 'us' (Japanese) and 'them' (Western) and/or the process of re-establishing and maintaining a sense of historical continuity with the traditions of Japan.

For example, cultural anthropologist Harumi Befu (1984, 1987) attempts a cultural-anthropological study of Japanese life space to explain why and how the *nihonjinron* has developed to 'rescue the Japanese identity' by employing the two paired concepts of 'Japanese/Western' and 'private/public'. The 'public' is defined as having to do with 'governance, the societal, the communal, and all else which involves the corporate interest of the body politic, particularly in the arena of social life traditionally regarded as "sacred"' (Befu 1984: 63). The 'private', on the other hand, refers to the realm of personal and family affairs and of individual interests in opposition to communal or societal affairs.

On the basis of these classifications, Befu maintains that, in the process of Westernisation that began in the second half of the nineteenth century, the 'Western' lifestyle has first come to dominate the 'public' areas, and that the 'Japanese' style has come to be confined to the 'private' area of life. Two sources of tension have arisen to constitute what Befu calls the 'crisis in [*sic*] Western dominance'. First, 'equation of the "Western" with the "public" and of the "Japanese" with the "private" has necessarily placed the "Western" style above the "Japanese" in the hierarchy of Japanese values' (ibid.: 64), because communal and societal concerns have traditionally been given priority over individual concern in Japan. Second, the 'Western' lifestyle has not only dominated 'public' places but has invaded extensively into the 'private' areas, such as in the case of Western-style private houses and furniture. Befu argues that Westernisation has brought about a 'shrinkage of the area of self-expression as Japanese' (ibid.: 66):

> Japanese are gradually losing areas in which they can express their identity as Japanese. In other words, Japanese are finding fewer and fewer opportunities to legitimize their being Japanese. Crisis arises in the fact that they must express their cultural identity with a cultural style which has been defined as politically inferior and also perceived by themselves as such.
>
> (Befu 1984: 66)

It is in this environment, Befu argues, that the *nihonjinron* plays a crucial role in challenging the dominance of the 'Western' style by demonstrating the uniqueness of Japanese culture, society and national character. In summary, the role of the *nihonjinron* is

> to rescue the 'Japanese' style from its inferior status and demonstrate the merit of the 'Japanese' culture by crystallizing the essence of Japanese culture and making this essence readily comprehensible to ordinary Japanese, and to remove Japan from the possibility of invidious comparison with the West through the claim of incomparable uniqueness of its essence.
>
> (ibid.: 73)

There is also a more historicist standpoint on Japan's threatened identity. Sydney Crawcour, for example, argues that the maintenance of a sense of historical continuity is an important reason for the development of the *nihonjinron*. He maintains that, in spite of the rapid and massive economic, political and social change, '*nihonjinron* has consistently asserted that Japanese personality and Japanese society have never changed' (1980: 186), referring to such frequently cited Japanese characteristics in the literature as 'the quasi-family group, the homogeneity of the Japanese race, special properties of the language (*kotodama*) and the vertical structure of society' (ibid.: 185).

Assessment

There is no evidence to suggest that the 'threatened identity' perspective is invalid, provided that this is employed as a 'supplementary' perspective. There are, however, some questions to be raised. For example, Befu's association of the 'public' with higher values and the 'private' with lower values should be questioned from the point of view of 'ordinary' people's perceptions of national identity, because ordinary people (who are not professional thinkers) do not usually concern themselves with the 'public' realm, as with the 'private', in their experience of Japaneseness. The important question here is: which social group is Befu talking about, intellectuals or ordinary people? But this is not to suggest that a symbolic study of life space is not useful. I have provided my own symbolic boundary analysis of Japanese identity in chapter 6.

This may certainly be a valid perspective on professional thinkers' concerns with Japanese uniqueness. The majority of 'ordinary' people, however, do not normally concern themselves with the problem of cultural identity as such, with the exception of those who regularly interact with foreigners. Although, if asked, most of our respondents favourably responded to comments stressing enduring Japanese elements in the wave of Westernisation, such a subject rarely enters into their everyday concerns. In fact, several respondents misunderstood the intention of my research and thought that, by discussing this subject, I was suggesting that they should be more aware of the identity and strengths of Japanese culture. Several respondents even appreciated being reminded of the importance of this subject when they were too busy with mundane everyday matters. Even those concerned about the 'destabilised' identity of the Japanese had more specific, and often practical, interests grounded in their personal lives; for example, an interest to shed light on problems in communicating with foreigners. Thus, one cannot explain the respondents' concern with Japanese uniqueness *solely* in terms of their concern about the threatened identity of Japanese culture.

The 'economic success' perspective

This perspective, widely held among thinking elites, regards the *nihonjinron* as an attempt to identify Japanese cultural uniqueness as a cause of Japan's economic success. The following remark is representative of such a view:

> As Japan's economic presence became increasingly difficult for many nations to ignore, many sought to bridge that gap by giving some plausible explanation for Japan's rapid growth. It is in this climate that a large number of books on Japan's apparent uniqueness began to appear, each seeking to expose the secret of Japan's rapid economic growth.
>
> (Mouer and Sugimoto 1980: 7)

Kawamura Nozomu also argues that the basic assumption of the *nihonjinron* is that 'national character is a valid concept which can be used as an independent variable to explain the direction in which Japanese society is moving' (1980: 44). The *nihonjinron* has consequently explained Japan's economic success in terms of what it defines as the unique national character of the Japanese.

Crawcour discusses this point further:

> Japanese intellectuals now attribute their country's economic success not to the effects of American-type modernization but to the operation of unique traditional virtues of Japanese society, culture and personality. It is widely believed that Japanese society has avoided most of the evils that have accompanied industrialization elsewhere (crime, drugs, social divisions, family breakdown) thanks to the operation of these peculiar virtues, and that to the extent that these problems do exist they are due to failure to preserve Japanese ways against foreign influences.
>
> (Crawcour 1980: 186)

Here, 'unique traditional virtues of Japanese society' refer to group loyalty, consensus, paternalistic management, social organisation based on vertical dependence and so on. Crawcour then criticises the *nihonjinron* for its neglect of important factors such as the 'availability of advanced technology from abroad, high rates of investment, abundant supplies of labour and a very favourable international environment' (1980: 187). The *nihonjinron* claims that Japan's 'economic success' is a cultural and moral victory of the Japanese, and this is all the more obvious when peculiar Japanese values are used to explain the apparent success in avoiding many of the serious social problems that are more conspicuous in the West such as the high rate of unemployment, adversarial trade unionism, violent crime and so on.

Assessment

The 'economic success' perspective has now become established (see Sawa 1987). Although this explanation may apply to a number of thinking elites, it is necessary, for the sake of a fairer understanding of the *nihonjinron* phenomenon, to distinguish between one's *intention* of writing on Japanese uniqueness and the *consequence*, often unintended, of such written work. Much of the *nihonjinron* discusses Japanese distinctiveness without explicitly indicating its superiority. In fact, some of the literature are even critical of Japanese peculiarities such as group orientation. But, once the association between group-oriented features of Japan's social culture and Japan's industrial strength has been popularly made, critics begin to assume that any literature on Japanese group orientation endorses a culturalistic and moralistic explanation of Japan's economic success.

How about the validity of the 'economic success' perspective as a way of thinking of the more 'ordinary' members of society? Prior to the interviews with the respondents, I myself supposed that this theory would explain the respondents' concern with Japanese uniqueness in view of the fact that the inundation of the *nihonjinron* literature in the 1970s coincided with the growing awareness of Japan's economic success among the Japanese. My research on educators and businessmen has yielded quite a different result. Most respondents interpreted the intention behind the *nihonjinron* in the opposite manner: they thought that the *nihonjinron*, especially those by academics and social critics, describe Japanese characteristics in a negative or self-denying manner. They were unhappy about the *nihonjinron*, which, they pointed out, had discouraged the Japanese from having a sense of national pride. Some even remarked that the *nihonjinron* should be replaced by another type of literature which gives a more positive meaning to Japanese peculiarities. Such a negative perception of the *nihonjinron* was prevalent both among educators and businessmen.

This is understandable in view of the fact that the literature on Japanese peculiarities produced in early post-war years was self-critical, reflecting the mood of the defeated nation, and that this set the tone for the subsequent discussions of Japanese character until the 1970s. Respondents' interest in Japanese distinctiveness did not begin abruptly with the *nihonjinron* boom of the 1970s, but rather many had already been exposed to some sort of literature on Japanese peculiarities before that. For example, the influence of Benedict's *The Chrysanthemum and the Sword* on older respondents was significant, as was discussed in chapter 7. Moreover, such a self-critical orientation was not absent in the *nihonjinron* of the 1970s and 1980s. Much of the *nihonjinron* was more 'neutral' than is often supposed in the sense that it emphasised Japanese distinctiveness without necessarily indicating its superiority. The negative image of the *nihonjinron* reflected and, at the same time, promoted the respondents' conscious rejection of the self-critical attitude of opinion leaders which they regarded as a remnant of post-war Japan.

It may be argued, therefore, that respondents' interest in the *nihonjinron* was not caused by their intention to reaffirm the idea that Japan's unique social culture is the cause of Japan's economic success. In other words, our findings do not support the proposition that one's exposure to the *nihonjinron* itself promotes nationalistic sentiment. Rather, it is one's perception of the *nihonjinron* in this contrary manner that can induce, as a counter-reaction, a more conscious attempt to see Japan's social culture positively, thereby eventually resulting in nationalistic sentiment which stresses the strengths of Japanese cultural distinctiveness. This 'reactiveness' has been recognised as an important background factor behind contemporary nationalism in Japan. (There is, however, an exception to this. Many respondents considered leading business elites' *nihonjinron* on the distinctiveness of Japan's business and management practices to be 'fair', positive and understanding of Japanese culture, as was discussed in chapters 7 and 8.)

The dominant ideology thesis

The dominant ideology thesis explains the apparent stability of contemporary capitalist society in terms of the successful ideological incorporation of the subordinate class into the existing social system.[1] From this perspective the *nihonjinron* is regarded as a case of the manipulation of ideas. Yamada Takao (1981a: 24–5) argues that the situation surrounding the *nihonjinron* should be understood in terms of conflicting political and social relations and examines the role of dominant ideology in post-war Japanese society. Dominant (or ruling) ideology is an instrument of class domination by which the dominant class manipulates the subordinate class.

The proponents of this thesis criticise the way in which the stability of Japanese society is explained in the *nihonjinron*, that is, in terms of the uniquely homogeneous and harmonious social culture of Japan. Rather, they argue, Japanese society is stabilised by dominant ideology, and the *nihonjinron* serves as such an ideology. Their criticism is based on the proposition that the nature of 'culture' can only be understood through a careful examination of the ways in which it is produced in class relations. For example, Kawamura Nozomu (1982) argues that it is 'thoroughly nonsensical' to regard the cultural features depicted in the *nihonjinron* as those unchanging Japanese characteristics which have continued throughout history and stresses the need to recognise the capitalist nature of Japanese society (1982: 145). Admitting that there is an element of 'Japaneseness' about class relations in Japan, he contends that such 'Japaneseness' should be understood in the context of the structural features of Japanese capitalism and redefined as social features conditioned by the historical situation and class relations. As a ruling ideology, the *nihonjinron* serves to implant particular cultural values, congruent with the values and interests of the dominant class, into the consciousness of the people. By accepting the legitimacy of the dominant system, the subordinate class is successfully incorporated into the existing social arrangements (Kawamura 1982: chs 3 and 4).

For the purpose of illustration, Kawamura cites the 'age of culture' study group organised in 1979 as an initiative of then Prime Minister, Ohira Masayoshi, to which several influential thinking elites were invited to express their views on the conditions of Japan. Kawamura argues that the strategic position of the *nihonjinron* is clearly laid out in the report published by the group in 1980 (ibid.: 143). Now that economic prosperity has been achieved, the report states, 'culture' should replace the previous goal of 'modernisation' and 'industrialisation'. In the previous period when Japan was trying to catch up, the Japanese 'denied or neglected their own traditional culture and looked elsewhere for their own goal' (quoted in Kawamura 1982: 147). In the 'age of culture', it is argued, 'the essential features of Japanese culture' should be re-evaluated (ibid.: 145). The report synthesises various theories set forth in the *nihonjinron*, characterising the essence of Japanese culture by its 'circular' structure in which there is no absolute distinction between

what are normally considered contradictory categories in the West.
Western culture is described as 'having a structure "dichotomising"
good and bad, god and devil, winner and loser, black and white'
(ibid.). On the basis of this fundamental epistemological difference,
the report contrasts Japanese and Western social culture:

> The West is oriented either towards 'individualism', which
> professes and seeks to establish the 'individual self' differenti-
> ated from others, or towards 'totalitarianism' which denies the
> 'individual'; on the other hand, the Japanese cultural essence
> may be called 'interpersonalism' which values the 'relationship
> between persons' and the 'relationship between the individual
> and the whole . . .'.
>
> (*The Age of Culture*, quoted in ibid.: 145)

The Japanese are positively related to one another by various social
ties such as kinship, ties based on one's place of origin, school ties and
company ties which provide the Japanese with a sense of security.
Japan, in this sense, is a '*nakama* (group) society' or an '*ie* (familial)
society', says the report (ibid.: 145). 'Positively re-evaluating those
Japanese values which place high value on warm human relations
nurtured in the traditions of Japanese society and harmony between
man and nature' (ibid.: 147), the report maintains that 'the high level
of our economic growth has not simply been an economic success but
a great cultural achievement as well' (ibid.: 152–3). Japanese culture
is regarded here as the major independent variable to explain the
'successful' social and economic development. Once the supremacy
of such Japanese cultural values is established in the *nihonjinron*, it
no longer takes much conscious effort for the *nihonjinron* to work
as a dominant ideology. Kawamura argues that 'what is being
discussed as "culture" has nothing to do with the aesthetic sense
of the Japanese but refers to nothing but the integrative power the
capitalist and the manager hold over the working class' (1982: 152).
Kawamura remarks further:

> To argue that modern Japan lacks class conflicts between
> capitalists and wage earners and solidarity within each class
> but is instead simply characterised by the presence of *oya-kata*
> [paternalistic leaders] and *ko-kata* [their followers] organised by
> vertical relationships, and to argue further that these charac-
> teristics derive from the essence of Japanese culture and the
> national character of the Japanese, is in perfect harmony with [the

interests of] capitalists and managers. It is quite natural, therefore, that these [*nihonjinron*] discussants are warmly welcomed by big businesses today. According to this position, loyalty and devotion expressed towards company groups as well as the centralised state which benefits the interests of companies result from the national character of the Japanese, not from the domination and coercion [by the dominant class].

(Kawamura 1982: 107)

Also, referring to a remark made by the head of the research institute affiliated to a big business company that Japan's economic competitiveness abroad is the result of harmony and consensus at home, Kawamura argues that such a remark 'completely ignores the class nature of "harmony" and "consensus" in the present-day company, where, in fact, the neglect of workers' rights and the oppression of, and interference into, unions are evident' (1982: 146–7).

The view that the *nihonjinron* developed as a dominant ideology is shared by several others (e.g. Yamaguchi 1984; Hijikata 1983; Halliday 1975; Dower 1975). Hijikata labels the *nihonjinron* as a 'soft and covert theory protecting [the interests of] the Establishment' (1983: 55), stating that 'because it does not seem like an outright reactionary ideology on the surface . . ., its subtle function is to deceive people to fall unwittingly into its trap' (ibid.: 167). Jon Halliday makes a similar point that the Japanese ruling class has successfully created an ideology that Japan is a 'classless society'. He says that 'an exceptionally sophisticated expression of this ideology [of Japan as a classless society] has been provided by the sociologist Nakane' (1975: 229).

The plain fact is that while the workers in a factory are *subjected* to this ideology [of 'vertical society'], management shows no 'enterprise solidarity'. The simplest evidence of this is the superb trans-enterprise organization of Japanese big business, which has the most powerful federations in the capitalist world. Group solidarity is an ideological weapon, where the capitalist class operates solidarity within itself and fragmentation among the working class.

(Halliday 1975: 230)

Halliday also remarks on the role of the government, which 'fosters the preservation of these conditions not only by promoting such ideology in schools, but by directly and indirectly creating the conditions where business can continue to exploit the working masses' (ibid.).

John Dower's following statement sums up the 'dominant ideology' criticism of the *nihonjinron*:

> Fragmentation of the working class is thus most correctly seen, not as a cultural phenomenon, but as an exceptionally successful means for controlling the proletariat, maintained by one of the most coherent and co-ordinated ruling blocs in the contemporary capitalist world.
>
> (Dower 1975: xxx)

Assessment

The dominant ideology thesis, which stresses the presence of classes with contradictory interests, orientates our attention to the neglected subject of classes in the *nihonjinron*. In fact, despite the view of Japanese society as a harmonious whole commonly held in the *nihonjinron*, we find a number of cases pointing to the presence of conflicting interests between classes. For example, hundreds of strikes are reported every year. Strikes involving tens of thousands of union members of the Japan National Railways (predecessor to the now privatised JR) may be a good example to point out the neglect in the *nihonjinron* of a class division, as is exemplified by Nakane's description of the JNR as an epitome of the paternalistic enterprise ('JNR as one family') (1967: 36–7).

There is, however, a logical limitation inherent in the dominant ideology thesis as a perspective to criticise the *nihonjinron*'s treatment of Japanese culture as a monolithic and harmonious whole. Dominant ideology theorists attach utmost importance to a class division within a society. It becomes evident, however, that their accounts of society are actually in harmony with the functionalist social theory to which Marxist and Marxian scholars object. The dominant ideology thesis explains the coherence and integration of society in terms of the incorporation of the subordinate class by a dominant ideology or the manipulation of a dominant set of ideas, values and beliefs. Its ideological opposite, Parsonian functionalism, too, explains the maintenance and continuity of a social system in terms of a shared set of values and beliefs. Socialisation ensures the internalisation of norms and values in the individual, who obtains psychological reward for accepting existing social arrangements. Social control of individuals is made possible by the conformity of individuals to the expectations of others in social interaction. The integration and stability of a social system and the lack of social conflict are thus seen as deriving from the acceptance of common culture.

Various scholars pointed out this theoretical similarity between these essentially opposing perspectives of Marxism and functionalism. Anthony Giddens argues that 'Marx always recognised the cohering effect of commonly held values and ideas ... and in fact built much of his theory upon such an assumption' (1968: 269). Abercrombie, Hill and Turner argue that both Marxist and functionalist theories have a common theoretical weakness: both are incapable of dealing in any convincing manner with the emergence of alternative cultures in society (1980: 30–58).

Such a similarity between the two essentially contradictory perspectives reveals the logical weakness of the dominant ideology thesis as a perspective to highlight a class division in Japanese society. The dominant ideology thesis ends up simply reinforcing the perception of Japan as a highly integrative and cohesive society sharing common values without showing the class-divided interests and values in any convincing manner.

Logically, this thesis could be defeated if a significant alternative culture (such as working-class culture) was found to exist. In the British cultural debate, the dominant culture thesis has been challenged by the alternative culture thesis which points to the presence of the significantly different working-class culture (see Abercrombie *et al.* 1980: 140–55). The Japanese cultural debate, however, is characterised by a lack of interest in whether or not working-class culture exists, probably because such a thing is not popularly assumed to exist, and we have no relevant data to discuss it with.

Of course, the subject of ideological manipulation as a means of ensuring conformity or compliance is not limited to the Marxist/Marxian discussion of class relations but may be extended to discussions of any type of social relations. The *nihonjinron* may be discussed as a case of 'management ideology' in a company organisation. The question here is how do we understand the coherence and integration of a company? Should we focus on the symbolic and moral manipulation or the sharing of common values, or both? And more specifically, how do we understand the willingness of our businessmen to be exposed to the *nihonjinron*?

As we found, businessmen were eager to gain a systematic understanding of business organisation and management or to learn the proper beliefs, values and norms of Japanese business organisation, and for such purposes abundant popular literature exists on Japan's business culture. The example, given in the earlier chapter, of a bank employee who approaches the *nihonjinron* 'out of an instinct to defend himself in the organisation' may be considered in this context. Are we to interpret his behaviour as a case of ideological manipulation? Or are we to understand that he voluntarily studies Japanese business culture in order to understand more objectively the situation in which he is placed? These are extremely difficult questions to test empirically. One might stress ideological manipulation, but how do we know that people do not share some sort of common values from the start or at the time of entrance into a company organisation? Conversely, one might stress common values, but how do people come to share them? By ideological manipulation? In short, 'ideological manipulation' in the context of a Japanese company is a topic in itself and requires further extensive research.

Explanations in terms of Japanese culture

Thus far the discussion has been concerned with general perspectives on the *nihonjinron*. There is another, more particularistic, view that attributes the Japanese's active concern with their identity to an intrinsic feature of Japanese culture. This type of cultural thinking deserves special attention because it is not only sometimes held by the thinking elites but is prevalent among ordinary, educated Japanese.

What may be called the cultural explanation ranges from a vague, inarticulate habit of thinking that simply regards the Japanese concern with self-identity as part of the Japanese national character to a more explicitly 'sociological' reasoning. The following remark by one of our respondents, a school headmaster, was typical of the former:

> It is the national character of the Japanese to be obsessed with the question of what is unique about the Japanese.

A more explicit reasoning considers one's active use of out-groups as reference groups to be intrinsic to the social structure of the Japanese group. It is a strong inclination for the members of a Japanese group to have an in-group exclusiveness while at the same time actively using out-groups as reference groups for comparative and normative purposes.[2] In a study of Japanese attitudes towards social spheres outside one's own group, social psychologist Inoue Tadashi (1979: 80) argues that it is important not merely to emphasise the in-group exclusiveness of the Japanese group but to indicate that the Japanese have traditionally depended upon value standards of groups other than their own to reflect upon their own group, that is, to be keenly concerned with the identity of their group in relation to the out-group.[3] The two seemingly contradictory aspects have existed side by side in Japanese society.

The prototype of a Japanese group with such features is often identified with the traditional social unit of the village community. Yanagita Kunio, a founding father of Japan's folklore studies, points out that an eagerness to be informed about the external world characterises the mentality of traditional villagers residing in a relatively isolated community. Villagers' travels to the city were not simply a result of their response to the gaiety of the city but more importantly reflected their willingness to acquire information about the outside world. Those villagers who had seen the city or the 'wider world' were considered the 'learned' (Yanagita 1962: 303). Also, village festivals provided important occasions to come into contact with travellers from various parts of the country and to obtain information about the world outside. Itinerants and strangers were treasured by villagers as those who could satisfy their intense curiosity.[4]

Of course, one's curiosity about other groups and one's self-reflection or self-examination of one's own group are not necessarily the same thing, but empirically the two have existed side by side in the Japanese perceptions of the external world (see chapter 6). Villagers living in the highly closed community lacked information about the world outside, a situation which induced them to be eager to be informed of the larger society outside their own communities and also to reflect upon themselves in a comparative light. As discussed in chapter 5, it is a widely-held view among scholars that communal features have disseminated beyond their original home, the village community, to form the broad characteristics of modern Japanese society during the process of industrialisation, thereby becoming an intrinsic part of Japanese social culture. The strong tendency of the Japanese to use other groups actively as reference groups is understood here to be intrinsic to the social structure of the Japanese group, the prototype of which is the traditional village community.

Assessment

Some fundamental questions may be raised as regards this cultural-istic view. In particular, the assumption that the strong tendency of the members of a closed community to use other groups as reference groups is peculiar to the pre-industrial community of Japan should be questioned, since such a tendency is expected to be widely observable in the world, if not universal. The inadequacy of the culturalistic view may also be shown by the fact that the respondents' orientations to the *nihonjinron* were not uniform but indeed diversified, and most of those actively receptive to the *nihonjinron* had specific, often practical, reasons for being so. Our respondents' interest in the *nihonjinron* was generally motivated and enhanced by their concern to understand and solve specific problems that immediately confronted them in their everyday life. It is therefore not plausible to suspect that the respondents' orientation to the *nihonjinron* was culturally determined. The majority of our respondents, however, tended to prefer a 'cultural explanation' themselves.

One is probably tempted to explain the strong concern of the Japanese with their self-identity in cultural terms because such a concern has usually been prominent in the past century or so, thereby giving the impression that this is an intrinsic characteristic of the Japanese. If the Japanese have persistently shown a keen interest in this question, it is necessary to look at it historically, and we find that such a concern, as manifested in the thinkers' discussions of Japanese identity, has always been a response to *specific* events and trends at each phase in history.[5] Such a long-standing concern should be regarded as a series of reactions to a series of historical events that have stimulated Japanese thinkers to define and redefine Japan's identity in relation to the more central civilisation, first of China and then of the West (see note 5, p. 243). We have, therefore, no grounds to believe that the Japanese thinkers' concern with Japanese uniqueness is culturally determined.

SUMMARY AND CONCLUSIONS

The explanations sketched in this chapter are flawed by one serious problem, that is, the failure to distinguish between the concerns of thinking elites who 'produce' works on national uniqueness and those of other social groups who 'consume' such works. It is one thing to explain the intellectuals' concern with national cultural uniqueness; quite another to understand why and how the other social groups respond to it. This may seem like an obvious point but not quite so in the dominant trends in Japanese studies. The fact that most existing explanations and criticisms of the *nihonjinron* given by Japanologists fail to make this distinction and tend to identify the two groups' concerns together illustrates the lack of a 'sociological' perspective. In other words, they fail to examine what it is that occurs between whom (that is, to whom, and by whom) within society? Ironically, a holistic view of Japanese society is held even among those who criticise the *nihonjinron* because of its assumption of Japan as a monolithic whole.

Thinking elites who write for nationally circulated publications may be interested in such large themes as Japan's national identity and Japan's role in the world, but they are men of ideas for ideas' sake. The following account of A.D. Smith on intellectuals and cultural nationalism is cogent:

> [Cultural nationalism] has always constituted the creation and special zone of intellectuals. For they, above all, feel the need for a resolution of those crises of identity which menace modern man, and which require of him a moral regeneration, a rediscovery and realisation of self, through a return to that which is unique to oneself, to one's special character and history, which cannot be severed from the individuality and unique history of one's own community.
>
> (Smith 1983: 94)

If the explanations discussed in this chapter are regarded as perspectives on professional thinkers, some of these explanations, as discussed, have valid points. There is little question that many professional thinkers engage in the *nihonjinron* out of their concern to resolve the crisis of cultural identity threatened by Westernisation and rapid social change. Also, it is very possible that behind some *nihonjinron* exists a motivation to associate the uniqueness of Japan's social culture with Japan's industrial strength. It may also be true that the *nihonjinron* has served as a management ideology to a certain extent, but I do not know whether the writers had the intention of developing such an ideology or their work had the unintended consequence of serving as a management ideology. It is important not to overgeneralise about thinkers' reasons for producing such works and also about the effects, intended or unintended, which such works have: different thinkers have different reasons for engaging in the *nihonjinron*, and their literature works differently for different people.

The existing explanations fail to explain why and how other social groups 'consume' works on Japanese uniqueness. As I already argued in chapter 7, other social groups, when responding to the ideas of intellectuals, tend to concern themselves with such ideas only so far as they are related to their immediate surroundings. For 'ordinary' people who are not men of ideas for ideas' sake, their interest in the *nihonjinron* arises from their concerns to understand and solve specific problems that confront them in their own immediate environments, working and otherwise. Such concerns are not necessarily instrumental but, more importantly, expressive. When the respondents found the *nihonjinron* useful, they may have used it in order to pursue their interests but, more importantly, to find meaning in, or to give meaning to, their daily activity. This is also true with supposedly instrumentally-minded businessmen, who, in fact, tend to be concerned to find meaning in their behaviour as businessmen. Different social groups are oriented differently towards the *nihonjinron* because its usefulness varies from one group to another. As we found, the *nihonjinron* was more useful for businessmen than educators.

What our findings suggest is that it is particularly important to pay attention to the role of one's immediate group in forming one's orientation to the ideology of nationalism. A number of sociologists pointed out, albeit in differing contexts, that the immediate group to which one belongs exerts a major influence on shaping one's ideological orientation (see Verba 1961: ch. 2). Karl Mannheim once remarked, 'Whatever changes the New Age may bring, person-to-person relationships and primary groups will remain the basic character-forming agencies of society' (1951: 181). Also, loyalty to one's immediate group may have significant latent effects on the political system by leading one to behave in such a manner as to support the larger social and political system. Hence, a well-known finding of wartime soldiers' behaviour in America and Germany that, whether the cause was democracy or Nazism, soldiers were motivated to fight for the society at large by the emotional rewards and affective security given by their immediate group. Shils and Janowitz also pointed out that the solidarity of the German army was found to be based only very indirectly and partially on broader political convictions or ethical beliefs. Rather, it depended on the degree of cohesion and the smooth functioning of primary group life (1948: 314). Also, several scholars have argued that one of the major reasons for a person's communist ideological orientation is that participation in the Communist party satisfies the person's need for affective ties (Selznick 1952: 283–7; Almond 1952: 272–9). These arguments, which emphasise the importance of the primary group for the political system and behaviour, can be interpreted as suggesting the importance of analysing one's relationship to one's immediate group in order to examine how one's orientation to a particular ideology such as nationalism is formed.

Chapter 10

'Resurgent cultural nationalism' and 'prudent revivalist nationalism'

TWO TYPES OF NATIONALISM IN CONTEMPORARY JAPAN

The word nationalism reminded many of our respondents of pre-war nationalism (*kokka-shugi*), that type of nationalism which had been imposed upon the people 'from above' and which had eventually led the nation into the Second World War. If nationalism has this negative image, it is natural that many respondents should have perceived it negatively, which was their first reaction. None the less, the majority of the respondents also expressed concern over the decline of national pride in post-war Japan, suggesting that it was necessary for the Japanese to promote a 'wholesome' (*kenzen na*) or 'prudent' nationalism. 'Wholesome' nationalism in contemporary Japan may broadly be divided into two types.

The first type of nationalism, which may be called 'resurgent cultural nationalism', has developed in the 1970s and 1980s in relation to the *nihonjinron*. 'Resurgent cultural nationalism' has centred around the thinking elites' activity, to which certain educated sections of the population have responded favourably. This type of cultural nationalism has concerned itself with the rediscovery, redefinition and reaffirmation of Japanese uniqueness. The preceding chapters have concentrated on this type of nationalism manifested in and generated by the *nihonjinron*. The second type of 'prudent' nationalism may be understood in relation to 'old nationalism' which, with Japan's defeat in 1945, apparently 'completed one full cycle of nationalism: birth, maturity and decline', as Maruyama (1953: 78) called it. The emperor system (*tennō-sei*)[1] and its concomitant symbols and practices, around which the 'old nationalism' had centred, came under attack during the period of post-war reform and have continued to exist only with negative connotations attached (see later). This type of contemporary nationalism may be called 'prudent revivalist nationalism' in the sense that the revival of the positive values of some of the symbols and practices of 'old nationalism' is regarded as a necessary, if not sufficient, element of the new, prudent, nationalism of Japan.

Since the aim of this study is to examine the type of contemporary cultural nationalism associated with the *nihonjinron* and since it is businessmen who have a major place in this type of nationalism, our discussion has tended to focus on businessmen and has not dealt fully with the educators' views of contemporary Japanese nationalism. In this chapter I shall attempt to bridge this gap.

In the following discussion, I shall first examine the educators' (especially older educators') perceptions of 'prudent revivalist nationalism' – because it is to them that 'revivalist' nationalism was a weighty matter – and then compare the educators and the businessmen. It will be seen that the educators' perceptions of contemporary Japanese nationalism tended to vary considerably depending on the age group. Age differences were also present among businessmen but not so significant as among the educators. In contrast to the younger educators who were rather indifferent to nationalism, the sense of nationalism among older educators was latent but strong, and it was 'prudent revivalist nationalism' that characterised the older educators' orientation. Then, I shall compare and contrast 'resurgent cultural nationalism' and 'prudent revivalist nationalism' as perceived by the respondents, and conclude by considering the possibility of a merger between the two.

It should be noted that most of the material for this study was collected before the death of the Shōwa Emperor (Emperor Hirohito) in January 1989. Whether the Japanese perceptions of the emperor system have undergone any significant changes after his death is a subject that requires further research.

THE HISTORICAL BACKGROUND

Since 'revivalism' involves the process of restoring something that was lost in the past, it will be necessary to begin with the historical background to 'prudent revivalist nationalism'.

Following Japan's defeat in 1945, ultra-nationalism swiftly vanished from the scene. Of particular importance in this regard was the Occupation's attack on nationalist elements and ideals in the ideological, political and economic spheres (see Morris 1960: ch. 1; Brown 1955: ch. 11). Since the study is concerned with the ideological aspects of cultural nationalism, the discussion here will be restricted to those same aspects. In order to eradicate the foundations of nationalistic ideology thoroughly, the Occupation authorities were quick to attack its thought-control structure, namely, the education system and State Shinto (*kokka shintō*).

The educational system was the first ideological instrument to come under attack because it was the chief instrument of transmitting nationalistic spirit to the people. In October 1945, the Occupation authorities adopted measures to eliminate militarism and ultra-nationalism from education. Japanese authorities were ordered to prohibit the teaching of any nationalistic ideology in schools and to remove all teachers and textbooks associated with it (see Brown 1955: 244). A subsequent order prohibited school courses in ethics (*shūshin*) and Japanese history (which taught the myth of imperial origin as history). *The Imperial Rescript on Education*, a symbol of pre-war nationalism, was also a target for attack. The reading of the *Rescript*, which had become a semi-religious ritual in pre-war schools, was officially prohibited in October 1946. In June 1948 the *Rescript* itself was rescinded after the Basic Law of Education was enacted (see Morris 1960: 2).

The next Occupation attack on the ideological foundations of pre-war nationalism was directed to State Shinto. A directive of 15 December 1945 was aimed 'to prevent a recurrence of the perversion of Shinto theory and beliefs into militaristic and ultra-nationalistic propaganda designed to delude the Japanese people and lead them into wars of aggression' (SCAP Instruction, no. 448 quoted in ibid.: 3). The propagation of nationalistic ideology in the rituals, practices and observances of Shinto or any other religion, faith or philosophy was prohibited. Government support of State Shinto was strictly prohibited. Government officials were forbidden to support Shinto establishments and teachings; Shinto doctrines were forbidden to be taught at school; and allocations of public funds were forbidden to Shinto institutions. Also, *kigensetsu*, the national holiday of 11 February instituted in 1873 (marking the anniversary of the legendary founding of the 'nation' by Emperor Jimmu in 660 BC), was formally outlawed in 1948. The government was also prohibited from circulating *Kokutai no hongi* (The Principles of the National Polity) and *Shinmin no michi* (The Way of the Subject), the former being influential nationalist commentaries on the uniqueness of the Japanese polity. The eradication programme was extended further to other nationalistic symbols, with prohibitions against the official use of 'terms whose connotation in Japanese is inextricably connected with State Shinto, militarism, and ultra-nationalism' (ibid.), such as *Hakkō Ichiu* (The Eight Corners of the World under One Roof) and *Dai Tōwa Sensō* (Greater East Asia War). *Kamidana* (Shinto altars) were prohibited in all public buildings. By this directive the Occupation legally dissociated State Shinto from the affairs of state and ordered the proponents of Shinto to cease teaching nationalistic doctrines. To complete the separation of the state from State Shinto, it was required for the emperor himself to deny his divinity. Japan's occupation under the Supreme Command for Allied Powers (SCAP) continued from 1945 to 1953 (ibid.: 2–5).

Criticism also came from among Japanese thinkers. Criticisms were directed at the very heart of the notion of *kokutai* (national polity), the symbols and practices associated with it (such as the *Kimigayo* anthem and the Rising Sun flag, visits to Shinto shrines, the ethics course in the school curriculum), and the social and cultural legacies of feudalism (see chapter 2).

Despite all this, by the early 1950s nationalism had already begun to re-emerge. Demands for the revival of the ethics course in the curriculum and for the formulation of a substitute for the old imperial *Rescript* were increasing. Ronald P. Dore summarises three arguments used in such demands. The first emphasises that any national system of education should concern itself with moral instruction. In the West this is provided by Christianity. In pre-war and wartime Japan this was provided by State Shinto. The vacuum left by the disappearance of the system of moral instruction should be filled by a new formulation of a system that could coexist both with Japan's tradition and post-war democracy. Second, moral degeneration had become a feature of post-war Japan due to the 'misinterpretation of democracy' and the 'confusion of liberty with licence'. The way to stop this, it was suggested, was to restore moral instruction in schools. The third argument was that it was necessary to restore a sense of national pride, which had been lost in defeat (Dore 1952: 147–9).

In 1950 the Ministry of Education made statements encouraging the singing of the 'national anthem' and the flying of the 'national flag' at schools on special ceremonial occasions. It was often argued that the new form of patriotism must be distinguished from pre-war and wartime aggressive nationalism. However, the development of post-war nationalism involved a revival of some pre-war symbols and practices. The Rising Sun flag was once again waved, the *Kimigayo* anthem was sung on every occasion of importance, and people began to visit the Shinto shrines again in droves. A proposal to revive the former *kigensetsu* national holiday of 11 February gained increased popular support (Morris 1960: 121–2, 134). It was at length formally revived in 1966 as 'National Foundation Day'.

It is not our aim to give a lengthy account of the events related to the evolution of Japanese nationalism since the early post-war years. Suffice to observe that the two opposing sentiments have existed side by side throughout the post-war period. On the one hand, particular caution has been given to prevent a revival of those symbols and practices reminiscent of pre-war and wartime ultra-nationalism. Of course, as Morris remarks, there is '[nothing] inherently sinister in a country's revival of interest in its cultural traditions', but 'there is often a very thin line of demarcation between this form of revival and a desire to restore earlier social and political patterns' (1960: 140). In other words, the development of the new nationalism was supposed to centre around the revival of the symbols that had formerly surrounded the emperor system. On this point, Maruyama Masao remarks:

> Certain people laugh at the over-sensitivity of someone who reads into every such event a revival of ultra-nationalism or fascism. . . . But from the dynamics of political behaviour we know that an accumulation of everyday acts, at first glance unrelated to politics, can suddenly be transformed into great political energy.

> (Maruyama 1963: 152–3)

For this reason, Maruyama suggests, it is only natural that hoisting the national flag, reviving the national anthem, worshipping at Shinto shrines and reintroducing pre-war contents into national education should have been hotly debated. On the other hand, there has always been an argument that it is necessary to take steps to restore a sense of national pride and patriotism. The three arguments summarised by Dore earlier have been regularly repeated by post-war educationalists. The evolution of nationalism in post-war Japan may, therefore, be best seen in terms of the Occupation-imposed and self-imposed restraints on nationalism and reactions against these restraints. Education is one of the social areas in which conflicts between the restraints on nationalism and reactions against such restraints have been particularly evident.[2]

On the basis of this historical background, let us turn now to an examination of the perceptions of our respondents – mainly educators – regarding 'revivalist' nationalism.

'PRUDENT REVIVALIST NATIONALISM' AMONG EDUCATORS

It is important to examine the respondents' perceptions of the 'revivalist nationalism' paying particular attention to age differences. Considering that experience (or lack of experience) of the Second World War and the after-effects of Japan's defeat affects the perception of nationalism and that different age groups have experienced war-related events differently, respondents may be classified into the older, intermediate and younger age cohorts. (For the age composition of respondents, see chapter 6.)

The older cohort (The war generation)

The older cohort, or those respondents born before 1932 (aged 55 and over at the time of the interview), had received a part or the whole of their lower-secondary education by the end of the war. Whether or not an individual was old enough to attend lower-secondary school in wartime Japan is considered to make a significant difference in the learning of the pre-war and wartime values of society – a point which many respondents indicated. This group was old enough to form ideas about society before the end of the war and also to have a relatively clear recollection of pre-war or wartime Japanese society. They are the 'war generation' (senchūha). However, their wartime experiences varied depending on the age and individual. Among our respondents, only five were old enough to be conscripted into the military, and all of those were stationed in Japan. The war involved the rest of this age cohort either as a result of war mobilisation through recruitment and voluntary commitment for work in communities and factories or in the forced evacuation of school children.

Most of the educators of this generation were actively defensive concerning the 'revivalist' type of nationalism, expressing the view that the school should not play a role in promoting nationalism. The following response of a high school headmaster born in 1929 was illustrative:

Nationalism! That's not something for us [educators] to organise.

The remark of another schoolteacher that 'nationalism should be generated spontaneously' was also typical of the defensive reaction of older educators to this subject. Such defensiveness of older educators reflected their conscious attempts to dissociate themselves from the role with which pre-war educators had been associated: the role of inculcating nationalistic spirit in young people, thereby leading Japan to ultra-nationalism and militarism. It also reflected their sensitivity concerning the presence of the many controversial issues that had characterised the post-war educational scene (such as the semi-compulsory practice of hoisting the 'national' flag and singing the 'national' anthem at school ceremonies;[3] the content of history textbooks; the issues concerning ethics courses). Educators are expected to take a position on these issues and thereby to reveal their political orientation. Little wonder, therefore, that educators, especially headmasters who held an administrative position, were actively defensive as regards the subject of nationalism.

At the same time, however, the majority of the older educators tended to support the positive reinterpretation of some of the symbols and practices of the 'old nationalism', which seems to be at odds with their initial display of aloofness from this subject. It is this mixed attitude that characterised the orientations of older educators. They were concerned to remove the negative values that had been attached to some (and only some) of the key symbols and practices of the 'old nationalism', regarding it as a necessary condition in order to rebuild the solid foundation of 'wholesome' nationalism in contemporary Japan. In other words, the reconstruction of the 'wholesome' nationalism, it was thought, should begin by restoring what had been lost. (There are exceptions such as that represented by Mr I, whose life history was discussed in chapter 7 and who was consciously opposed to revivalism.)

The extent to which they supported symbols and practices of the 'old' nationalism varied from one individual to another. None of the respondents discussed the imperial institution except to state briefly that it was indispensable for Japan because first, the emperor was the 'symbol' of the nation, second, the imperial institution was a time-honoured tradition, third, the emperor was a fatherly figure for the Japanese, or fourth, no one else could replace the emperor in his role as the 'representative' of the nation (on such occasions as hosting foreign heads of state). Of course, the first statement that the emperor is the symbol of the nation is inclusive of others, but when this is said, it is often intended to emphasise a distinction between the pre-war emperor as a 'divine' source of authority and the post-war emperor defined in the post-war Constitution of 1947 as 'the symbol of the State and of the unity of the people, deriving his position from the will of the people with whom resides sovereign power'. However, no one could specify what had changed and what had not changed regarding the emperor as the 'symbol' of the nation. The unwillingness of respondents to discuss the emperor was partly due to the conservative tradition of not discussing this matter openly and partly because they had never seriously thought about the emperor.[4]

In discussions on 'revivalist' nationalism, respondents tended to refrain from mentioning the emperor system as such but rather to centre on some of the concrete symbols and rituals that had formerly surrounded the emperor system, in particular, the *Kimigayo* anthem and the Rising Sun flag – the two symbols that have come to be regarded in the post-war period as the very symbols of the pre-war nationalism and militarism. The compulsory practice of using these symbols in formal rituals such as school ceremonies has been, and still is, an object of criticism by a number of groups such as opposition political parties, the Japan Teachers' Union and liberal thinkers. Disagreements have continued to exist over whether or not these are the 'official' national anthem and flag.[5] The majority of the older educators felt duty-bound to see that the 'national' flag should be hoisted and the 'national' anthem sung on formal school ceremonies.

Why were older educators so concerned with the symbols and practices of the 'old nationalism'? There is little question that this was caused in part by the nostalgia they felt towards their younger days. Socialisation may be divided into three stages: socialisation of the young in the family, formal socialisation at school and adult socialisation. Each stage is important in its own way, but as far as the values of the nation and nationalism are concerned, most respondents regarded the middle school stage (from age 12 to 15) as having been most influential:

Values and ideas implanted in the middle school days cannot be easily forgotten. My wife is only five years younger than I am but thinks very differently about society. She was only a primary school pupil during the last years of the war. (A remark of a headmaster born in 1930)

Pre-war values were consciously or unconsciously relegated to the back of the minds of older educators in the self-critical period following Japan's defeat. However, a sentiment that has been suppressed can be rekindled and gradually brought back into consciousness with the gradual diminution of the self-critical mood of the nation. This was what seemed to have occurred with older respondents. The majority of the educators of the 'war generation', who had been old enough to internalise pre-war moral and social values, were sympathetic towards and/or highly evaluative of certain pre-war values and practices, such as respect for one's seniors and teachers, respect for the 'national' flag and anthem, the teaching of morals in class, strict discipline and so on.[6]

The positive orientation of older educators to certain symbols and practices associated with 'old nationalism' was more than just a simple, nostalgic response to the past. Rather, it reflected their more active awareness concerning the present issues regarding these national symbols. First, several of the older educators not only felt nostalgic about certain moral values they had acquired as youths but considered it desirable to revive them to a certain extent in order to discipline pupils. A few older educators went so far as to evaluate positively pre-war ethics courses. One may be tempted to conclude that this is an indication of their desire to revive the worship of the emperor. But it must be carefully understood that, when they remember such symbolism, they do not think much of the emperor *per se* but rather of traditional moral values and social ideals in general. This is shown by the fact that it was when they discussed the lack of discipline among present-day pupils that they touched upon the nationalistic symbolism of pre-war Japan. The following remark of a primary school headmaster (born in 1927) was illustrative:

Pupils today do not respect their teachers. They don't even know how to use proper language to their seniors. They talk to their teachers as if chatting to their friends. What is worse, younger teachers encourage this trend. This is indeed regrettable!

For some older educators, juvenile delinquency and the deteriorating standard of social manners among pupils were perceived in the same context as the issues of such 'old' nationalist symbols as the 'national' flag and anthem, and ethics courses. This tendency was particularly evident at a technical high school. (Technical schools normally get less studious pupils and have more serious disciplinary problems.) A headmaster (born in 1927) of a technical high school remarked on the militaristic disciplining of pupils in wartime Japan:

> I do not admire militarism but I think it is important to teach pupils how to use proper language to their teachers and respect their seniors and so forth in the manner education was done when I was younger.

It is not the pre-war 'emperor' as such but the system of moral values and social relations (which the 'emperor' symbolised) that they admired. Superficially, it may appear to be a question of how one thinks of the emperor as a national symbol; essentially, it deals with the affirmation of traditional moral values. But one could argue that this was, after all, the essence of the emperor system (*tennō-sei*). The notion of the emperor system itself refers to the political, social, cultural, psychological and other characteristics of Japanese society which the emperor, as a source of 'traditional authority', represented. In particular, it refers to a specific pattern of interpersonal relationships such as filial piety towards one's parents, loyalty to the power holder, paternalism, organic or quasi-familial and quasi-communal social relations and so on. In this, we are restating the interpretation, in a particular context, of a general view expressed by Emile Durkheim ([1912] 1964), who argues to the effect that religious society is only human society. Religion in the broad sense remains at the heart of any community, embodying a system of communal beliefs and practices renewed constantly by the group constituted by worshippers. Modern society, too, needs the periodic regeneration or ritual affirmations of the moral values necessary to a well-governed and 'good' society. Nationalistic rituals of pre-war Japan were exactly this kind of ceremonial in which the society reaffirmed the moral values of the society and renewed its devotion to those values by an act of 'communion'.

The pre-war emperor system certainly embodied these values, but it is too simplistic to argue that one's favourable orientation to these values will necessarily make one a nationalist desiring the revival of the old-style emperor system. All that can be stated here is that, when the headmaster of a technical high school discussed practices reminiscent of pre-war nationalism and school disciplinary matters together, he was suggesting that some of the pre-war style school rituals were useful practices to discipline pupils with particular reference to respect for one's seniors and the maintenance of order in society.

Furthermore and more importantly in terms of the number of responses, the older educators' revivalist concern was a *reaction* against the remaining *après-guerre* sentiment which had limited any expression of nationalism. The 'self-critical' or 'self-deprecating' attitude had long dominated in the post-war period. The majority of the older respondents, both educators and businessmen, expressed their frustration over the continuing self-imposed restraints on expressions of national pride. They argued that symbols and practices associated with 'old nationalism' (such as the emperor system, the 'national' flag and anthem, and the content of Japanese history teaching) had been held in disrepute for too long and that they should now be reinterpreted and constitute a foundation for Japan's new nationalism, provided that prudence was maintained. The following remark of a high school headmaster typified this reactive sentiment:

Pre-war nationalism went too far and led the country to the war. After the war, we went too far again, this time in the opposite direction, denying the values of anything that had to do with the pre-war system and thereby leaving the nation with only its outward form and without its heart. Thus, we have to put our national sentiment on its proper track.

Such reactive sentiment was directed against what respondents called 'progressive intellectuals' (*shimpo-teki chishikijin*), who had led post-war public opinion, and the Japan Teachers' Union. These had, in the view of respondents, gone too far in criticising symbols and practices connected with 'old nationalism'. The following remark of a schoolteacher born in the late 1920s was illustrative:

There is an atmosphere in which, if we praised our country, we would be called a rightist by so-called progressive intellectuals.

Other remarks also indicated the *reactive* nature of their support of the 'old' nationalist symbols. Another high school teacher said:

How absurd it is that we have to take the trouble to debate over something so natural and obvious! What's wrong with teaching our pupils morality and giving pupils the opportunity to sing our national anthem?

Also, a high school headmaster (born in 1929) remarked:

> There are no other countries in the world where you get criticised
> for flying the national flag and singing the national anthem. In
> Japan there are people who would not even let us do that. I
> envy Americans because they can fly their national flag at
> every important place and sing their anthem on every important
> occasion without causing much hassle.

It should be noted that the educational scene in Nakasato is
largely free of active opposition groups. The extent to which
people actively oppose the symbolism of 'old nationalism' varies
considerably depending on the region, since each region experienced
the war differently, has a different sort of internal politics, and has a
different political culture and history.[7]

The intermediate and younger cohorts

It is not easy to characterise the intermediate age group, or those
respondents born between 1933 and 1938 (aged between 49 and 54
at the time of the interview), because they did not appear to have any
special characteristics of their own regarding 'revivalist' nationalism.
They spent their childhood (or, to be more precise, a part or the whole
of their primary schooling) during the war but are supposed to have
been rather too young to form ideas about the wider world outside
their immediate groups such as family, peer group and school. All
one could do to characterise them is to state that they had the mixed
characteristics of the older and younger cohorts.

The majority of the younger teachers born after 1939 (aged 48
and under) tended to be indifferent to the subject of nationalism
in general and 'old' nationalism in particular. They neither strongly
supported nor opposed the symbolism of pre-war nationalism.
Unlike most older educators, who considered the positive reinterpretation of 'old' nationalist symbols to be necessary in order to rebuild
a solid foundation for contemporary nationalism, the younger generation had no strong sense of attachment to these classic symbols.
For them, national symbols did not have to centre around these
classic ones. But, unlike businessmen, younger educators had not
yet found, or were not concerned to find, any significant substitute
that might become a foundation upon which to express a renewed
sense of national pride and identity.

A comparison of educators and businessmen

An age difference was also found to exist among businessmen. Younger businessmen, like younger educators, tended to be indifferent towards 'revivalist nationalism'. Older businessmen's attitude towards 'revivalist' nationalism also tended to be favourable, mirroring their age-group counterparts in education. The observations about older educators apply on the whole to older businessmen also, except that they were not so actively conscious as older educators. That is, older businessmen tended not to express their sentiment about symbols associated with 'old' nationalism unless asked explicitly about their perceptions of them. The majority of the businessmen of the 'war-generation', too, considered it desirable to give more favourable meaning to certain 'old' symbols and practices. The lack of an 'active consciousness' among businessmen may be due to the fact, that, whereas there are those events and controversies in the work place of educators which reminded them regularly of such issues, such a reminder was relatively absent in the immediate working environment of businessmen. In other words, the older businessmen's favourable orientation to 'prudent revivalist' nationalism was less manifest than that of older educators.

'RESURGENT CULTURAL NATIONALISM' AND 'PRUDENT REVIVALIST NATIONALISM': A COMPARISON

Nationalism consists of two related yet distinct aspects: the aspects of 'identity' and 'solidarity'. The former is concerned with the exploration, formulation and emphasis of a nation's identity; the latter with the creation, maintenance and enhancement of solidarity among members of a nation. Let us now compare and contrast, as a way of summary, 'resurgent cultural nationalism' and 'prudent revivalist nationalism' from the standpoints of these two aspects of nationalism.

'Resurgent cultural nationalism'

What I call 'resurgent cultural nationalism' has centred around the thinking elites' formulation of ideas of Japanese distinctiveness (the *nihonjinron*), to which certain educated sections of the population have favourably responded. If national identity may be formulated

on the basis of the differentiation of a nation from others and/or
the affirmation of a specific vision of the historical continuity
of a nation, 'resurgent cultural nationalism' has promoted the
sense of the specificity of Japanese identity among the educated
(especially businessmen) mainly through the process of symbolic
boundary-marking of 'our own realm'. It has largely centred around
the 'spatial' dimension of national identity. (This is not to suggest
that the 'time' dimension is unimportant in 'resurgent cultural
nationalism', as was shown in chapter 5 by the academics' concern
to articulate the continued presence of social traditions in modern
Japanese society.) Businessmen, as the diffusers and recipients of
the *nihonjinron*, however, are on the whole predominantly concerned
with 'spatial' differentiation (see chapter 8).

In order to consider the 'solidarity' aspect of 'resurgent cultural
nationalism', two levels of collective experience may be classified:
the societal and intermediate-group levels. At the societal level,
one's interest in the *nihonjinron* does not intrinsically lead to the
maintenance and enhancement of national solidarity considering
that, first, such an 'intellectual' interest has been confined to
limited sections of the highly educated population. 'Resurgent
cultural nationalism' has remained a predominantly elite affair.
Second, the *nihonjinron* does not produce any tangible symbols and
practices through which the members of a nation can collectively
experience the 'communal time and space'. Rituals are an important
means of maintaining and enhancing the solidarity of a nation,
whether organic or associational. To borrow Durkheim's words,
'society cannot make its influence felt unless it is in action, and it
is not in action unless the individuals who compose it are assembled
together and act in common' ([1912] 1964: 418). The type of concern
with national identity manifested in the *nihonjinron* phenomenon does
not lead to the experience of any sort of rituals at the societal level.
At the level of the intermediate group or in the specific context of
the company, however, it has helped to maintain and enhance group
solidarity in the organic sense, as was seen in chapter 8. Thus, from
the 'solidarity' point of view, 'resurgent cultural nationalism' has
enhanced 'fragmentary nationalism' in the context of the company
but has not worked to enhance a sense of national solidarity at the
societal level.

'Prudent revivalist nationalism'

Although the *nihonjinron* significantly promotes the spatial sense of 'us' (the Japanese) against 'them' (the non-Japanese) among certain elite sections of the population, it does not affirm a stable vision of historical continuity. By contrast, 'revivalist nationalism' serves to reaffirm the nation's identity mostly through the 'time' dimension. The emperor system, in particular, is a symbol of particular importance to the historical longevity of the Japanese nation. Although, as mentioned earlier, most respondents, both educators and businessmen, hesitated to discuss the emperor system, its historical continuity is one exceptional aspect of the emperor system that many respondents were willing to stress. A headmaster born in the late 1920s discussed this point:

> Stories about the origin of our emperors are not true, but no one can deny the fact that the imperial family has continued for long, longer than anything else. As such it is an ideal national symbol. Nothing else can substitute the imperial family for this very reason. There is no compelling reason why it should not be respected as something to symbolise the Japanese nation. It would be so unrealistic if we did not do so.

A businessman in his early forties remarked on the *gengō* (the Japanese era according to which each emperor's reign constitutes one era reckoning, for example, 1985 as the sixtieth year of the Shōwa):

> The *gengo* system can be quite inconvenient. In discussing history, you have to be good at arithmetic to know when the fifteenth year of the Meiji or the twelfth year of the Shōwa are in the Western calendar system. Also, when you travel abroad and fill in your date of birth in the embarkation card, you have to recalculate the year in which you were born according to the Western era. I had looked at the negative side of Japan's era system, but since I learnt that in Taiwan they also have their own era system, I have come to think that the *gengō* system is not such a bad idea because it is one good way to give one a sense of belonging to a nation with a distinctive history.

In other words, the emperor system, as a 'primordial' symbol, gives the Japanese a comforting sense of historical continuity.

Also, symbols associated with 'old' nationalism are effective in conjuring up one's emotive sense of attachment to the nation. A schoolteacher in his late fifties remarked:

> I have heard stories from a former pupil of mine, now a middle-management executive, that he had once been moved to tears to hear the Japanese anthem when he was alone in a foreign country. He said, 'That was the time when I really felt how wonderful it was to be a Japanese'.

Thus, from the 'identity' point of view, 'revivalist nationalism' serves primarily to reaffirm a 'primordial' sense of the historical continuity of the nation. From the 'solidarity' perspective, 'prudent revivalist nationalism' offers much to consider. The pre-war emperor system was designed to create and enhance the solidarity of the Japanese through the notion of Japanese society as an organic whole, which rested comfortably on both its social base (the family system) and religious base (Shinto) as well as the successful synthesis of these secular and religious cultures. But, considering that in post-war Japan the *ie* (family) system has disintegrated and Shinto has lost its significance and the synthesis of the two is highly unlikely, one wonders if the emperor system has any significant role to play in contemporary Japan. Most respondents considered that the emperor system had retained its symbolic and integrative role without being able to specify what had changed and what had not changed about it. As regards the more concrete symbols and practices of 'old' nationalism which surrounded the emperor system, most older respondents regarded some of them as necessary for the integration of Japan, suggesting that the use of such symbolism in rituals was an important means of enhancing the sense of belonging to the Japanese nation. For example, several educators pointed out the importance of school rituals in this context where the 'national' anthem was played and the 'national' flag was hoisted and where pupils collectively experienced the sense of belonging to Japan. A headmaster said:

> Those pupils who grow up eating Western food and sleeping in a Western-style bed have no such opportunity to think of their country in their everyday life. Considering this, it's not such a bad idea to give them opportunities at school ceremonies to remind them occasionally of their sense of belonging to the nation.

Thus, from the 'solidarity' perspective, 'revivalist nationalism' is intended to reaffirm the solidarity of a nation through the collective experience of rituals and other symbolic practices.

A MERGER BETWEEN THE TWO TYPES OF NATIONALISM?

We conclude this study with some further remarks on the emperor system (*tennō-sei*). The aim of the present study is to examine the type of cultural nationalism associated with the *nihonjinron*, not the type of nationalism related to the emperor system. Besides, the emperor system is too large a topic to be fully dealt with within the scope of this study. None the less, it will be worthwhile at least to touch briefly upon the emperor system insofar as it is considered to be related to the *nihonjinron* and to raise some questions about it, considering that the emperor system was at the heart of 'old nationalism' and that there is literature to suggest a linkage of the *nihonjinron* with the emperor system.

As has been suggested earlier, neither the *nihonjinron* type of cultural nationalism nor 'revivalist nationalism' provides an independent basis for inclusive nationalism or has a strong appeal to large sections of the population. The question one might ask here is: will there be an eventual 'merger' between the *nihonjinron* type of cultural nationalism and 'revivalist nationalism'? In fact, there is a view which suggests that the *nihonjinron* will eventually be linked to the emperor system.

I shall consider the relationship of the *nihonjinron* to the emperor system by way of an assessment of such a view.

'The linkage view'

According to what for the sake of convenience may be called the 'linkage view', the type of nationalism associated with the *nihonjinron* will eventually be linked to the emperor system. Such a prediction is made on the basis of the compatibility assumed to exist between the ideology of the *nihonjinron* and the ideology of the emperor system.

Three areas of 'compatibility' may be pointed out. First, the *nihonjinron*'s assumption concerning the uni-racial composition of the Japanese is seen as compatible with the emperor ideology, which regards the imperial family as descended directly from the Sun Goddess and blessed with an unbroken lineage. The pre-war nationalistic ideology was formed through the manipulation of the notions of the family system (*ie*) as well as ancestor worship (Shinto), according to which all Japanese families – and therefore all Japanese subjects – had stemmed from the imperial family as the main family, thereby being united in worshipping the common ancestor. Such a familial nation is, by definition, 'uni-racial' (in the sense of the common origin of the Japanese).

Second, one's attachment to the communal and familial group, a notion emphasised in the *nihonjinron*, is also supposed to be inseparable from the emperor system. The intuitive, 'non-logical' and 'non-rational' modes of communication, which are regarded popularly and by scholars as the product of the homogeneous composition of the 'Japanese race', are another area of affinity felt with the emperor ideology, which is a highly non-rational system of ideas. The emperor ideology, 'invented' on the basis of social culture (familism) and religious culture (Shinto), was designed to appeal to the affects, not the reason, of the people. That it was also a taboo to think logically and rationally about the emperor before and during the Second World War is indicative of the non-rationalistic nature of the emperor ideology.[8]

The third area of compatibility is related to the first and the second. To regard the Japanese as a 'uni-racial', familial nation is to regard Japanese society as a monolithic whole, thereby characterising Japan as a 'classless' society, a point emphasised in the *nihonjinron*. The organic (not associational) concept of the state, a main feature of the emperor ideology, is intended to transcend classes (see e.g. Hijikata 1983).

The proponents of this view argue that the type of interest and sentiment promoted by the *nihonjinron* will eventually be integrated into the more elaborate ideology of the emperor system. For example, Hijikata Kazuo (1983: 55) argues that the episodic manner of reference to everyday cultural experience, a method commonly employed in the *nihonjinron*, is a most effective method for elites to establish a specific political thesis among the 'ordinary' people. He maintains that the essence of Japanese national culture will eventually be sought in the ideology of the emperor system and that this is manifested in the way Japanese culture is discussed in the *nihonjinron* which 'disguises itself as an academic activity' (ibid.: 56), but is actually a means of ideological manipulation. Hijikata maintains that the revival of nationalism is facilitated by the presence of the emperor ideology which is dormant but alive in the mentality of the people (ibid.: 65–71).

Regarding the nature of the emperor system in post-war Japan, Yamada Takao maintains that 'the emperor system which the ruling strata are manipulating today is not a revived version of the pre-war type emperor system characterised by divine authority and absolutism but the post-war type which is a kind of bourgeois monarchy "harmonised" perfunctorily with the notion that sovereignty rests with the people' (1981b: 121–2). Although there are a minority of right-wing groups who demand the revival of the pre-war style emperor system as the political and legal authority, the major trends are to be found among 'business circles and conservative ideologues [who] value the emperor as [a source] of spiritual and cultural authority' (ibid.), or as a source of dominant ideology, to reinforce monopoly of capital and the integration of the national community. (On dominant ideology, see chapter 8). To illustrate this point, Yamada refers to speeches made at the Convention of the Western Japan Keizai Dōyūkai (employers' Committee for Economic Development) in 1978, where participating business leaders stressed the necessity for the 'enrichment of national consciousness' through the 'formation of wholesome national sentiment towards the imperial family' (quoted in Yamada 1981a: 45). The following statement made by a member of the Fukui Keizai Dōyūkai is illustrative:

> It is the imperial family that has elevated and maintained the standard of our traditional culture since antiquity. . . . How we pass on this precious heritage of our country, the imperial family, to succeeding generations is not only our responsibility to our children and grandchildren but also fundamental to guarding this free society. . . . More adequate consideration should be given in education to the imperial family which has an important meaning [in our lives].
>
> (Quoted in ibid.: 44–5)

Jon Halliday depicts *tennōism* (emperorism) as 'the main specific feature of Japanese bourgeois ideology', arguing that 'the key feature is *not* "Emperor *worship*" as such, but the "validation" of authoritarianism' (1975: 263), because

> Tennōism arbitrarily 'legitimates' the flow of authority from the top. Subordinates must obey their 'superiors' without question, and rights are severely circumscribed. Tennōism creates a climate where reason and justice are ostracized: where the term

'benevolence' covers a panoply of terror and violence in family, school, army and factory.

(Halliday 1975: 263)

Halliday then shows how the *nihonjinron* and the emperor ideology play a similar role in promoting the interests of the capitalists. Earlier (in chapter 9) we saw Halliday arguing that 'group solidarity is an ideological weapon' (1975: 229–30) and referring to Nakane Chie's theory of 'vertical society' as a 'sophisticated expression' of the ideology that Japan is a classless society. Similarly, the ideology of *tennōism*

> serves capitalists, and meshes with the attempt to deny the existence of classes in Japan. All being subjects of the Emperor, questions such as one's location in the production process alleg-edly become irrelevant. Tennōism attempts to eliminate the right to stake demands; the denial of class operates to deny the possibility of class interests, and thus the ground on which demands might be advanced.

(Halliday 1975: 264)

There are two different levels of argument here, the general and the Marxist. At the general level, the 'linkage theory' maintains that the *nihonjinron* will eventually be absorbed and incorporated into the emperor system on the basis of the assumption that the emperor ideology encompasses the basic characteristics of Japanese social culture similar to those emphasised in the *nihonjinron*. At the Marxist level of argument, criticisms are directed against bourgeois nationalism which threatens working-class solidarity. The following assessment will be restricted to the general level of discussion, as the subject of Marxist perspectives on cultural nationalism is another topic too large to be included in this study.

Fragmentary nationalism in contemporary Japan

The 'linkage perspective' sketched in the previous section on the relationship of the *nihonjinron* ('resurgent cultural nationalism') to the emperor system ('revivalist nationalism') is simplistic and should be doubted on the following grounds.

First, the 'linkage view' is based on a simplistic assumption that those favourably oriented to the *nihonjinron* will also support con-servative ideology in general and the emperor system in particular. An interest in the *nihonjinron* does not necessarily lead to an interest in the emperor system, as is typically shown in the case of the younger businessmen, who were strongly attracted to the thinking elites' ideas of Japanese cultural uniqueness but uninterested in the emperor system. The reverse is also true, as is shown in the case of older educators who were positively oriented to 'old' nationalist symbolism but not to the *nihonjinron*. In other words, nationalism in contemporary Japan is *fragmentary* in the sense that different social groups and different individuals have different perceptions of and attitudes towards the ways in which Japanese national identity and solidarity should be reaffirmed and reconstructed.[9] This is because different social groups and individuals relate ideas of national identity in different ways to their practical activities and concerns.

It has proven important in the course of our discussion to examine carefully one's immediate circumstances in order to analyse one's orientation to a particular ideology. The orientation of an individual to a particular ideology is largely dependent upon that individual's specific concern in his or her immediate setting. For example, businessmen tended to be positively oriented to the *nihonjinron* because ideas of the distinctiveness of Japanese social culture provided them with useful perspectives on Japanese management and business practices in the international context. One of the reasons why older educators tended to be positively oriented to 'old nationalism' was that they found some of the practices associated with the emperor system (such as rituals designed to enhance the virtues of filial piety and respect for one's seniors) had a practical use in disciplining pupils. Other social groups – farmers, manual workers, artists, religious groups, bureaucrats, politicians and so on – are expected to have their own perceptions of national identity and their own versions of nationalism.

Second, and as a continuation of the first point, the 'linkage view' is based on the assumption that various types of nationalism in contemporary Japan – one of which is that type of nationalism associated with the *nihonjinron* – will eventually be integrated into a coherent system of ideologies and policies and that the ideology of the emperor system will serve this integrative role. However, is it not also possible to suppose that nationalism in Japan will *remain* 'fragmentary'? The task of primary nationalism was certainly to create 'national' identity – where there was only the 'ethnic' identity of the Japanese – and to unify the nation by 'inventing' the nation's tradition. Where national identity and unity are already evidently present, is it not too simplistic to assume that any idea that touches upon the communal and familial aspects of Japanese society, the non-logical modes of thinking and uni-racial consciousness, will eventually be absorbed into a more comprehensive system of nationalist ideology, which, according to the proponents of the 'linkage view', is the emperor system?

The above leads to the third point, namely, that the 'linkage view' simplistically assumes that the *nihonjinron*'s emphasis on the 'familial' and 'communal' characteristics of Japan's social culture will *necessarily* be absorbed into the emperor system.[10] Although it is true that these social characteristics were inseparable elements of the emperor system for about three quarters of a century before 1945, it is equally true that after 1945 the traditional family institution (*ie*) and village community (*mura*) themselves have disintegrated. Furthermore, familial and communal characteristics have come to be associated predominantly with the company organisation, and the 'familial' and 'communal' Japanese company organisation has proven to have performed productively without an appeal to the emperor system. This suggests that the emphasis on communal and familial social relations does not necessarily lead to an absorption of such characteristics into the emperor system. Also, the 'linkage view' simplistically identifies communalism and familism as unchanging features of the emperor system and fails to take into account that a tradition can be 'reinvented' to adjust to changing social, cultural and political conditions. But it is not the purpose of the present study to predict how the emperor institution will be 'reinvented'.

In addition to these three questions raised against the 'linkage theory', which regards the 'revivalist nationalism' associated with the emperor system as the major foundation of contemporary Japanese nationalism, there is another point that may be considered with regard to revivalism. We cannot ignore the presence of groups of people who explicitly oppose the revival of 'old' nationalism. Although there is little doubt that some of the symbolic rituals of 'old' nationalism often 'function' to enhance national solidarity, we should also keep in mind that rituals also work in the opposite way. Robert Bocock argues that rituals 'may also make some groups feel less part of the national group in that they are made conscious of the fact that they do not share some of the values which seem to lie behind the group's ritual' (1974: 98), such as respect for established authority and military virtues. As an example, he cites some groups in Britain (such as radical youth) who find their sense of separatedness from the 'mainstream' society reinforced when they witness rituals involving the royal family (e.g. Trooping the Colour, the Queen's Christmas Day speech, the State Opening of Parliament). The same is true with similar ritual occasions in Japan. There have always been and still are significant numbers of people whose opposition to nationalistic values are reinforced precisely because of the existence of these 'nationalistic' rituals. For example, there are a number of people who oppose ritualistic occasions associated with nationalism such as ceremonies on the 'National Foundation Day', the official visits of cabinet ministers to the Yasukuni Shrine (where the war dead, including war criminals, are enshrined), the display of the 'national' flag and the singing of the 'national' anthem at school ceremonies and so on. For them, such rituals are nothing but a reminder of their opposition to nationalism.

The question we have been considering is: will there be an eventual merger between 'resurgent cultural nationalism' and 'prudent revivalist nationalism'? All we can conclude at present on the basis of the available material is that it is too simplistic to expect such a merger on the basis of the similarities between the two value systems. Whether the emperor institution will serve to integrate other forms of nationalism such as the type of cultural nationalism associated with the *nihonjinron* will depend on a number of factors. But such a prediction is not the concern of this study.

FINAL REMARKS

In concluding this study, it may be helpful to offer a couple of remarks of clarification concerning the term nationalism and the phenomenon of cultural nationalism. First, although the social scientific nature of the term nationalism should be clear from the preceding discussion, clarification here may assist in avoiding misinterpretation, since this term is also used in popular discourse in various ways with differing connotations depending on national and historical circumstances. 'Nationalism' refers broadly to the sentiment among a people that they compromise a community with distinctive characteristics and the will to maintain and enhance that distinctiveness within an autonomous state. Employing the concept of nationalism in this manner, this study has focused on a selected aspect of nationalism, enquiring into the process of cultural nationalism by which the national cultural identity has been reinvented, maintained and promoted in contemporary Japanese society.

The evaluation of nationalism differs depending on the individual and the social group as well as the wider socio-economic and historical context. Sometimes nationalism may serve as a guard against the symbolic or physical violence of assertive foreign powers; sometimes it may become a source of oppression itself. Similarly, cultural nationalism may help to reaffirm and preserve the diversity of world cultures against the homogenising effect of dominant foreign cultures or civilisations. But it also has the potential to hinder international understanding through an execessive emphasis on the nation's uniqueness.

Second, in relation to cultural nationalism, it is not my purpose to claim that Japan's cultural nationalism is necessarily stronger than that of other countries. Rather, the issue of cultural nationalism is equally relevant in other parts of the world, including the countries of Europe and north America. In fact, cultural nationalism as the project of creating, preserving and strengthening a people's national identity is an integral feature of the classical view of the modern international order.

Notes

1 INTRODUCTION (pp. 1–8)

1 For a useful exposition of cultural nationalism, see Hutchinson 1987, especially ch. 1.

2 According to a survey by the Nomura Research Institute (1978: 3), approximately seven hundred books were published between 1946 and 1978 on the theme of Japanese peculiarities, 58 per cent of which were published after 1970 and 25 per cent of which appeared in the peak period between 1976 and 1978. (The percentages have been calculated by Sugimoto and Mouer [1982: 13] on the basis of this survey.) This is, however, an underestimate of the range of the *nihonjinron* literature, as this survey only counts those titles with the designation 'Japanese' or with obviously Japanese concepts. The *nihonjinron* as an attempt to articulate Japanese uniqueness and as an exemplifier of a cultural mode of thinking far exceeds this figure.

3 For example, the journal *Gendai Shakaigaku* (Review of Contemporary Sociology) (vol. 7, no. 1, 1980) featured the *nihonshakairon* (discussions of Japanese society). The monthly journal *Shisō no Kagaku* (The Science of Thought) carried critical articles on the *nihonjinron* continuously from 1984 to 1985. Sugimoto Yoshio and Ross Mouer organised a conference on this topic in Australia in 1980 and published the conference papers in *Social Analysis* (no. 5/6, 1980). Also, the National Museum of Ethnology in Japan held a conference on this and related topics in 1983. The English report of the conference is published in Umesao Tadao, Harumi Befu and Josef Kreiner (eds) *Senri Ethnological Studies: Japanese Civilization in the Modern World* (no. 16, 1984).

4 An exception may be those ideological critics who claim that the *nihonjinron* have been produced for the ruling class to dominate the subordinate sections of the population, but they simply confine themselves to an ideological critique without engaging in an empirical examination.

5 One exception is Peter Dale (1986), but he only mentions the German experience, and in a sketchy manner.

6 On the definition of nationalism, see, for example, Smith (1971, 1973). There are a number of other ways of classifying the types

of nationalism. For a summary of the typologies, see, for example, Smith (1971: chs 8 and 9); Breuilly (1982). See also Seton-Watson (1977); Snyder (1964, 1976).

7 The term intelligentsia was first used in Russia in the nineteenth century to refer to those who held professional occupations with their university degrees, but its meaning has been subsequently extended to include all those engaged in non-manual or new-middle-class occupations. The intellectuals, on the other hand, comprise the much smaller group of those who possess this distinctive feature: 'direct concern with the culture of a society' (Bottomore 1964: 70). The boundaries between the two groups are difficult to determine with precision. For example, the lower levels of the group of intellectuals merge with middle-class occupations such as journalism.

8 It is Professor Percy Cohen who first used the term 'thinking elites' during our conversation. My thanks to him for these insights.

9 One possible criticism that I foresee being directed against this study is the claim that I underestimate the role of the state in cultural nationalism. It is not claimed in these pages, however, that the role of the state is unimportant. There is no question that the state plays an important role in cultural nationalism in contemporary Japan. After all, the state runs education to a considerable extent, and businessmen are tied to the state in one way or another. But the role of the state is too large a topic to be included in this study, requiring treatment in a separate work (see chapter 10, n. 2).

2 THE *NIHONJINRON* (pp. 9–38)

1 On anti-intellectualism in England, see, for example, Bottomore, who remarks: 'In Britain, intellectuals have not possessed such great social prestige as in France, nor have they been so prominent in political life, either by membership of parliament, or by any collective activity of social thought and criticism' (1964: 75).

   For the British antipathy towards modern sociology, see, for example, Abercrombie *et al.* (1984: 8–10). In addition to the traditionalism, empiricism and individualism of British culture, the authors give three other reasons for the British objection to sociology: the hostility of the academic establishment towards the new discipline, the misconception of sociology as simply jargon, and the charge that it is politically biased towards the left. Marsland (1988) wrote a lengthy criticism of the anti-management bias of sociology. The day following the publication of Marsland's book, the *Daily Mail* carried a nearly page-long review article, entitling it 'Sociologists . . . the saboteurs of Britain' (31 March 1988, p. 6). This itself is another example of the English dislike of sociology.

   I also suppose that different attitudes towards sociology in England and other countries are caused in part by the different types of social development England and other countries have experienced. Whereas other societies, which have experienced *conscious* industrialisation, have given a role to scholars of society to play in the development of society, the original, piecemeal and *unconscious* process of industrialisation in England has given no such opportunity. Even in France, Saint-Simon's concern with industrial society was to bring it about consciously.

2 There has been an increasing growth of interest among the Japanese in the other parts of Asia in the 1980s. It is questionable whether this is the instrumental concern of the Japanese with remarkable economic performance in the newly industrialising countries or their 'romantic' interest in the 'simpler' way of life in still developing areas.

3 Among the many books on intercultural communication are Condon and Saito (eds) (1974), Condon (1980) and Naotsuka (1980). The Japanese translation (1966) of Edward Hall's *The Silent Language* (1959) was also widely read.

4 This may be shown by the fact that both Nakane and Doi reiterated their theories at a conference on intercultural communication held in 1972. The conference papers are compiled in Condon and Saito (eds) (1974).

5 *Mono no aware* is usually translated as 'the pathos of things'. But R.A. Miller argues that philologically *mono* does not refer to objects in the external world: 'For him (Motoori) . . . *mono no aware* had nothing to do with "things"; it was rather a feeling or sensibility (*aware*) modified by "some, certain, some . . . or other" (*mono*)' (1971: 217).

6 Some of the earlier exponents of a group model who had international impact are Embree (1939) and Benedict (1946).

7 There are numerous other works on groupism. For example, folklorist Araki Hiroyuki's *The Patterns of Behaviour of the Japanese* (1973) is another representative work on groupism.

8 'Contextualism' is Hamaguchi's own translation for his notion *kanjin-shugi*. I prefer 'interpersonalism' because it is more faithful to the original meaning. See Hamaguchi (1977, 1980, 1982).

9 A conscious distinction is not usually made between 'group orientation' and 'interpersonalism' (or 'contextualism'). Sociologist Hazama Hiroshi uses the term 'groupism', noting that 'the "desirable" relationship between the individual and the group in the context of [Japanese] groupism is not that of antagonism but of identification [and fusion]' (1971: 16).

10 The Japanese personality traits are characterised in the *nihonjinron* as maternal (feminine) and tolerant and harmonious; Western personality traits as paternal (masculine), intolerant, and aggressive and antagonistic.

Psychologist Kawai Hayao (1976), following the tradition of Carl G. Jung's psychoanalytic theories, argues that Japan is a 'mother-dominated' society. Kawai contrasts the 'maternal principle', which is based on the notion of the mother's indiscriminate or egalitarian love, and the 'paternal principle', which stresses the primacy of individual rights. Based on the assumption that the different degrees of balance and tension between the two principles account for the different social and cultural features observed in Japan and the West, Kawai characterises Japan as a mother-dominated society as contrasted with the father-dominated society of the West. He argues, for example, that, behind some social problems in Japan such as the presence of a large number of children refusing to go to school, there exists a characteristic feature of the 'mother-dominated society', which is the incomplete development of ego. This theory is related closely to Doi's theory of *amae*. Sabata Toyoyuki (1964) also describes Japan as a 'feminine society', the characteristics of which include reliance on affectivity rather than on reason and logic. Another manifestation of the maternal–paternal dichotomy is the polytheism (animism) of Japan and the monotheism of the West.

11 There are also Sabata's model (1966) of the 'carnivorous' (and therefore assertive) Western mentality and the 'vegetarian' (and therefore less assertive) Japanese mentality, and Tamaki's rice agriculture model of Japanese society (1977).

12 Although the popularity of this book is certainly attributable to its content, it may also be due to the mystery surrounding the identity of BenDasan. BenDasan has never made a public appearance even at the bestowal ceremony when he won the 1970 Ōya Prize, Japan's very distinguished award for essay-form literature. He says in his book that he is a Jew born and raised in Japan, but a popular view holds that he is a well-known Japanese social critic.

13 Robert Miles (e.g. 1982a, 1982b, 1987) criticises this usage of the 'race' concept. Miles argues from a Marxist perspective that it is necessary to distinguish between phenomenal forms ('the surface appearance of the way in which the world is organised') and essential relations ('the real, underlying relations'), or to recognise that the former may actually obscure the latter (1982a: 31). Miles thus considers it *the* task of sociology to identify the ideological, political and economic processes (with special emphasis given to the nature of capitalism and class formation) by which the category of 'race' has been created and reproduced; otherwise, he says, sociologists would end up legitimating the 'false problematic' of race.

14 My definition of race is a slight modification of that of Van den Berghe who defines race as 'a human group that defines itself and/or is defined by other groups as different from other groups by virtue of innate and immutable physical characteristics' (1978: 9).

15 There is abundant literature on the origins of the Japanese, such as Jinruigaku Kōza Hensan Iinkai (eds) (1978) and Hanihara (1984).

16 On the Korean minority in Japan, see Lee and DeVos (1981).

17 Since the mid-1980s migrant workers (mostly working illegally) from South-east Asian countries such as Bangladesh, Pakistan and the Philippines have increased in number. Debates on whether Japan should allow foreigners to work as manual workers have become prevalent among opinion formers.

18 A.D. Smith also indicates, albeit from a different perspective, that race thinking developed out of ethnic sentiment. He remarks that, although 'both racism and nationalism refer back, ultimately, to the same basic unit, the ethnic group and its traditional correlate, ethnocentrism', they have developed in the opposite directions: nationalism has

strengthened 'the cultural basis of the community, while dropping the old ideas of centrality and superiority' because 'in an increasingly interdependent world, it has become simply impossible in the long run for particular ethnic states to operate as if other ethnic states possessed no value at all'; racism 'has emphasised the ideas of centrality, group rightness and superiority, but dropped the cultural basis of ethnocentric prejudice. Instead, it has elevated to first place ethnocentrism's rather secondary physical prejudices' (Smith 1979: 90–2).

19 Consider, for example, Robert Knox's *The Races of Men* (1850). Gobineau's *Essai sur L'inégalité des Humaines* ([1853–55] 1915) and many other books published between that time and the end of the Second World War. On the doctrine of racism, see, for example, Banton (1970, 1977) and Van den Berghe (1978).

20 The concept of property seldom, if ever, appears in the study of ethnicity and nationalism, and everyday use of this term is normally restricted to objects of material value, but it can be expanded to include symbolic property. For the application of the notion of property to social relations, see Hollowell (1982). I am indebted to Professor Tsurumi Kazuko for suggesting the use of this concept to describe the Japanese perception of their uniqueness.

21 For the literature on the relationship between blood type and personality traits, see Hayashida (1976: 128–81).

22 On pre-war studies on blood type, see Hayashida (1976: 144–59).

23 According to Nomi's survey (1973: 256), only 5 per cent of his respondents consider that there is no relation between blood type and personality.

24 Both Nomi and Suzuki realise the multifaceted nature of personality, considering it impossible to identify rigorously standard personality characteristics for each of the four blood types.

25 Interestingly, both Nomi and Suzuki point out the similarity between the Japanese and the Germans.

26 For a cogent discussion of functionalism or the holistic approach, see Percy S. Cohen (1968: ch. 3).

27 Piers and Singer (1953) argue that guilt 'inhibits and condemns transgression' and shame 'demands achievement of a positive goal'. This is related to Freud's identification of shame as the motivation associated with 'the ego ideal involving a positive achievement' and guilt as the motivation associated with superego formation (see DeVos 1960: 288). George DeVos criticises such dichotomy as an oversimplified division between shame and guilt. DeVos points out that Western scholars are blind to the strong sense of guilt among the Japanese because they 'tend to look for guilt, as it is symbolically expressed, in reference to a possible transgression of limits imposed by a generalized ideology or religious system . . .' (ibid.). DeVos saw the prototype of Japanese guilt in the sense of obligation in the child to recompense for the mother's self-sacrifice. Guilt for the Japanese is thus understood to arise at least in part from 'one's empathetic feelings for the pain and sacrifice suffered by another person' (see Lebra 1976: 13).

28 See also Tsurumi (1947).

29 See, e.g. Lebra (1976).
30 For example, Watsuji (1951) and Tsuda (1948).
31 I myself was attracted to intercultural communication in the mid-1970s and eventually participated in the discussion of 'peculiar' patterns of behaviour of the Japanese. Looking back, I, like many others, was under the influence of the spirit of the times then. The present work is, therefore, one result of my learning process during the past decade.

3 IDEAS OF NATIONAL DISTINCTIVENESS (pp. 39–67)

1 A section of this chapter appeared in altered form in Japanese as 'Cultural nationalism and two types of ideas of national distinctiveness', *Sophia University Studies in Sociology* 15 (1990).
2 On Ottomanism and Turkism, see Kushner (1977: 3–5); Lewis (1968: 323–43).
3 The development of Turkism was inspired by several sources. On this, see Lewis (1968: 343–9); Kushner (1977: 5).
4 In India both cultural and political nationalism appeared at different stages. See McCully (1966: 191–8); Heimsath (1964: 139–43); Desai (1966: 199, 323–34, 347ff); Hutchinson (1987: 42–5).
5 I owe these examples to Hutchinson (1987: 14).
6 ibid.: 15.
7 On *kokugaku*, see, e.g. Matsumoto (1957); Haga (1963); Ōkubo (1963); Maruyama (1952); Harootunian (1988).
8 Prior to the development of *kokugaku*, another school of thought emerged to systematise Japan's history. In the second half of the seventeenth century Tokugawa Mitsukuni (1628–1700), the daimyō of the Mito district, established an academy chiefly concerned with historical scholarship and to that aim historians were gathered around him. The most notable achievement of this school was the compilation of *Dai Nihonshi*, a voluminous work of history of Japan from the foundation of the imperial dynasty to the late fourteenth century. There is little question that this school stimulated intellectual interest in traditions of Japan.
9 *Kojiki* covers the period from the mythical creation of Japan to the reign of Emperor Suiko (AD 554–628).
10 The social backgrounds of the *kokugaku* scholars discussed here are as follows: Keichū was a Buddhist monk; Kada no Azumamaro was born the son of a Shinto priest; Kamo no Mabuchi was a Shinto priest; Motoori Norinaga was of merchant family background.
11 We should not overgeneralise about the interests of various *kokugaku* scholars. Whereas Mabuchi was certainly interested in the simple, archaic and uncorrupt, Norinaga was not necessarily drawn to these themes. Norinaga's interest was extended to cover later works such as *The Tale of Genji* (early eleventh century) and *Kokinshū* (early twelfth century). I thank Kate Nakai for her useful comments on *kokugaku*.
12 Some of the *nihonjinron* have been written by historians, but their perspective is not necessarily historical.

13 This is based on my content analysis of end-of-the-year editorials in five London-based newspapers from 1945 to 1984.

14 I do not suggest, however, that historical memories are completely irrelevant in secondary nationalism. In a recent article qualifying his historicist theory of ethnicity and nationalism, Smith admits that historical memories are not so directly relevant as a national symbol in the long-formed and well-established nations of the West as in smaller and more contested nations, remarking that 'citizens tend to take their [historical] myths and memories for granted; only a minority speak of Saxon liberties or Gallic ancestry, let alone Varangian forbears' (Smith 1988: 10).

15 According to the Kohn dichotomy of 'Western' (political and associational) nationalism and 'Eastern' (cultural and organic) nationalism, the former includes England, British Dominions, France, the Netherlands and Switzerland; the latter central and eastern Europe and Asia.

16 German Romanticism was 'an interpretation of life, nature, and history and this philosophic character distinguished it from romanticism in other lands' (Kohn 1960: 49).

17 Influenced by Herder's legacy, Fichte and other German Romantics advanced a more simplified idea on the language question. For them, nations are language groups and nationalism is a linguistic movement.

18 Although the notion of mysterious *Volksgeist* characterised true Romanticism and was frequently mentioned in the writings of the eighteenth and nineteenth centuries, it was not accepted by all nationalist thinkers. For example, when Brockhaus posited national individuality and language and common descent as the chief constituent factors of the nation, he did not use the Romanticists' expression of 'national soul'. In a study of key terms of nationalism, Kemiläinen (1964: 130) remarks that national 'spirit' did not always mean something mystical and transcendental because, when 'spirit' or 'soul' was mentioned, national modes of thinking and behaving were often meant.

19 On cultural nationalism in Denmark, see Thyseen (1980).

20 For a comparison of Herder's and Rousseau's ideas of nationalism, see Barnard (1983).

21 This is not to suggest that Indian nationalism is different in kind rather than degree from other nationalisms. For, as John Hutchinson points out (in a personal correspondence), it is common, if not universal, for nationalists to argue that their nation has made a unique contribution to a wider civilisation. For example, 'the Irish see themselves as apostles of Catholic Christianity; the Russians as the preservers of Orthodoxy; the Arabs as the vanguard of Islam and of science and philosophy in the Middle Ages. Even German nationalists in the early nineteenth century spoke of their destiny to unify Europe under the aegis of Christianity rather than rationalism and militarism like the French'.

22 My thanks to John Hutchinson for pointing this out.

23 Herder did not deny the role of institutions. In fact, he recognised the formative role played by institutions (e.g. religious, educational, familial) in the nation's infancy, and also, as Berlin (1976: 163) points

out, Herder regarded national identity as constantly changing through non-metaphysical factors such as educational institutions, relationships with neighbouring countries and climate. I am indebted to John Hutchinson for pointing this out.

24 One of the explicit challenges on the common-sense notion of society is presented by Michael Mann. Mann argues that 'human beings are social, not societal' (1986: 14).

4 THEORIES OF ETHNICITY AND NATIONALISM (pp. 68–86)

1 Portions of this chapter appeared in Japanese as 'Developments in and problems concerning theories of ethnicity', *Japanese Sociological Review* 37, 4 (1987), and are reproduced by permission of the Japan Sociological Society.

2 For a concise discussion of ambiguity surrounding the Japanese territory to the north-east of Hokkaidō, Japan's northernmost main island, and to the south of Kyūshū, its southernmost main island, see Lehmann (1982: 7–8).

3 See Okamura (1981: 452–65).

4 I am grateful to Professor Percy S. Cohen for his insightful comments on the relationship between the culturalist and boundary perspectives on ethnicity, which he illustrated with this example.

5 I have benefited from Epstein's (1978: 2) reading of Geertz.

6 The term 'modernism' is first used in this sense by Smith (1984: 452–61). The term 'historicism' has been used in a number of ways and, therefore, carries diverse connotations. I use this term to refer to the view that social and cultural phenomena are best understood in the context of historical development.

7 A useful summary and evaluation of Smith's thesis is provided in Hutchinson (1987: chs 6 and 7).

8 For a critical assessment of Armstrong's approach, see Smith (1984).

9 For a critical discussion of Deutsch's thesis, see also Smith (1983: 8–13).

10 For criticism of Gellner's theory of nations and nationalism, see Smith (1971, 1981, 1983, 1986).

11 Hobsbawm and Ranger are not the only ones who have pointed this out. Yanagita Kunio also wrote that 'much of what we now think of as "tradition" is of unexpectedly recent origin' (1969: 32–48). But Yanagita's position differs fundamentally from that of Hobsbawm and Ranger, who go even so far as to promote things of dubious historical origin as links in the present with the past. (I am grateful to Professor Tsurumi Kazuko for her comments on Yanagita.) For a more detailed examination of the 'invention of tradition' perspective, see Yoshino (1987), out of which this chapter has developed.

12 Customs barriers (*sekisho*) remained in the Tokugawa period, but only as a policing device, not for economic purposes. See Lehmann (1982: 51).

5 MODERN JAPANESE SOCIETY AS *GEMEINSCHAFT* (pp. 87–103)

1 For various explanations of social order, see Percy Cohen (1968: 18–33).
2 See Tsurumi (1970: 104–5).
3 The Japanese word *kokka* (consisting of two characters meaning 'country' and 'family') means both nation and state. This dual meaning is indicative of the historical process in which the state came to be identified with the nation as symbolised by the central political and social–cultural authority, the emperor.
4 The leaders of the Freedom and Popular Rights Movement, under the influence of liberal theorists such as Rousseau and Mill, were active in the 1870s and 1880s, demanding the establishment of a representative assembly elected by the people. See Ienaga *et al.* (1957).
5 On the different types of Shinto, see Tsurumi (1979b).
6 There are also other elements constituting the emperor system and its ideology. Tsurumi Kazuko (1970: 184–212) regards the emperor system and its ideology as a composite of social and belief systems such as militarism, constitutionalism, familism, the village community and the organismic concept of the state.
7 On familistic enterprise, see, e.g. Abegglen (1958); Marshall (1967); Dore (1973a); Hirschmeier and Yui (1975); Clark (1979); Odaka (1984).
8 The other 5 to 6 per cent of the population included artisans, merchants, priests and outcastes. (Sekiyama 1958: 312).
9 On the quasi-parent–child relationship, see Yanagita (1963a: 370–90) and Sakurai (1974: 194–207).
10 For example, there were the *heso-oya*, who was asked to cut the umbilical cord for a newly born baby and remained a guardian; the *nazuke-oya*, who named the child; the *eboshi-oya*, who presided at a young man's coming of age; the *kane-oya*, who presided at a young woman's coming of age; and the *yori-oya*, who was chosen by a young man's parents to find him a job, among others. For a useful account of quasi-parents in English, see Tsurumi (1979a).
11 On *wakamono-gumi*, see Sakurai (1968); Segawa (1972); Nakayama (1958).
12 For the relationships between vertical and horizontal social relations, see Tsurumi (1979a).
13 Max Weber also pointed out the importance of the transmission of traditions through the training of juniors by seniors at school ([1921] 1982: 298–305).
14 On the communal characteristics of the modern Japanese company see, e.g. Abegglen (1958); Brown (1966); Odaka (1984).
15 *Nemawashi* is a process of prior informal negotiation and persuasion among concerned parties before a proposed matter is presented to a formal meeting. Although such an informal process is not unique to Japan, informal activities are given far greater weight in Japan than in Western countries. *Ringi* is a procedure of circulating a memorandum

within a company to obtain approval of all those concerned for a proposed idea.

16 It is possible to explain these group-oriented characteristics of the Japanese company without resorting to culturalism or traditionalism. Ronald Dore's 'late development thesis' (1973b) is one such attempt. Dore's analysis centres around the different historical circumstances of early and late developers.

17 The Japanese family underwent considerable structural change in the post-war period, during which the lineal family system (*ie*) steadily disintegrated. The average family size decreased from 4.98 in 1930, to 4.97 in 1955, to 3.45 in 1975 and to 3.33 in 1980. In terms of family structure the nuclear family type spread to over 60 per cent of the total by 1975, indicating a change from the pre-war family type based on the parent–child relationship to one based on the couple's marital relationship. Families were freed of the formal constraints imposed by the pre-war extended family system as a result of the 1947 revision of the Civil Code. The abolition of the landlord–tenant system in early post-war years did much to bring about the weakening sense of 'family status', which was then linked to the reduced authority of the head of the household and the faded pre-eminence of the patriarch. The lineal family system (*ie*) disintegrated (Fukutake 1982: 123–9).

The disintegration of the *mura* (village community) was brought about by the twin forces of industrialisation and urbanisation and profound changes in agriculture. The proportion of non-farming households increased from 39 per cent of the total number of sample settlements in 1960, to 54 per cent in 1970 and to 77 per cent in 1980. Furthermore, nearly 70 per cent of the 'farming' families gain more than half of their income from outside agriculture (as of 1980), thereby causing differentiation among a small number of full-time farmers, a large number of part-time farmers, and non-agricultural residents who have increased in number in response to the creation of factories in formerly agricultural regions and as a result of urban housing sprawl. In these circumstances, the villages have ceased to exist as highly closed, self-autonomous and cohesive communities with a sense of common purpose (ibid.: 131–7).

6 PERCEPTIONS OF JAPANESE UNIQUENESS AMONG EDUCATORS AND BUSINESSMEN (pp. 104–32)

1 Although the administrative boundaries of the city of Nakasato encompass a wide area, it is largely mountainous and most of its population is concentrated on a coastal plain in an area barely ten kilometres across. The city grew out of a medieval 'castle town' and is now a provincial centre. The local economy, in addition to agriculture, is dominated by light industries, both traditional and modern.

2 Supplementary research was conducted in early 1991.

3 An interview normally began with casual chatting followed by more focused discussions on particular topics. The topics normally discussed

were: the distinctiveness of Japanese culture and society as perceived by the respondents; literature on the *nihonjinron* they had read; their impressions and evaluations of the *nihonjinron*; reasons for their concern (or lack of concern) with the *nihonjinron*; their role in relation to the 'production', 'reproduction' and 'consumption' of ideas on Japanese culture; their ideas of thinking elites and intellectuals; their perception of sociology, nationalism, Japanese history, and Japan and the world. Questions were also asked about their personal history and their role in relation to the family, the community and the society at large, their interest in and contact with foreign countries. Questions were also asked about their perceptions of the social and cultural characteristics of Nakasato in comparison with those of the rest of Japan. These topics were used only as a general guide. Usually I raised a topic, and the respondent proceeded to give his (or her) views, with occasional additional questions from myself. The discussion frequently wandered away from the assigned topic, but little attempt was made to restrict such digressions, since all the reactions of the respondent were held to be significant data. The formal discussion normally took about an hour and a half, and was followed by further casual chatting. Following the initial interviews, several supplementary meetings with willing respondents were made. With those not willing to meet for an interview, telephone conversations and/or letters were exchanged to fill in gaps in the information and to make sure about the accuracy of my understanding of their responses.

4 Of all the respondents, I first contacted high school headmasters. I initially encountered a little difficulty in arranging meetings with the headmasters, although the effort to approach them taught me a good deal about how they regarded this subject, especially how they regarded their role in relation to the production, reproduction and consumption of ideas concerning Japanese society and culture. For example, in my first approach to some of the headmasters, I used the term *chishikijin* (intellectuals) to be taken to refer indirectly to them. I was told by the head of the headmasters' association (through whom I was to be later introduced to the other headmasters) that this had initially caused a somewhat defensive attitude on the part of some headmasters. I discovered that some of them had an ambivalent attitude towards their position in relation to intellectuals or thinking elites. On the one hand, they think that high school headmasters are not intellectuals; on the other hand they think that they should seriously and responsibly think about social and cultural affairs. I thus decided to include in the interview the respondents' perceptions of who are intellectuals and thinking elites, which produced an interesting result.

5 The usual definition of a manager in a Japanese company is someone who is not a member of the company union. Ordinary members of the company are required to be union members; normally section heads and higher ranks are excluded from union membership. The line between a union member and a manager is drawn rather arbitrarily between the standard ranks of sub-section head and section head. Although there is a statutory distinction between

directors and employees in Japanese companies, directors tend to be regarded simply as those who have worked their way up to the highest standard ranks from the lower positions. (For a good account of ranks in a Japanese company, see Clark 1979: 104–34.)

6 In family firms directors are normally also large shareholders, and board and management are less clearly differentiated (see Clark 1979: 3, 110).

7 Miles also points out the importance of analysing the association of race with the other symbols of nationalism. Discussing the subject in the British context, Miles argues that it is important to examine the interrelations between the imagery evoked by race and the values and beliefs which underlie nationalism (1982b: 284–7).

8 Some of the characteristics and institutions discussed here are not only English but British. But I am concerned here with English people's perceptions of their national identity.

9 A glimpse at a variety of the state-of-Britain literature – one of the most widely read of which is Anthony Sampson's *The Changing Anatomy of Britain* (1982) – would show us something about the British tendency to perceive their distinctiveness in terms of objectified institutions. Sampson's approach is typically institutional and objectifying: the author discusses one British institution after another such as the monarchy, parliament, the Conservative Party, the Labour Party, trade unions, schools, universities, police, scientists and engineers, the City, farmers and the press. Sampson quotes Hugh Trevor-Roper who remarks that 'whatever qualities we have as British people [do not] come from the blood or from race' (ibid.: xvii). Trevor-Roper states that it is institutions that form their national identity.

10 For example, the tea ceremony (*cha no yu*) seems to be an epitome of traditional Japanese culture, which embraces such very Japanese values as harmony, reverence, purity and tranquillity. The tea ceremony, the tea house, the garden, the physical and spiritual aspects of the ceremony all combine harmoniously to provide a sense of tranquillity and to cultivate an ideal attitude towards man and nature, ideal as defined in Japanese culture. Also, the simplicity of the tea house is a perfect example of Japanese architectural space. But, as a middle-aged businessman said: 'Who in today's Japan can afford to appreciate the spiritual beauties of the tea ceremony except a small number of people who have a special interest in it?'

11 Listening to and singing *enka* (popular ballads) is another aspect of everyday culture which several respondents remarked upon as a source of their Japanese identity. Singing *enka* at a *karaoke* bar is a very popular mode of enjoyment among many Japanese.

12 One reason why race thinking has been equated with genetic determinism in the West may be understood as follows. Whereas the notion of 'racially exclusive possession of particular culture' appropriately characterises the 'particularistic' cultural sentiment of the Japanese who have long perceived themselves to be on the 'periphery' in relation to the 'central' civilisations of China and the West (where the 'universal' norms have been perceived to exist), genetic determinism

as an ideology to rationalise Western dominance points to the more universal (and superior) aspects of human ability and activity that are perceived to have comprised the base of the 'universal' civilisation of the West. Viewed in terms of universal criteria, the difference between Westerners (Caucasians) and others is a question of difference in ability: hence, the 'vertical' sense of *superiority*. By contrast, the Japanese sense of difference associated with the notion of 'racially exclusive possession of particular culture' is primarily a matter of 'horizontal' *difference* (difference of a kind). The fact that the Western civilisation has tended to be perceived by Westerners and non-Westerners alike as being 'universal' and that this civilisation has been associated with the white race may be considered a reason for the equation of racial sentiment with genetic determinism in the West.

I may have given the impression that the Japanese sense of uniqueness is exclusively that of difference of a kind, but, where intelligence level is referred to, it involves a sense of superiority. The Japanese are not unconscious of their intelligence level. In fact, about half the respondents suggested that the Japanese intelligence level is very high, referring, for example, to cross-cultural comparisons of mathematical scores and the high scholastic performance (as they perceive it) of Japanese scientific researchers working in the USA. However, I could not find any clear-cut evidence to claim that their perception of Japanese intelligence is 'racial' in nature. Rather, they vaguely suggested that it has much to do with the Japanese way of life that stresses diligence.

13 Race relations in Britain have witnessed substantial changes in common with other aspects of British society since the 1960s, and this in itself may make it appropriate to reappraise this theory as a perspective on British race relations.

14 *Kareta bunshō* means 'sentences written in the refined style', but it connotes much more than that. It carries the nuance of having mastered an art or reached a stage at which technical skills no longer preoccupy the mind of an artist or artisan. *Ikina niisan* is literally 'a stylish fellow' but this does not do justice to the richness of the original expression. *Iki* is considered one of the 'untranslatables' because it originally connotes a particular style characteristic of urbanites in early modern Japan.

Any language has culture-bound expressions, and in this sense Japanese is no exception. What is characteristic about the Japanese is that they consciously emphasise the existence of those idioms considered beyond the comprehension of non-Japanese.

15 To be more specific, the 'outward-looking' and 'inward-looking' periods have alternated in Japanese history at least until the Second World War. Contrast, for example, the period from about the seventh century towards the end of the ninth century when a massive wave of Chinese influences swept over Japan and the subsequent period from the tenth century onwards when imported cultures were endogenised; also the westernising climate of the first two decades after the Meiji Restoration of 1868 and the following two decades which saw the revival of traditional values.

16 Of course, it is also possible to emphasise the presence of the Japanese spirit behind some of these activities such as judo, which many Japanese do not consider a sport but as a way of spiritual practice.

17 Discussions of this sort increased in the early 1980s in elite journals such as *Chūō Kōron*. There are also books such as Yamazaki *et al.* (1983).

7 THE DIFFUSION OF IDEAS OF JAPANESE UNIQUENESS (pp. 133–157)

1 As a way of analysing the ways in which non-elite members of society are or are not manipulated by the elite, William Kornhauser (1959) points out the importance of examining the role of intermediate groups. Intermediate groups mean groups which are neither the primary group (the family) nor the state.

2 The difference between businessmen and educators was found to be statistically significant, on the assumption that we have taken random samples from the two populations, which we have not. (For my decision not to use random samples, see chapter 6.)

I am grateful for Watanabe Shin and Jeff Burton for their great help and guidance in compiling statistics.

3 Some of the other reasons include chance factors (such as those indicated by the statement 'I happened to find these books at bookshops') and demonstration effects (such as those revealed by the statement 'I read it because it was a best seller at that time').

4 That businessmen are knowledgeable about the content of the *nihonjinron* was shown by the fact that a couple of businessmen pointed out that the type of *nihonjinron* dealt with in this research is the one that was popular some time ago and that there had been a shift of emphasis in the state-of-Japan discussions in the past few years.

5 Like educators, some businessmen also gave other, more passive reasons. But, unlike educators, the majority of them also gave more active reasons in addition to passive ones.

6 There were respondents whose contact with non-Japanese was mainly through their after-work evening classes in English.

8 LEADING BUSINESS ELITES, NATIONALISM AND CULTURAL NATIONALISM (pp. 158–184)

1 This is also illustrated by the fact that, as anthropologist Aoki Tamotsu (in Hall and Aoki 1988) once observed, Japanese businessmen were already well informed of anthropological works on cultural differences, such as Edward Hall's *The Silent Language* (1959, 1966), even before Japanese cultural anthropologists took notice of this book. It may well be that academic anthropologists did not concern themselves with this work because they did not recognise its academic worth; as Hall himself admits, this was the way his work was first received

by American anthropologists. Rather, this example is intended to show the eagerness of Japanese businessmen to learn cultural differences systematically.

2 On the relationship of nationalism to business ideology in early modern Japan, see, e.g. Marshall (1967); Hazama (1972, 1980); Morikawa (1973); Hirschmeier and Yui (1975).

3 Business nationalism on the whole became less evident from about 1910 to the 1930s, but did not disappear altogether from the scene. Hazama (1980: 68) points out two new trends in business nationalism that emerged during this period. One of these trends concerns the attempt to nationalise industrial technology as was manifested, for example, in the ideas of managers such as Kodaira Namihei (1874–1951) and Noguchi Shitagau (1873–1944) who sought to nationalise Japanese industries which had depended heavily on foreign-made technology. The other concerns the expansionist ideology represented by the ideas of the so-called 'new *zaibatsu*' leaders such as Kuhara Fusanosuke (1869–1965) and Ayuhara Gisuke (1880–1967), whose business interests were closely connected with the military industries.

4 An expression of business nationalism in terms of an appeal to Japan's unique social culture is not entirely new, and even received sporadic mention prior to the 1970s. For example, Idemitsu Sazō (1885–1981), a nationalistic entrepreneur who engaged in sales of petroleum, sought the source of Japan's national greatness in harmonious human relations in the familistic enterprise and the world of harmony centring around the emperor, contrasting the 'spiritual' country of Japan with the 'materialistic' countries of the West (Morikawa 1973: 6–7). Of course, the idea of familism had long been a feature of Japanese management, but it was not until the 1970s that familistic social characteristics were positively evaluated both in Japan and abroad, and recognised as a source of Japanese identity and pride.

5 This is certainly not to suggest that autobiographies by successful businessmen are unique to Japan; cf. *Iacocca: An Autobiography* (New York: Bantam Hardcover, 1984).

6 Cultural relativism as an explicit anthropological perspective originates with Ruth Benedict (1934) and Melville Herskovits (1947).

7 First, defence of the values of the less developed world could result in justifying the technologically backward stage of ex-colonial countries. George Stocking summarises this position by stating that cultural relativism, which 'buttressed the attack against racialism [can] be perceived as a sort of neo-racialism justifying the backward techno-economic status of once colonized peoples' (1982: 176). Second, one of the arguments by anti-relativists holds that cultural relativism perpetuated a kind of 'inverted racism'. Spiro remarks that cultural relativism was used 'as a powerful tool of cultural criticism, with the consequent derogation of Western culture and of the mentality which it produced. Espousing the philosophy of primitivism . . . the image of primitive man was used . . . as a vehicle for the pursuit of personal utopian quests, and/or as a fulcrum to express personal discontent

with Western man and Western society' (1978: 336).

8 Business elites' concern with the promotion of the distinctiveness of their nation's culture is not unique to Japan. If we extend our focus beyond the contemporary world, a close look at the activities of English industrialists in the mid-nineteenth century suggests an interesting parallel with contemporary Japan, albeit with a differing degree and in a different context. In the period between the 1830s and 1850s – long before William Morris and the arts and crafts movement of the 1880s and 1890s – we find a group of English manufacturers and industrialists who, dissatisfied with the deteriorating standard of design brought about by mechanisation and conscious of the high standard of continental design, showed an interest in maintaining and raising the standard of design in England and, in so doing, asserted the Englishness of English design (see Kusamitsu 1982). Some manufacturers (such as Josiah Wedgewood and Herbert Minton, manufacturers of pottery) perceived that it was necessary for workers to acquire sufficient skill and knowledge in order for British manufacturing to compete in taste with its continental counterparts. Edmund Potter, a Calico printing manufacturer, expressed a keen interest in producing designs with a refined English style in the age of mechanisation. Potter (1852, quoted in ibid.: 72) praised the sober, quiet and modest kind of taste in beauty of the English middle class and stated that 'in this brand of the business, the English printer is most decidedly superior to his French competitors'. Unlike people such as William Morris, the prime motive of industrialists in the mid-nineteenth century was to produce and sell goods in great quantities, but it is worthy of attention that some of them also exhibited an interest in promoting an English taste. Since it is also only a minority of manufacturers of that period who showed such a concern in the promotion of the distinctiveness of English design, I do not argue that they were the main promoters and social bearers of English cultural nationalism. Rather, my aim is to show in a non-Japanese context an example of industrialists concerning themselves with the promotion of an interest in the distinctiveness of their national culture and art (see Kusamitsu 1982).

I am grateful to Kusamitsu Toshio for introducing me to this English example.

9 Tsurumi (1970: 80–137) refers to the army as the emperor system in microcosm and discusses how the army, along with the school, built up a most effective programme of inculcating the values of nationalism and of the emperor system before and during the Second World War.

9 EXPLANATIONS OF THE *NIHONJINRON* (pp. 185–202)

1 For a useful examination of dominant ideology, see Abercrombie, Hill and Turner (1980). In the last fifty years or so, Marxists have been confronted with the apparent stability of capitalist society and the relative absence of working-class consciousness. In order to explain this 'unexpected' development of history, modern Marxist theorists turned their attention to the ideological control of the working class by the ruling

class, supposing that, if capitalism was not overthrown because of its economic contradictions, then it must be stabilised by its superstructure (see, e.g. Gramsci 1971; Althusser 1969, 1971; Miliband 1969).

2 The normative and comparative functions of reference groups are to establish behavioural standards and to provide guidelines for making self and other judgements. The former use is represented by Merton, the latter Hyman.

3 Inoue is not specifically concerned with the *nihonjinron* but with the more general question of the strong tendency of the Japanese to use out-groups as reference groups.

4 For a summary of Yanagita's ideas, see Tsurumi (1977: 197–228). Tsurumi (1972: 26) points out that this state of mind of villagers living in a highly closed community corresponds to what Paul Hazard (1953) calls the 'psychology of uneasiness', by which is meant that uneasiness caused by a sense of deficiency prevents people from developing indifference and is the ultimate force that motivates people to look for something different.

5 Japanese uniqueness is a theme that has periodically concerned thinkers in modern Japan. Following the first two decades of Westernisation in the Meiji period (1868–1911), the next two decades witnessed a strong interest among intellectuals in exploring indigenous and distinctively Japanese ideas, leading to *kokusui hozon* (preservation of national essence) movement. By the turn of the century emphasis on Japanese distinctiveness took on a more active tone, reflecting the mood of the victorious nation after the Sino-Japanese War (1894–5). This nationalist ideology, called *nihonshugi* (Japanism), not merely rejected foreign religions and values and advocated the worship of imperial ancestors but urged the people to enhance national solidarity and to honour the military. The period following Japan's victory in the Russo-Japanese War (1904–5) was characterised by a desire to rationalise the nation's greatness rather than by a mere search for its uniqueness. Notions such as *bushidō* (the way of samurai) and *kokutai* (peculiar unity of the Japanese people centred on the imperial family) were emphasised. The ways in which Japanese thinkers interpreted the nation's uniqueness thus varied from one historical time to another. Such changes are reflected in changes in the editorial content of the leading nationalist journal *Nihonjin* (The Japanese). Prior to the Sino-Japanese War, this journal represented the views of the 'preservation of national essence'. Before and during the Russo-Japanese War, it reflected the views of Japanism. In 1907, the journal changed its name to *Nihon oyobi Nihonjin* (Japan and the Japanese) and assumed a new editorial policy which stressed spiritual superiority but assumed a more tolerant attitude towards foreign ideas and institutions, reflecting the relatively peaceful and prosperous mood of the nation (see Brown 1955: 155–6). The late 1930s and early 1940s saw another boom of national character literature, this time called *nihongaku* (study of Japan), reasserting Japanese uniqueness and greatness. The post-war period saw two cases of intense national self-appraisal, as we saw in chapter 2. (For a useful exposition of ideology in the Meiji period, see Gluck 1985).

10 'RESURGENT CULTURAL NATIONALISM' AND 'PRUDENT REVIVALIST NATIONALISM' (pp. 203–225)

1 The term *tennō-sei* (the emperor system) was originally coined by Marxist historians in 1932 to refer to the absolutist political system which emerged after the Meiji Restoration of 1868 and which Marxists aimed to overthrow by revolution. Following Japan's defeat in 1945, however, the term came to be widely used as an objective social scientific term to refer more generally to the political system centring around the imperial symbols. See Kamishima in Kuno and Kamishima (eds) (1974: 453).

2 The Ministry of Education's guidelines on the content and goals of the school curriculum, which are reviewed approximately every ten years, are indicative of the state's stance or intentions on nationalism and their change in time. The new guidelines announced by the Ministry on 10 February 1989 and to be put into effect in 1992 reveal an ever stronger emphasis on nationalism. At the same time, the guidelines emphasise the need of preparing pupils for a new role of the Japanese in the age of 'internationalisation', showing ironically that nationalism – in the sense of 'raising consciousness of being a Japanese and cultivating national identity' and stressing Japan's culture and tradition – is promoted in the name of the 'internationalisation' of Japan. Under the new guidelines, the main emphasis should be on moral education from primary to high school, a move regarded by education authorities as a remedy for problems at school such as the presence of a sizeable number of pupils who find it socially and psychologically difficult to go to school, bullying among pupils and teenage suicide; teachers will be instructed to educate pupils to 'venerate' (*keiaisuru*) teachers – a phrase reminiscent of Confucian ethics; teachers will be obligated to deepen their pupils' 'understanding and veneration for the emperor'; and schools will be *required*, for the first time in the post-war period, to hoist the *Hinomaru* flag and to sing the *Kimigayo* anthem at entrance and graduation ceremonies.

The previous guidelines only stated that it is 'desirable' to use these symbols at school ceremonies and left it to the discretion of schools and the board of education of each administrative region; but the revision made this practice mandatory to the extent that teachers who refuse to comply will be subjected to punishment. Also, the state will, for the first time, require the primary school curriculum on history to include forty-two selected historical figures including admiral Tōgō Heihachirō whose exploits in the Russo-Japanese War (1904–5) were used to promote militarism in textbooks during the Second World War. The new guidelines are also concerned to dissociate Japan's image from its deeds in the Second World War, making it possible for textbooks to skimp on details regarding Japan's aggression against China.

The Ministry of Education has long sought to de-emphasise the issues surrounding the Second World War, as is exemplified by the remark made by the former Education Minister, Nishioka Takeo: 'There are many things to reflect on in connection with World War

II, but it's not constructive to drag it on forever' (quoted in *Mainichi Daily News*, 11 February 1989).

I do not know, however, whether the role of the state has increased, for it may be that the state is only responding to the change in the public's perceptions of Japanese nationalism, national pride and confidence, which are, in turn, strongly congruent with other factors such as the thinking elites' activity to rearticulate and reassert Japanese uniqueness and the sentiment and activities of other educated sections of the population who respond to such thinking elites' activities. I do not know, either, the degree to which the state enhances national sentiment compared to social groups such as intellectuals, media people, businessmen and so on. It is also necessary to consider the point that the state's programme to enhance nationalism makes some groups more active in their opposition to it. The Japan Teachers' Union (*Nikkyōso*) and many liberal-minded sections of the population denounce the new revisions as a return to pre-war methods of teaching and injecting nationalistic spirit among the public. Again, I do not know the extent to which and the ways in which such opposition alters the development of nationalism and national sentiment. All these questions require further extensive research.

3 It was officially taught before 1945 that the word *Kimigayo* meant the emperor's reign. After 1945, however, the Ministry of Education gave no formal interpretation as to the precise meaning of the word *Kimigayo*, thus even allowing for quite another meaning, 'the people'. The Ministry did not formally deny the pre-war interpretation, either.

Scholars are divided in their views on the historical background of the *Kimigayo* anthem and the Rising Sun flag. See, for example, the special issue of *Kikan Kyōikuhō* (1985).

4 Even many opinion formers only began to consider seriously what the post-war emperor system had meant for the Japanese and what role the emperor system would play in the future when the Shōwa Emperor (Emperor Hirohito) fell seriously ill in September 1988 and the prospect of a new emperor became a reality.

5 *Kimigayo* and *Hinomaru* (The Rising Sun) have never been officially adopted as the national anthem and flag, though they have been widely identified as such. Those who do not regard them as the 'official' national symbols consciously call them *Kimigayo* and *Hinomaru* rather than *kokka* (national anthem) and *kokki* (national flag).

6 It is supposed that respondents do not normally disclose their real feelings at the interviews. We should not, therefore, depend too much on what respondents stated at the interview. But one advantage of conducting research in a provincial city was that the respondents knew one another personally and quite often exchanged views among themselves. I was able from time to time to obtain information concerning the views of some respondents from the other respondents and thereby to understand their views in perspective. For example, one headmaster said that he still admired pre-war nationalist values but that his former colleague, now a headmaster of another school, who was three years older and had been enrolled at the military academy

in the last days of the war, was even more strongly influenced by the nationalistic thought and more strongly supportive of the revival of nationalism today. But this headmaster himself was rather defensive at the interview and did not display as many signs of nationalistic sentiment as his former colleague suggested.

7 Prefectural differences in the support of the emperor system and its concomitant symbols are in some ways related to the ways in which different prefectures experienced the Second World War. For example, Okinawa, where bitter fighting actually took place, and Hiroshima show low degrees of support. Also, support of the use of the Rising Sun flag and the *Kimigayo* anthem at school ceremonies is on the whole negatively correlated with the relative proportion of the membership in the Japan Teachers' Union in each prefecture. JTU is in general strongly opposed to the emperor-related symbols, though each prefectural union has different policies. In all of those prefectures with a JTU membership of less than 30 per cent (i.e. Tochigi, Gifu, Shimane, Yamaguchi, Tokushima, Kagawa, Ehime, Nagasaki), *Kimigayo* is sung at more than 90 per cent of the primary and secondary schools. Furthermore, each region has its own political history and internal politics – and this explains partly why the JTU is strong in some prefectures and not in others – but an examination of this requires a full separate study. The prefecture, the capital city of which is Nakasato, shows a percentage very close to the national average as regards those who responded that 'the emperor should be respected' but shows percentages above the national average as regards the display of the Rising Sun flag and the singing of *Kimigayo* at school ceremonies. For a full discussion of regional differences in support of the emperor system and its related symbols, see Araki (1986: 150–78).

8 It was a taboo to think rationally about the emperor in pre-war and wartime Japan. As one famous event that illustrates this, Minobe Tatsukichi (1873–1948), professor of law at Tokyo Imperial University, developed a theory of the emperor as an organ of the state. The theory was condemned by the military in 1935 as lese-majesty, and his books were banned. Minobe was forced to resign from the House of Peers. On the non-rationalistic nature of the emperor ideology, see Tsurumi (1970).

9 Writing in the early 1950s, Maruyama Masao ([1952] 1974) remarked on fragmentation as one of the characteristic features of post-war Japanese nationalism.

10 It is too simplistic to assume that one's interest in communal and familial features of Japanese society necessarily leads to one's support of the emperor system. We may point out the presence of scholars such as Kamishima Jirō who has developed a theory of modern Japanese society as a 'secondary village community' but maintains a critically objective attitude towards the question of the emperor system.

Bibliography

Abegglen, James C. (1958) *The Japanese Factory: Aspects of its Social Organization*, Glencoe, Ill.: Free Press.

Abercrombie, N., Hill, S. and Turner, S.T. (1980) *The Dominant Ideology Thesis*, London: George Allen and Unwin.

——(1984) *The Penguin Dictionary of Sociology*, Harmondsworth: Penguin Books.

Aida, Yūji (1962) *Āron shūyōjo* (The Ahlone Concentration Camp), Tokyo: Chūkō Bunko, translated as *Prisoners of the British: A Japanese Soldiers' Experiences in Burma*, by H. Ishiguro and L. Allen, London: Cresset Press, 1966.

——(1972) *Nihonjin no ishiki kōzō* (The Structure of Japanese Consciousness), Tokyo: Kōdansha.

Almond, Gabriel (1952) *The Appeals of Communism*, Princeton, NJ: Princeton University Press.

Althusser, Luis (1969) *For Marx*, London: New Left Books.

——(1971) 'Ideology and ideological state apparatuses', in *Lenin and Philosophy and Other Essays*, London: New Left Books.

Anderson, Benedict (1983) *Imagined Communities: Reflections on the Origins and Spread of Nationalism*, London: Verso.

Aoki, Tamotsu (1990) *'Nihonbunkaron' no henyō: sengonihon no bunka to aidentitii* (The Transformation of 'Theories of Japanese Culture': Culture and Identity in Post-war Japan), Tokyo: Chūōkōronsha.

Araki, Hiroyuki (1973) *Nihonjin no kōdōyōshiki* (The Patterns of Behaviour of the Japanese), Tokyo: Kōdansha.

Araki, Moriaki (1986) *'Tennō to tennōsei'* (The emperor and the emperor system) in Rekishigaku Kenkyūkai (ed.).

Armstrong, Bruce (1989) 'Racialisation and nationalist ideology: the Japanese case', *International Sociology* 4, 3: 329–43.

Armstrong, John A. (1982) *Nations before Nationalism*, Chapel Hill: University of North Carolina Press.

Aruga, Kizaemon (1943) *Nihon kazokuseido to kosakuseido* (The Japanese Family System and Tenant System), Tokyo: Kawaide Shobō.

——(1950) Review of *The Chrysanthemum and the Sword* by Ruth Benedict, 'Nihonshakaikōzō niokeru kaisōsei no mondai' (The issue of stratification in Japanese social structure), *Minzokugaku kenkyū* (Ethnological Studies) 14, 4: 13–23.

——(1959) 'Nihon no ie' (The Japanese Family), in Nihon Jinrui Gakkai (ed.) *Nihon minzoku* (The Japanese Nation), Tokyo: Iwanami Shoten.

Banton, Michael (1967) *Race Relations*, New York: Basic Books.

——(1970) 'The concept of racism', in S. Zubaida (ed.) *Race and Racialism*, London: Tavistock.

——(1977) *The Idea of Race*, London: Tavistock.

——(1983) *Racial and Ethnic Competition*, Cambridge: Cambridge University Press.

Barnard, F.M. (ed.) (1969) *J.G. Herder on Social and Political Culture*, Cambridge: Cambridge University Press.

——(1983) 'National culture and political legitimacy: Herder and Rousseau', *Journal of the History of Ideas* 44, 2: 231–53.

Barth, Fredrik (1969) 'Introduction', in F. Barth (ed.) *Ethnic Groups and Boundaries*, London: Allen & Unwin.

Barzan, Jacques ([1937] 1965) *Race: A Study in Superstition*, New York: Harper & Row.

Befu, Harumi (1980) 'The group model of Japanese society and an alternative', *Rice University Studies* 66, 1: 169–87.

——(1984) 'Civilization and culture: Japan in search of identity' in T. Umesao, H. Befu and J. Kreiner (eds).

——(1987) *Ideorogii toshite no nihonbunkaron* (The Theory of Japanese Culture as an Ideology), Tokyo: Shisō no Kagakusha.

BenDasan, Isaiah (1970) *Nihonjin to Yudayajin* (The Japanese and the Jews), Tokyo: Yamamoto Shoten, translated as *The Japanese and the Jews* by Richard L. Gage, Tokyo: Weatherhill, 1972.

Benedict, Ruth (1934) *Patterns of Culture*, Boston: Houghton Mifflin.

——([1942] 1983) *Race and Racism*, London: Routledge & Kegan Paul.

——(1946) *The Chrysanthemum and the Sword*, Boston: Houghton Mifflin, translated as *Kiku to katana* (The Chrysanthemum and the Sword) by Hasegawa Matsuharu, Tokyo: Shakai Shisōsha, 1948.

Berkes, Niyazi (1954) 'Ziya Gökalp: his contribution to Turkish nationalism', *The Middle East Journal* 8, 4: 375–90.

Berlin, I. (1976) *Vico and Herder*, London: The Hogarth Press.

Bester, J. (1973) 'Foreword' in Doi (1973).

Bocock, Robert (1974) *Ritual in Industrial Society: A Sociological Analysis of Ritualism in Modern England*, London: Allen & Unwin.

Bonet, Paul (1975) *Fushigi no kuni, Nihon* (Japan, the Strange Country), Tokyo: Diamondosha.

Bottomore, Thomas B. (1964) *Elites and Society*, Harmondsworth: Penguin.

Brass, P. (1979) 'Elite groups, symbol manipulation and ethnic identity among the Muslims of South Asia', in D. Taylor and M. Yapp (eds) *Political Identity in South Asia*, London: Curzon Press.

Breuilly, John (1982) *Nationalism and the State*, Manchester: Manchester University Press.

Brown, Delmer M. (1955) *Nationalism in Japan: An Introductory Historical Analysis*, New York: Russell & Russell.

Brown, William (1966) 'Japanese management: the cultural background',

Monumenta Nipponica 21: 47–60.

Burke, Kenneth (1969) *A Grammar of Motives*, Berkeley and Los Angeles: University of California Press.

Chin, Shun Shin (1978) *Nihonjin to Chūgokujin* (The Japanese and the Chinese), Tokyo: Shōdensha.

Clark, Gregory (1977) *Nihonjin: yuniikusa no gensen* (The Japanese Tribe: Origins of a Nation's Uniqueness), trans. M. Muramatsu, Tokyo: Saimaru Shuppankai.

Clark, Rodney (1979) *The Japanese Company*, New Haven: Yale University Press.

Cobban, Alfred (1964) *Rousseau and the Modern State*, London: Allen & Unwin.

Cohen, Abner (1969) *Custom and Politics in Urban Africa*, Berkeley: University of California Press.

——(1974) 'Introduction: the lessons of ethnicity', in A. Cohen (ed.) *Urban Ethnicity*, London: Tavistock.

Cohen, Percy S. (1968) *Modern Social Theory*, London: Heinemann.

——(1976) 'Race relations as a sociological issue', in G. Bowker and J. Carrier (eds) *Race and Ethnic Relations*, London: Hutchinson.

Condon, John (1980) *Ibunkakan komyunikēshon* (Intercultural Communication), Tokyo: Saimaru Shuppankai.

Condon, John and Saito, Mitsuko (eds) (1974) *Intercultural Encounters with Japan*, Tokyo: Simul Press.

Crawcour, Sydney (1980) 'Alternative models of Japanese society: an overview' in R. Mouer and Y. Sugimoto (eds).

Curtin, P.D. (1965) *The Image of Africa: British Ideas and Action 1780–1850*, London: Macmillan.

Dale, Peter (1986) *The Myth of Japanese Uniqueness*, London: Croom Helm.

Desai, A.R. (1966) *The Social Background of Indian Nationalism*, Bombay: Bombay Publishing Company.

Deutsch, Karl (1966) *Nationalism and Social Communication*, 2nd edn, New York: MIT Press.

DeVos, George (1960) 'The relation of guilt toward parents to achievement and arranged marriage among the Japanese', *Psychiatry* 23: 287–301.

Doi, Takeo (1971) *Amae no kōzō* (Structure of Dependence), Tokyo: Kōbundo, translated as *The Anatomy of Dependence* by John Bester, Tokyo: Kodansha International, 1973.

Dood, W.A. (1971) 'Tanzania' in *The Encyclopedia of Education*, Macmillan and Free Press.

Dore, Ronald P. (1952) 'The ethics of the new Japan', *Pacific Affairs*, June: 147–59.

——(1973a) *British Factory–Japanese Factory: Origins of Diversity in Industrial Relations*, Berkeley: University of California Press.

——(1973b) 'The late development effect', University of Sussex, Institute of Development Studies.

Dower, John W. (1975) 'Introduction' in J. Halliday.

Drucker, P.F. (1971) 'What can we learn from Japanese management?', *Harvard Business Review*, March–April: 110–22.

Durkheim, Emile ([1893] 1960) *The Division of Labour in Society*, trans. G. Simpson, Glencoe: Free Press.

——([1912] 1964) *The Elementary Forms of the Religious Life*, trans. J.W. Swain, London: Allen & Unwin.

——([1922] 1956) *Education and Sociology*, trans. S.D. Fox, Glencoe: Free Press.

Ebuchi, K. (1983) 'Shōchōtaikei toshiteno nyū-esunisiti' (New ethnicity as a symbolic system), *Girei to shōchō: bunkajinruigakuteki kōsatsu* (Rituals and Symbols: A Cultural–Anthropological Enquiry), Kyūshū Daigaku Shuppankai.

Eisenstadt, S.N. (1972) 'Intellectuals and tradition', *Daedalus* (a special issue on intellectuals and tradition), Spring 1972: 1–19.

Embree, John F. (1939) *Sue Mura: A Japanese Village*, Chicago: Chicago University Press.

Epstein, A.L. (1978) *Ethos and Identity*, London: Tavistock.

Fichte, J.G. (1922) *Addresses to the German Nation*, (1807–8), trans. R.F. Jones and G.H. Turnbull, Chicago: Open Court Publishing Co.

Firth, Raymond (1973) *Symbols: Public and Private*, London: Allen & Unwin.

Foucault, Michel (1972) *The Archaeology of Knowledge*, trans. Alan Sheridan, New York: Pantheon Books.

Francis, E.K. (1974) 'The nature of the ethnic group', *American Journal of Sociology* 52, 5: 393–400.

Fukutake, Tadashi (1982) *The Japanese Social Structure*, trans. Ronald P. Dore, Tokyo: University of Tokyo Press.

Geertz, Clifford (1963) 'Integrative revolution', in C. Geertz (ed.) *Old Societies and New States*, New York: Free Press.

——(1984) 'Distinguished lecture: anti anti-relativism', *American Anthropologist* 86, 2: 263–78.

Gellner, Ernest (1973) 'Scale and nation', *Philosophy of the Social Sciences* 3: 1–17.

——(1983) *Nations and Nationalism*, Oxford: Basil Blackwell.

Gendai Shakaigaku (1980) A special issue on the *nihonshakairon* (The theory of Japanese society) 7, 1.

Giddens, Anthony (1968) '"Power" in the recent writings of Talcott Parsons', *Sociology* 2, 3: 257–72.

Glazer, Nathan and Moynihan, D.P. (1963) *Beyond the Melting Pot*, New York: MIT Press.

——(1974) 'Why ethnicity?', *Commentary* 58, 4: 33–9.

——(eds) (1975) *Ethnicity: Theory and Experience*, Cambridge, Mass.: Harvard University Press.

Gluck, Carol (1985) *Japan's Modern Myths: Ideology in the Late Meiji Period*, Princeton, NJ: Princeton University Press.

Gluckman, Max (1940) 'The analysis of a social situation in modern Zululand', *African Studies* 14: 1–30.

Gobineau, J.A. de (1915) *The Inequality of Human Races* (trans. of part of *Essai sur l'inégalité des Races Humaines* [1853–54]), London: Heinemann.

Gramsci, Antonio (1971) *Selections from the Prison Notebooks*, London: New Left Books.

Haga, Noboru (1963) *Bakumatsu kokugaku no tenkai* (Development of *kokugaku* at the End of the Tokugawa Period), Tokyo: Hanawa Shobō.

Hall, Edward (1959) *The Silent Language*, New York: Doubleday, translated as *Chinmoku no kotoba* (The Silent Language) by M. Kunihiro *et al.*, Tokyo: Nanudō, 1966.

Hall, Edward and Aoki, Tamotsu (1988) 'Bunka no sa wo ikani koeruka' (How can we go beyond cultural differences?), *Chūō Kōron*, January: 210–15.

Hall, John W. (1971) 'Thirty years of Japanese studies in America', *Transactions of the International Conference of Orientalists in Japan*, The Institute of Eastern Culture, 16: 22–35.

Hall, R.K. (ed.) and Gauntlett, J.O. (trans.) (1949) *Kokutai no Hongi: Cardinal Principles of the National Entity of Japan*, Cambridge, Mass.: Harvard University Press.

Halliday, Jon (1975) *A Political History of Japanese Capitalism*, New York: Pantheon Books.

Hamaguchi, Eshun (1977) *'Nihonjinrashisa' no saihakken* (Rediscovering 'Japaneseness'), Tokyo: Nihon Keizai Shimbunsha.

——(1980) 'Nihonshakairon no paradaimu kakushin wo mezashite' (Towards a paradigmatic change in the theories of Japanese society), *Gendai Shakaigaku* (Reviews of Contemporary Sociology) 7, 1: 29–45.

——(1982) *Kanjinshugi no shakai nihon* (Japan: the Interpersonalistic Society), Tokyo: Tōyō Keizai Shinposha.

Hanihara, Kazuo (1984) *Nihonjin no kigen* (The Origins of the Japanese), Tokyo: Asahi Shimbunsha.

Hannan, M.T. (1979) 'The dynamics of ethnic boundaries in modern states', in J.W. Meyer and M.T. Hannan (eds) *National Development and the World System*, Chicago: University of Chicago Press.

Harootunian, H.D. (1978) 'The consciousness of archaic form in the new realism of kokugaku', in T. Najita and I. Scheiner (eds) *Japanese Thought in the Tokugawa Period 1600–1868: Methods and Metaphors*, Chicago: University of Chicago Press.

——(1988) *Things Seen and Unseen: Discourse and Ideology in Tokugawa Nativism*, Chicago: University of Chicago Press.

Hatch, E. (1983) *Culture and Morality: The Relativity of Values in Anthropology*, New York: Columbia University Press.

Haugland, Kjell (1980) 'An outline of Norwegian cultural nationalism in the second half of the nineteenth century', in R. Mitchison (ed.).

Hayashida, Cullen T. (1976) 'Identity, race and the blood ideology of Japan', Ph.D. dissertation, University of Washington.

Hayes, Carlton (1931) *The Historical Evolution of Modern Nationalism*, New York: Smith.

Hazama, Hiroshi (1963) *Nihonteki keiei no keifu* (The Genealogy of Japanese-style Management), Tokyo: Nōritsu Kyōkai.

——(1971) *Nihonteki keiei – shūdan shugi no kōzai* (Japanese-style Management: Strengths and Weaknesses of Groupism), Tokyo: Nihon Keizai Shimbunsha.

——(1972) 'Nihon ni okeru keiei rinen no tenkai' (The development of business creed in Japan), in K. Nakagawa (ed.) *Gendai keieigaku zenshū*

(Collected Works on Contemporary Studies in Management), vol. III: *Keiei rinen* (Business Creed).

——(1980) 'Nihonjin no kachikan to kigyōkatsudō' (The Japanese sense of values and company activities), *Gendai no esupuri* (Esprit d'Aujourd'hui) 160: 59–79, originally published in Hazama (ed.) *Nihon no kigyō to shakai* (The Japanese Company and Society), Tokyo: Nihon Keizai Shimbunsha, 1977.

Hazard, Paul (1953) *The European Mind, 1680–1715*, trans. J.L. May, London: Penguin.

Hechter, Michael (1975) *Internal Colonialism: The Celtic Fringe in British National Development 1536–1966*, London: Routledge & Kegan Paul.

——(1978) 'Group formation and the cultural division of labor', *American Journal of Sociology* 84, 2: 293–318.

Heimsath, Charles H. (1964) *Indian Nationalism and Hindu Social Reform*, Princeton, NJ: Princeton University Press.

Herskovits, Melville (1947) *Man and His Works*, New York: Alfred A. Knopf.

Hickox, M.S. (1984) 'The problem of early English sociology', *The Sociological Review* 32, 1: 1–7.

Hijikata, Kazuo (1983) *'Nihonbunkaron' to tennō-sei ideorogii* ('Theories of Japanese Culture' and the Emperor Ideology), Tokyo: Shin-Nihon Shuppansha.

Hirschmeier, Johannes and Yui, Tsunehiko (1975) *The Development of Japanese Business, 1600–1973*, London: Allen & Unwin.

Hobsbawm, Eric J. (1983) 'Introduction: inventing traditions', in Hobsbawm and Ranger (eds) (1983).

——(1990) *Nations and Nationalism since 1780*, Cambridge: Cambridge University Press.

Hobsbawm, Eric J. and Terence Ranger (eds) (1983) *The Invention of Tradition*, Cambridge: Cambridge University Press.

Hoetink, H. (1975) 'Resource competition, monopoly, and socioracial diversity', in L.A. Despres (ed.) *Ethnicity and Resource Competition in Plural Societies*, The Hague: Mouton Publishers.

Hollowell, P.G. (ed.) (1982) *Property and Social Relations*, London: Heinemann.

Hostler, C.W. (1957) *Turkism and the Soviets*, London: Allen & Unwin.

Hsu, Francis L.K. (1975) *Iemoto: The Heart of Japan*, New York: John Wiley & Sons.

Husband, Charles (1982) 'Introduction: "race", the continuity of a concept' in Husband (ed.) *'Race' in Britain*, London: Hutchinson.

Hutchinson, John (1987) *The Dynamics of Cultural Nationalism: The Gaelic Revival and the Creation of the Irish Nation State*, London: Allen & Unwin.

Ienaga, Saburō *et al.* (eds) (1957) *Jiyūminken shisō* (The Ideas of Freedom and People's Rights), Tokyo: Aoki Shoten.

Iizuka, Kōji (1952) *Nihon no seishin-teki fūdo* (The Mental Climate of Japan), Tokyo: Hyōronsha.

Inoue, Tadashi (1979) *'Sekentei' no kōzō* (The Anatomy of *'Sekentei'*), Tokyo: NHK Books.

Inoue, Tetsujirō (1908) *Rinri to kyōiku* (Ethics and Education), Tokyo: Kōdōkan.

Inukai, Michiko (1972) *Watashi no Yōroppa* (My Europe), Tokyo: Shinchōsha.

Isaacs, Harold (1975) *The Idols of the Tribe: Group Identity and Political Change*, New York: Harper & Row.

Ishida, Eiichirō (1967) *Bunkajinruigaku nōto* (Essays on Cultural Anthropology), Tokyo: Perikansha.

——(1969) *Nihonbunkaron* (Lectures on Japanese Culture), Tokyo: Chikuma Shobō, translated as *Japanese Culture: A Study of Origins and Characteristics*, by T. Kachi, Tokyo: University of Tokyo Press, 1974.

Ishida, Takeshi (1954) *Meji seiji shisōshi kenkyū* (Studies in Political Thought in the Meiji Period), Tokyo: Miraisha.

Itasaka, Gen (1978) *Nihongo no hyōjō* (Japanese Language Expression), Tokyo: Kōdansha.

Jinruigaku Kōza Hensan Iinkai (ed.) (1978) *Jinruigaku kōza* (Lectures in Anthropology), vol. VI: *Nihonjin* (The Japanese) II, Tokyo: Yūzankaku.

Kabir, H. (1956) *Education in New India*, London: Allen & Unwin.

Kamenka, Eugene (ed.) (1976) *Nationalism: The Nature and Evolution of an Idea*, London: Edward Arnold.

Kamishima, Jirō (1961) *Kindainihon no seishin kōzō* (The Mental Structure of Modern Japan), Tokyo: Iwanami Shoten.

——(1980) 'Nihonshakai no tokusei' (The Characteristics of Japanese Society) in *Shin Nihonjinron*, Tokyo: Kōdansha.

Katsuta, Shūichi (1973) *Katsuta Shūichi chosakushū* (Collected Works of Katsuta Shūichi), vol. II: *Kokumin kyōiku no kadai* (The Tasks of National Education), Tokyo: Kokudosha.

Kawai, Hayao (1976) *Bosei shakai Nihon no byōri* (Pathology of the Maternal Society of Japan), Tokyo: Chūō Kōronsha.

Kawamura, Nozomu (1980) 'The historical background of arguments emphasizing the uniqueness of Japanese society', in Mouer and Sugimoto (eds).

——(1982) *Nihonbunkaron no shūhen* (Some Arguments on Theories of Japanese Culture), Tokyo: Ningen no kagakusha.

Kawashima, Takeyoshi (1950) Review of *The Chrysanthemum and the Sword* by Ruth Benedict, 'Hyoka to hihan' (Evaluations and criticisms), *Minzokugaku kenkyū* (Ethnological Studies) 14, 4: 1–8.

——(1950) *Nihon shakai no kazoku-teki kōsei* (The Familial Structure of Japanese Society), Tokyo: Nihon Hyōronsha.

——(1957) *Ideorogii toshiteno kazokuseido* (The Family System as an Ideology), Tokyo: Iwanami Shoten.

Kazamias, Andreas M. (1966) *Education and the Quest for Modernity in Turkey*, Chicago: University of Chicago Press.

Kedourie, Elie (1960) *Nationalism*, London: Hutchinson.

Kedourie, Elie (ed.) (1971) *Nationalism in Asia and Africa*, London: Weidenfeld & Nicolson.

Kemiläinen, Aira (1964) *Nationalism: Problems Concerning the Word, the Concept and Classification*, Jyväskylä: Kustantajat Publishers.

Kikan Kyōikuhō (1985) *Hinomaru/Kimigayo* (A special issue of *Kikan Kyōikuhō*).

Kimura, Shōzaburō (1978) *Yōroppa kara no hassō* (Thoughts from Europe), Tokyo: Kōdansha.

Kindaichi, Haruhiko (1975) *Nihonjin no gengo hyōgen* (Linguistic Expression of the Japanese), Tokyo: Kōdansha.

Kishida, Kunio (1947) *Nihonjin kikeisetsu* (A Theory of the Abnormalities of the Japanese), Tokyo: Hyōronsha.

Knox, Robert (1850) *The Races of Men*, London: Renshaw.

Kobayashi, Shigeru (1971) *Soshiki soseigaku* (Reviving Organisation), Tokyo: Goma Shobō.

Kohn, Hans (1955) *Nationalism: Its Meaning and History*, Princeton, NJ: D. Van Nostrand.

——(1960) *The Mind of Germany: The Education of a Nation*, New York: Scribners.

Kornhauser, William (1959) *The Politics of Mass Society*, London: Routledge & Kegan Paul.

Koyasu, Nobukuni (1977) *Norinaga to Atsutane no sekai* (The World of Norinaga and Atsutane), Tokyo: Chūō Kōronsha.

Kunihiro, Masao (1973) 'Indigenous barriers to communication', *The Japan Interpreter* 8, 1: 96–108.

——(1972) *Kokusai eigo no susume* (An Encouragement of International English), Tokyo: Jitsugyō no Nihonsha.

——(1976) 'The Japanese language and intercultural communication', *The Japan Interpreter* 10, 3/4: 267–83.

Kuno, Osamu and Kamishima, Jirō (eds) (1974) *'Tennōsei' ronshū* (Collection of Articles on the 'Emperor System'), Tokyo: Sanichi Shobō.

Kuper, Leo (1974) *Race, Class and Power*, London: Duckworth.

Kusamitsu, Toshio (1982) 'British industrialisation and design 1830–1851: with special reference to printing and figure-weaving in the Lancashire and West Riding textile industries', Ph.D. thesis, University of Sheffield.

Kushner, David (1977) *The Rise of Turkish Nationalism 1876–1908*, London: Frank Cass.

Leach, Edmund D. (1954) *Political Systems of Highland Burma*, London: London School of Economics.

Lebra, Takie Sugiyama (1976) *Japanese Patterns of Behavior*, Honolulu: University of Hawaii Press.

Lee, Chansoo and George DeVos (1981) *Koreans in Japan: Ethnic Conflict and Accommodation*, Berkeley: University of California Press.

Lehmann, Jean-Pierre (1982) *The Roots of Modern Japan*, London: Macmillan.

Lewis, Bernard (1968) *The Emergence of Modern Turkey*, 2nd edn, London: Oxford University Press.

Mann, Michael (1986) *The Sources of Social Power*, vol. I, Cambridge: Cambridge University Press.

Mannheim, Karl (1951) *Freedom, Power and Democratic Planning*, London: Routledge & Kegan Paul.

——(1954) *Ideology and Utopia*, London: Routledge & Kegan Paul.

Marshall, Byron K. (1967) *Capitalism and Nationalism in Prewar Japan: The Ideology of the Business Elite, 1868–1941*, Stanford: Stanford University Press.

Marsland, David (1988) *Seeds of Bankruptcy: Sociological Bias Against Business and Freedom*, London: The Claridge Press.

Maruyama, Masao (1952) *Nihon seiji shisōshi kenkyū* (Studies in Japanese Political Thought), Tokyo: Tōkyō Daigaku Shuppan, translated as

Studies in the Intellectual History of Tokugawa Japan by Mikiso Hane, Tokyo: University of Tokyo Press, 1974.

——(1963) *Thought and Behaviour in Modern Japanese Politics*, London: Oxford University Press.

Maruyama, Masao *et al.* (1953) *Nihon no nashonarizumu* (Nationalism in Japan), Tokyo: Kawaide Shobō.

Masuda, Yoshio (1967) *Junsui bunka no jōken* (The Conditions of Pure Culture), Tokyo: Kōdansha.

Matsumoto, Michihiro (1975) *Haragei no ronri* (The Logic of *Haragei*), Tokyo: Asahi Shuppansha.

——(1978) 'Haragei', *Asahi Evening News*, 9 October 1978.

——(1984) *Haragei*, Tokyo: Kōdansha.

Matsumoto, Sannosuke (1957) *Kokugaku seiji shisō no kenkyū* (Study of the Political Thinking of *Kokugaku*), Tokyo: Yūhikaku.

——(1973) 'Kokugaku shisō no keisei to tokushitsu' (The formation and characteristics of *kokugaku* thought) in K. Tsurumi (ed.) *Sōgōkōza, nihon no shakai bunka shi* (Social and Cultural History of Japan), vol. III.

Matsuo, Shōichi (1981) 'Joron: sengo handō ideorogii kōsei to wareware no rekishigaku' (Introduction: reactionary ideological offensive in the post-war period and our historical studies) in K. Yamada and S. Matsuo (eds) *Sengoshi to handō ideorogii* (Post-War History and Reactionary Ideology), Tokyo: Shin-Nihon Shuppan.

Matsushima, Shizuo (1967) 'Keiei kanri no nihonteki tokushitsu' (Japanese-style characteristics of management and administration) in H. Mannari and M. Sugi (eds) *Sangyō shakaigaku* (Industrial Sociology), Tokyo: Yūhikaku.

Matsushita, Kōnosuke (1982) *Nihon to nihonjin ni tsuite* (On Japan and the Japanese), Tokyo: PHP Kenkyūjo.

McCully, Bruce T. (1966) *English Education and the Origins of Indian Nationalism*, Gloucester, Mass.: Peter Smith.

McKay, J. (1982) 'An exploratory synthesis of primordial and mobilizationist approaches to ethnic phenomenon', *Ethnic and Racial Studies* 5: 395–420.

Mead, Margaret (1959) *An Anthropologist at Work: Writings of Ruth Benedict*, Boston: Houghton Mifflin Co.

Merton, Robert (1951) *Social Theory and Social Structure*, New York: Free Press.

Miles, Robert (1982a) *Racism and Migrant Labour*, London: Routledge & Kegan Paul.

——(1982b) 'Racism and nationalism in Britain' in Charles Husband (ed.) *'Race' in Britain*, London: Hutchinson.

——(1987) 'Recent Marxist theories of nationalism and the issue of racism', *British Journal of Sociology* 38, 1: 24–43.

Miliband, R. (1969) *The State in Capitalist Society*, London: Weidenfeld & Nicolson.

Miller, R.A. (1971) *Japanese and the Other Altaic Languages*, Chicago: University of Chicago Press.

Mitchison, Rosalind (ed.) (1980) *The Roots of Nationalism: Studies in Northern Europe*, Edinburgh: John Donald Publishers.

Minami, Hiroshi (1950) Review of *The Chrysanthemum and the Sword* by Ruth Benedict, 'Shakaishinrigaku no tachiba kara' (From the points of view of social psychology), *Minzokugaku kenkyū* (Ethnological Studies) 14, 4: 9–12.

——(1953) *Nihonjin no shinri* (The Psychology of the Japanese), Tokyo: Iwanami Shoten, translated as *The Psychology of the Japanese People* by Albert R. Ikuma, Tokyo: University of Tokyo Press, 1971.

——(1973) 'The introspection boom: wither the national character', *Japan Interpreter* 8: 160–75.

——(1980) *Nihonjinron no keifu* (The Genealogy of the *Nihonjinron*), Tokyo: Kōdansha.

Mitsubishi Corporation (1983) *Japanese Business Glossary/Nihonjingo*, Tokyo: Tōyōkeizai Shinpōsha.

Mannari, Hiroshi (1980) 'The Japanese factory reconsidered', *Rice University Studies* 66, 1: 189–200.

Moriguchi, Kenji and Hamaguchi, Eshun (1964) 'Nihonbunka kenkyū no tenbō to bunken risuto: sengo wo chūshin to suru nihonbunkaron no keifu' (An overview and bibliography of studies in Japanese culture: the genealogy of theories of Japanese culture focusing on the post-war period), *Shisō no kagaku* (The Science of Thought), April.

Morikawa, Hidemasa (1973) *Nihongata keiei no genryū: keiei nashonarizumu no kigyō rinen* (The Origins of Japanese-style Management: Business Nationalism as Business Creed), Tōyōkeizai Shinpōsha.

Morita, Akio (1986) *Made in Japan: Akio Morita and Sony*, New York: Signet, translated as *Made in Japan: waga taikenteki kokusai senryaku* (My Own Experience of International Business Strategy) by M. Shimomura, Tokyo: Asahi Shimbunsha, 1987.

Morris, Ivan (1960) *Nationalism and the Right Wing in Japan: A Study of Post-War Trends*, London: Oxford University Press.

Mouer, Ross and Sugimoto, Yoshio (eds) (1980) *Japanese Society: Reappraisals and New Directions*, a special issue of *Social Analysis*, no. 5/6.

Mouer, Ross and Sugimoto, Yoshio (1986) *Images of Japanese Society*, London: Kegan Paul International.

Murakami, Yasusuke, Kumon Shunpei and Sato Seizaburō (1979) *Bunmei toshite no ie-shakai* (Familial Society as a Pattern of Civilization), Tokyo: Chūō Kōronsha.

Nairn, Tom (1977) *The Break-Up of Britain: Crisis and Neo-Nationalism*, London: New Left Books.

Naotsuka, Reiko (1980) *Ōbeijin ga chinmokusuru toki* (When Westerners Fall Silent), Tokyo: Taishūkan.

Nakane, Chie (1967) *Tate shakai no ningen kankei: tan-istu shakai no riron* (Human Relations in Vertical Society: A Theory of a Unitary Society), Tokyo: Kōdansha.

——(1970) *Japanese Society*, Berkeley and Los Angeles: University of California Press.

Nakayama, Tarō (1958) *Nihon wakamono shi* (A History of Young People in Japan), Tokyo: Nichibunsha.

Nielsen, F. (1980) 'The Flemish movement in Belgium after World War II', *American Sociological Review* 45: 76–94.

Nietzsche, Friedrich ([1886] 1990) *Beyond Good and Evil*, trans. R.J. Hollingdale, Harmondsworth: Penguin Books.

Nihon Seisansei Honbu (ed.) (1965) *Sengo keieishi* (History of Post-War Management), Tokyo: Nihon Seisansei Honbu.

Nippon Steel Corporation, Personnel Development Office (1984) *Nippon: The Land and Its People*, 2nd edn, Tokyo: Gakuseisha.

Nippon Steel Human Resources Development Co. Ltd (1987) *Talking About Japan/Nihhon wo kataru*, Tokyo: ALC.

Nisshō Iwai Corporation (1987) *Ibunka kōshōjutsu: kokusai bijinesu no genba kara* (Skills in Cross-Cultural Negotiation: From the Scene of International Business), Tokyo: Kōbunsha.

Nitobe, Inazo (1899/1990) *Bushido: The Soul of Japan; An Exposition of Japanese Thought*, Tokyo: Shokwabo.

Nomi, Masahiko (1973) *Ketsuekigata ningengaku* (The Study of People Through Blood Types), Tokyo: Sankei Shimbun.

Nomura Sōgō Kenkyusho (Nomura Research Institute) (1978) *Nihonjinron: kokusai kyōchō jidai ni sonaete* (*Nihonjinron:* For an Age of International Cooperation), A special issue of *Refarensu* (Reference), no. 2.

Norman, E.H. (1975) *Origins of the Modern Japanese State: Selected Writings of E.H. Norman*, edited by John Dower, New York: Pantheon Books.

Odaka, Kunio (1984) *Nihonteki keiei* (Japanese-style Management), Tokyo: Chūkō Shinsho.

Okakura, Tenshin (Kakuzō) (1906) *The Book of Tea*, New York: Duffield.

Okamura, J.K. (1981) 'Situational ethnicity', *Ethnic and Racial Studies* 4: 452–65.

Ōkubo Tadashi (1963) *Edo jidai no kokugaku* (National Learning in the Edo Period), Tokyo: Shibundō.

Parsons, Talcott (1937) *The Structure of Social Action*, New York: McGraw-Hill.

——(1951) *The Social System*, New York: Free Press.

Piers, Gerhert and Singer, Milton B. (1953) *Shame and Guilt*, Springfield, Ill.: Charles C. Thomas.

Pitt-Rivers, Julian (1977) 'Race in Latin America: the concept of "raza"' in John Stone (ed.) *Race, Ethnicity and Social Change*, North Scituate, Mass.: Duxbury Press.

Plamenatz, J. (1976) 'Two types of nationalism' in E. Kamenka (ed.)

Poggi, G. (1978) *The Development of the Modern State*, London: Hutchinson & Co.

Ragin, C.C. (1979) 'Ethnic political mobilization: the Welsh case', *American Sociological Review* 44: 619–35.

Reischauer, Edwin (1978) *The Japanese*, Cambridge, Mass.: Harvard University Press.

Reiss, H.S. (ed.) (1955) *The Political Thought of the German Romantics, 1793–1815*, London: Blackwell.

Rekishigaku Kenkyūkai (ed.) (1986) *Tennō to tennōsei o kangaeru* (An Examination of the Emperor and the Emperor System), Tokyo: Aoki Shoten.

Rex, John (1970) *Race Relations in Sociological Theory*, London: Routledge & Kegan Paul.

Rex, John and Mason, David (eds) (1986) *Theories of Race and Ethnic Relations*, Cambridge: Cambridge University Press.

Sabata, Toyoyuki (1964) *Nihon wo minaosu: sono rekishi to kokuminsei* (Rediscovering Japan: Its History and National Character), Tokyo: Kōdansha.

——(1966) *Nikushoku no shisō: Yōroppa seishin no saihakken* (The Philosophy of Carnivorous People: Rediscovering the European Spirit), Tokyo: Chūō Kōronsha.

Sakuma, M. (1983) *Nihonteki keiei no kokusaisei: ibunka eno tekiō wa kanō ka* (How International is Japanese-style Management?: Is Cross-Cultural Adaptation Possible?), Tokyo: Yūhikaku.

Sakurai, Tokutarō (1968) 'Wakamono-gumi no soshiki to kinō' (The organisations and functions of young men's group), *Nihonjin no sei to shi* (Life and Death of the Japanese), Tokyo: Iwasaki Bijutsusha.

——(1974) 'Kesshū no genten' in K. Tsurumi and S. Ichi (eds) *Shisō no bōken* (Adventures in Thought), Tokyo: Chikuma Shobō.

Sakuta, Keiichi (1971) 'Kyōdōtai to shutaisei' (Community and individuality) in H. Furuta *et al.* (eds) *Kindai nihon shakai shisōshi* (The History of Social Thought in Modern Japan), vol. II, Tokyo: Yūhikaku.

Sampson, Anthony (1982) *The Changing Anatomy of Britain*, Sevenoaks: Hodder & Stoughton.

Sawa, Takamitsu (1987) 'Kokkashugi taitō no kehai' (Signs of growing nationalism), *Asahi Shimbun*, 27 May.

Segawa, Kiyoko (1972) *Wakamono to musume o meguru minzoku* (Folklore on Young Men and Women), Tokyo: Miraisha.

Sekiyama, Naotarō (1958) *Kinsei nihon no jinkō kōzō* (The Population Structure of Early-Modern Japan), Tokyo: Nishikawa Kōbunkan.

Selznick, Philip (1952) *The Organizational Weapon*, New York: McGraw Hill.

Servan-Schreiber, J.-J. (1968) *The American Challenge*, trans. R. Steel, London: Hamish Hamilton.

Seton-Watson, Hugh (1977) *Nations and States: An Enquiry into the Origins of Nations and the Politics of Nationalism*, London: Methuen.

Shils, Edward (1957) 'Primordial, personal, sacred and civil ties', *British Journal of Sociology* 7: 113–45.

——(1972) 'Intellectuals, tradition, and the traditions of intellectuals: some preliminary considerations', *Daedalus*, Spring: 21–33.

——(1977) 'Social science and public opinion', *Minerva* 4, 3/4: 273–85.

Shils, Edward and Janowitz, Morris (1948) 'Cohesion and disintegration in the Wehrmacht', *Public Opinion Quarterly* 12: 280–315.

Shindo, Sadakazu (1987) *Hito o ikasu: watashi no jissen keieiroku* (Making the Most of Human Resources: My Experiences in Management), Tokyo: Daiamondosha.

Shinoda, Yūjirō (1977) *Nihonjin to doitsujin* (The Japanese and the Germans), Tokyo: Kōbunsha.

Shintō, Hisashi (1988) *Naratte oboete maneshite suteru* (Learn, Master, Imitate, and Unlearn), Tokyo: NTT Shuppan.

Singh, Karan (1963) *Prophet of Indian Nationalism: A Study of the Political Thought of Sri Aurobindo Ghosh 1893–1910*, London: Allen & Unwin.

Smith, Anthony D. (1971) *Theories of Nationalism*, London: Duckworth.

Smith, Anthony D. (1973) *Nationalism*, A trend report and bibliography, *Current Sociology* 21, 3, The Hague: Mouton.
——(1979) *Nationalism in the Twentieth Century*, Oxford: Martin Robertson.
——(1981) *The Ethnic Revival*, Cambridge: Cambridge University Press.
——(1983) *State and Nation in the Third World*, Brighton: Harvester Press.
——(1984) 'Ethnic persistence and national transformation', *British Journal of Sociology* 35: 452–61.
——(1985) 'Ethnie and nation in the modern world', *Millennium* 14: 127–42.
——(1986) *The Ethnic Origins of Nations*, Oxford: Basil Blackwell.
——(1988) 'The myth of the "modern nation" and the myths of nations', *Ethnic and Racial Studies* 11, 1: 1–26
Snyder, Louis L. (1964) *The Dynamics of Nationalism*, D. Van Nostrand.
——(1976) *The Varieties of Nationalism: A Comparative View*, London: Thomas Nelson & Sons Ltd.
Spiro, M. (1978) 'Culture and human nature' in G. Spindler (ed.) *The Making of Psychological Anthropology*, Berkeley: University of California Press.
Stocking, G.W., Jr (1982) 'Afterward: a view from the center', *Ethnos* 47: 172–86.
Sugimoto, Yoshio and Mouer, Ross (1982) *Nihonjin wa 'nihonteki' ka* (Are the Japanese 'very Japanese'?), Tokyo: Tōyō Keizai Shinpōsa.
Suzuki, Takao (1975) *Tozasareta gengo: nihongo no sekai* (The Closed-off Language: the World of Japanese), Tokyo: Shinchō Sensho.
Suzuki, Yoshimasa (1973) *O-gata ningen* (O-type People), Tokyo: Sanshinsha.
Taira, Kōji (1970) *Economic Development and the Labor Market in Japan*, New York: Columbia University Press.
Taiyō Kōbe Bank (1988) *The Nipponjin/The Scrutable Japanese*, Tokyo: Gakuseisha.
Takasugi, Ichirō ([1950] 1977) *Kyokko no kage ni* (In the Shadows of Auroras), Tokyo: Tozanbō.
Tamaki, Akira (1977) *Inasaku bunka to nihonjin* (Rice Production Culture and the Japanese), Tokyo: Gendai Hyōronsha.
Tanizaki, Junichirō (1974) *Bunshō dokuhon* (Manual of Prose Composition), in *Tanizaki Junichirō zenshū* (Collected Works of Tanizaki Junichirō), vol. XXI, Tokyo: Chūō Kōronsha.
Thyssen, A. Pontoppidan (1980) 'The rise of nationalism in the Danish monarchy 1800–1864, with special reference to its socio-economic and cultural aspects', in Mitchison (ed.).
Tilly, C. (ed.) (1975) *The Formation of Nation States in Western Europe*, Princeton, NJ: Princeton University Press.
Toshiba Co., Personnel Development Department (1985) *Toshiba's Practical Cross-cultural Dialogs*, Tokyo.
Tsuda, Sōkichi (1948) *Nihonjin no shisō-teki taido* (The Thinking Attitude of the Japanese), Tokyo: Chūō Kōronsha.
Tsujimura, Akira (1981) *Sengo nihon no taishū shinri* (The Psychology of the Masses in Post-war Japan), Tokyo: Tōkyō Daigaku Shuppan Kai.
Tsukasa, Shintarō (1951) *Mono no mikata ni tsuite* (On the Ways of Looking at Things), Tokyo: Kawaide Shobō.

Tsunoda, Ryusaku, Wm. Theodore de Bary, and Keene, Donald (comps) (1958) *Sources of Japanese Tradition*, New York: Columbia University Press.

Tsunoda, Tadanobu (1978) *Nihonjin no nō: nō no hataraki to tōzai no bunka* (The Japanese Brain: Functions of the Brain and the Cultures of the East and the West), Tokyo: Taishūkan.

Tsurumi, Kazuko (1947) '"Kiku to katana": amerikajin no mita nihonteki dōtokukan' (*The Chrysanthemum and the Sword*: Japanese morals as seen by an American'), *Shisō* (Thought), March.

——(1970) *Social Change and the Individual: Japan Before and After Defeat in World War II*, Princeton, NJ: Princeton University Press.

——(1972) *Kōkishin to nihonjin* (Curiosity and the Japanese), Tokyo: Kōdansha.

——(1977) *Hyōhaku to teijū to* (Itinarants and Settlers), Tokyo: Chikuma Shobō.

——(1979a) 'Aspects of endogenous development in modern Japan, Part 1: social structure: a mesh of hierarchical and coequal relationships in villages and cities', Research Paper Series A-36, Institute of International Relations, Sophia University.

——(1979b) 'Aspects of endogenous development in modern Japan, Part II: religious beliefs: state shintoism vs. folk belief', Research Paper Series A-37, Institute of International Relations, Sophia University.

Ulich, Robert (1961) *The Education of Nations: A Comparison in Historical Perspective*, Boston: Harvard University Press.

Umesao, T., Befu, H. and Kreiner J. (eds) (1984) *Japanese Civilization in the Modern World*, a special issue of *Senri Ethnological Studies*, no. 16.

Van den Berghe, Pierre L. (1978) *Race and Racism*, 2nd edn, New York: John Wiley & Sons.

Van Heerikhuizen, Bert (1982) 'What is typically Dutch?: sociologists in the 1930s and 1940s on the Dutch national character', *The Netherlands' Journal of Sociology* 18: 103–25.

Verba, Sidney (1961) *Small Groups and Political Behavior: A Study of Leadership*, Princeton, NJ: Princeton University Press.

Vogel, Ezra (1979) *Japan as Number One*, Cambridge, Mass.: Harvard University Press, translated as *Japan azu nambāwan* by Hironaka Wakako and Kimoto Akiko, Tokyo: TBS Buritanika, 1979.

Wallerstein, I. (1974) *The Modern World System*, New York: Academic Press.

Wallman, Sandra (1978) 'The boundaries of "race": process of ethnicity in England', *Man* 13, 2: 200–15.

——(1981) 'Refractions of rhetoric: evidence for the meaning of "race" in England', in R. Paine (ed.) *Politically Speaking: Cross-cultural Studies of Rhetoric*, Philadelphia: Institute for the Study of Human Issues.

——(1986) 'Ethnicity and the boundary process in context' in Rex and Mason (eds).

Wallman, Sandra (ed.) (1979) *Ethnicity at Work*, London: Macmillan.

Watanabe, Shōichi (1974) *Nihongo no kokoro* (The Soul of the Japanese Language), Tokyo: Kōdansha.

——(1980) *Nihon soshite nihonjin* (Japan and the Japanese), Tokyo: Shōdensha.

Watsuji, Tetsurō (1950) Review of *The Chrysanthemum and the Sword* by Ruth Benedict, 'Kagakuteki kachi ni taisuru gimon' (A question about its scientific value), *Minzokugaku kenkyū* (Ethnological Studies) 14, 4: 23–7.

——(1951) *Uzumoreta nihon* (Japan Buried), Tokyo: Shinchōsha.

Wetherall, William (1981) 'Public figures in popular culture: identity problems of minority heroes' in C. Lee and G. DeVos.

Weber, Max (1948) *From Max Weber, Essays in Sociology*, edited by H. Gerth and C.W. Mills, London: Routledge & Kegan Paul.

——(1982) *Seiji ronshū* (Collected Works on Politics), vol. I, translated by T. Nakamura *et al*. from *Gesammelte Politische Schriften* (1921), Tokyo: Misuzu Shobō.

Yamada, Takao (1981a) 'Sengoshi ni okeru kokumin-tōgō no shodankai' (The stages of national integration in post-war history) in K. Yamada and S. Matsuo (eds) *Sengoshi to handō ideorogii* (Post-war History and Reactionary Ideology), Tokyo: Shin-Nihon Shuppan.

——(1981b) 'Nihon kokkashugi shisō no konnichiteki ichi' (The present-day situation surrounding nationalistic thought in Japan), *Zen'ei* (Vanguard), October: 121–34.

——(1985) 'Sengo yonjū-nen to "aikokushin" ideorogii' (Forty years after the war and the 'patriotic' ideology), *Kagaku to shisō* (Science and Thought) 56: 166–77.

Yamaguchi, Kazutaka (1984) Review of '*Nihonbunkaron' to tennōsei ideorogii* ('Theories of Japanese culture' and the emperor ideology) by Hijikata Kazuo, *Kagaku to shisō* (Science and Thought) 52: 156–62.

Yamaguchi, Masayuki (1980) 'Nihonteki kyōdōtai no hōkai to "kindaika"' (The decline of the Japanese-style community and 'modernisation'), *Kagaku to shisō* (Science and Thought) 38: 227–43.

Yamazaki, M. *et al*. (1983) *Nihon wa sekai no moderu ni naruka* (Can Japan be an [Alternative] Model for the World?), Tokyo: Bungei Shunjū.

Yanagita, Kunio (1950) Review of *The Chrysanthemum and the Sword* by Ruth Benedict, 'Jinjōjin no jinseikan' (Ordinary people's view of life), *Minzokugaku kenkyū* (Ethnological Studies) 14, 4: 28–35.

——(1962) 'Toshi to nōson' ('The city and the agricultural village') in *Teihon Yanagita Kunio shū* (Collected Works of Yanagita Kunio), vol. XVI, Tokyo: Chikuma Shobō.

——(1963a) 'Oyakata kokata' (The patron and the client), *Teihon*, vol. XV, Tokyo: Chikuma Shobō.

——(1963b) 'Ie kandan', *Teihon*, vol. XV, Tokyo: Chikuma Shobō.

——(1963c) 'Meiji Taishō shi' (A history of the Meiji and Taishō Periods), *Teihon*, vol. XXIV, Tokyo: Chikuma Shobō.

——(1969) 'Mukashi-fū to tōsei-fū' (Old-fashioned ways and modern ways) in *Momen izen no koto* (Days Before Cotton), Tokyo: Kadokawa Shoten.

——(1971) 'Nihon nōmin-shi' (A history of Japanese peasants), *Teihon*, vol. XVI, Tokyo: Chikuma Shobō.

Yasuda, Saburō (1980) 'Nihonshakairon no tenbō' (An overview of theories of Japanese society), *Gendai shakaigaku* (Review of Contemporary Sociology) 7, 1: 3–14.

Yinger, Milton J. (1976) 'Ethnicity in complex societies', in Coser, L.A.

and Larsen, L.O. (eds) *The Uses of Controversy in Sociology*, New York: Free Press.

Yoshino, Kōsaku (1987) 'Minzoku riron no tenkai to kadai: "minzoku no fukkatsu" ni chokumenshite' (Developments in and problems concerning theories of ethnicity: in the face of the 'ethnic revival'), *Shakaigaku hyōron* (Japanese Sociological Review) 37, 4: 2–17.

Index